NEOLIBERALISM

Thanks to the rise of neoliberalism over the past several decades, we live in an era of rampant anxiety, insecurity, and inequality. While neoliberalism has become somewhat of an academic buzzword in recent years, this book offers a rich and multilayered introduction to what is arguably the most pressing issue of our times. Engaging with prominent scholarship in media and cultural studies, as well as geography, sociology, economic history, and political theory, author Julie Wilson pushes against easy understandings of neoliberalism as market fundamentalism, rampant consumerism, and/or hyper-individualism. Instead, Wilson invites readers to interrogate neoliberalism in true cultural studies fashion, at once as history, theory, practice, policy, culture, identity, politics, and lived experience. Indeed, the book's primary aim is to introduce neoliberalism in all of its social complexity, so that readers can see how neoliberalism shapes their own lives, as well as our political horizons, and thereby start to imagine and build alternative worlds.

Julie A. Wilson is Associate Professor, Allegheny College, Department of Communication Arts and Theatre. She is the author (with Emily Chivers Yochim) of *Mothering through Precarity: Women's Work and Digital Media*.

KEY IDEAS IN MEDIA AND CULTURAL STUDIES

The *Key Ideas in Media and Cultural Studies* series covers the main concepts, issues, debates and controversies in contemporary media and cultural studies. Titles in the series constitute authoritative, original essays rather than literary surveys, but are also written explicitly to support undergraduate teaching. The series provides students and teachers with lively and original treatments of key topics in the field.

Cultural Policy
by David Bell and Kate Oakley

Reality TV
by Annette Hill

Culture
by Ben Highmore

Representation
by Jenny Kidd

Neoliberalism
by Julie A. Wilson

NEOLIBERALISM

Julie A. Wilson

 Routledge
Taylor & Francis Group

NEW YORK AND LONDON

First published 2018
by Routledge
711 Third Avenue, New York, NY 10017

and by Routledge
2 Park Square, Milton Park, Abingdon, Oxon OX14 4RN

*Routledge is an imprint of the Taylor & Francis Group, an
informa business*

© 2018 Taylor & Francis

Library of Congress Cataloging-in-Publication Data
Names: Wilson, Julie A., 1975– author.
Title: Neoliberalism / Julie A. Wilson.
Description: New York, NY : Routledge, 2017. | Series:
   Key ideas in media and cultural studies
Identifiers: LCCN 2017005752 | ISBN 9781138654624
   (hardback) | ISBN 9781138654631 (pbk.)
Subjects: LCSH: Neoliberalism. | Neoliberalism—
   Economic aspects. | Neoliberalism—Social aspects.
Classification: LCC JC574 .W557 2017 | DDC 320.51/3—dc23
LC record available at https://lccn.loc.gov/2017005752

ISBN: 978-1-138-65462-4 (hbk)
ISBN: 978-1-138-65463-1 (pbk)
ISBN: 978-1-315-62308-5 (ebk)

Typeset in Times New Roman
by Apex CoVantage, LLC
Printed at CPI on sustainably sourced paper

For Megan, Zach, and Lee

CONTENTS

ACKNOWLEDGMENTS

My name is on the cover, but this book was written by many. First and foremost, it was written in dialogue with so many students at Allegheny College whose radical openness, intellectual curiosity, and willingness to share their daily hurts and dreams are the conditions of possibility for this book. I owe them everything. Specifically, they pushed me to write this book as more than a critique of neoliberalism. They wanted resources for imagining and building a new world. They also wanted a book that was written for them, not academics. I have tried my very best to meet these demands and have been forever transformed in the process of doing so.

Megan Bart, Zach Cramer, and Lee Scandinaro: you were the seed for this book. It was your longing for new political horizons that inspired me to start teaching about neoliberalism as our conjuncture in the first place.

Briann Moye and Brigit Stack, my brilliant and dedicated research assistants: thank you for sharing my brain, for running down my ideas, for writing up potential case studies, and for living with me through this project. I hope you can see here just how much you've meant and contributed. To the Andrew W. Mellon Collaborative Undergraduate Research in the Humanities Grant: thank you for making this invaluable collaboration possible in the first place and for supporting my work with students over the past five years.

Tory Kaigan-Kuykendall, Jeremy Loewer, Peter McCaffrey, Brogan McGowan, Kristen Migliozzi, Rachael Robertson, Jessica Schombert, Xzavier Scott, and Erin Yates: thank you for wading through *The New Way of the World* with me. Our conversations were formative; you sharpened and elevated this project more than you can know.

Hayley Anderson, Greg Bras, Caitlin Brown, Aaron Donahoe, Arianna O'Connell, Jordan Palmer, Rochelle Rogalski, Jon Scroxton, Alex Trunfio, and Nadiya Wahl: without your efforts at the end of this process, I am not sure the book would have made it into this form. Your engagement with and commitment to this project are gifts for which I will always be grateful. Sophie Dodge: the love with which you move through the world has been the biggest inspiration. Samantha Samakande: you are the wisest person I know; I really tried to let your spirit animate the final articulation.

I could have never started teaching about neoliberal culture if it wasn't for the intellectual brilliance and generosity of my teacher, mentor, and friend, Laurie Ouellette. This work is indebted, too, to Sarah Banet-Weiser, Jo Littler, and Roopali Mukherjee, whose writing on neoliberal politics and culture also has contributed so much to my thinking and teaching over the years.

I am so grateful to Erica Wetter for suggesting I write this book. Your enthusiasm for this project and faith in me have been so empowering. To Mia Moran, thank you for getting me to the finish line. I couldn't have done it without you.

To my comrades in the Marxism reading group, Bill Bywater, Jay Hanes, David Miller, Laura Quinn, Barbara Shaw, Vesta Silva, Eleanor Weisman, Sharon Wesoky, and Jon Wiebel: thank you for making space for us to think together about neoliberalism. To my fellow commoners in Meadville, Pennsylvania, including Mark Ams, Ian Carbone, Heather Fish, Don Goldstein, Taylor Hinton, Julie Hunter, Kerstin Martin, Stephanie Martin, Vanessa Shaffer, Greg Singer, Autumn Vogel, and Peter Zimmer: thank you for working by my side day in and out to make a new world. We're doing it!

To my mom, Ann Wilson, and sister, Dana Wilson: I am so grateful for your love and support. I am who I am because of you.

And, finally, to Emily Yochim and Joe Tompkins, my persons: nothing is possible without you. Thank you for believing in me and for contributing so much intellectual energy to this project along the way—from talking to me pretty much everyday about neoliberal politics to reading and editing every word. As with everything I write, it's as much yours as mine.

INTRODUCTION
LIVING IN COMPETITION

Today's public secret is that everyone is anxious.
—Institute for Precarious Consciousness[1]

If you are like most of my students, you're anxious. This anxiety
might be felt when you sit down to write a paper. You feel so much
pressure, words refuse to come, and when they do, they most always
seem inadequate. Questions race through your mind: Will I perform
well enough on this assignment? Is my GPA competitive? Will this
major actually translate into a job? How will I ever be able to repay
my student loans? Am I good enough? Do I even belong here? You
most likely experience these anxieties and uncertainties as yours and
yours alone. They are deeply private thoughts and feelings that should
not be shared, except perhaps with a therapist or a best friend. However, as we are going to find out throughout this book, these personal,
intimate anxieties do not belong to or emerge from you. They are not
natural or inherent to you. They come from the world you inhabit. In
other words, they are social and historical. Even though you experience them as private, perhaps even a source of shame or stigma, they
are common, something most all of us undoubtedly share.

The purpose of this book is to help you understand in a deep and meaningful way why life today appears and feels as it does by cultivating a thick, holistic, and critical understanding of neoliberalism. Generally speaking, neoliberalism is a set of social, cultural, and political-economic forces that puts competition at the center of social life. According to neoliberalism, government's charge is not the care and security of citizens, but rather the promotion of market competition. In the neoliberal imagination, public social infrastructures (such as social security, unemployment benefits, public education) are believed to squash entrepreneurialism and individualism and breed dependency and bureaucracy. Competition, on the other hand, is heralded to ensure efficiency and incite creativity. Spurred by competition, individuals, organizations, companies, and even the government itself, will seek to optimize and innovate, creating a truly free social world where the best people and ideas come out on top. Put a little differently, neoliberalism aims to create a market-based society, where there are only competing private enterprises. Since the late 1970s, neoliberal ideas have increasingly guided the policies and practices of governments and other social institutions, and as a result, we have come to live in competition with ourselves, others, and our social world.

In theory, neoliberalism and its commitment to creating a competitive society make a lot of sense. However, might our anxieties register a dark side? Might they be symptomatic that something here is not quite right?

It is vital that we clear something up right away. *Neoliberalism is not simply a new form of political liberalism.* It should not be confused with left causes and political parties. Rather, the "liberalism" in neoliberalism refers to a belief in individual liberties, property rights, and free markets. For example, in the United States context, which is the primary focus of this book, both the Republican and Democratic parties are predominantly liberal. They both agree that a good society is a capitalist society rooted in individual property rights and market freedoms. As we will explore more fully in the following chapters, neoliberalism refers to the reinvention of liberal ideas and commitments in ways that have profoundly transformed the fabric of identity and social life. In a neoliberal society, the capitalist market is no longer imagined as a distinct arena where goods are valued and exchanged; rather, the market is, or ideally should be, the basis for *all* of society. Thus, neoliberalism works aggressively to infuse competition into the nooks and crannies of who we are and the environments we inhabit. Every aspect of our lives, even those facets that do not necessarily have anything to do with money or the economy, become geared toward market competition, from our education to our friendships to our very sense of self and self-worth.

This generalization of market competition produces anxieties. What else should we expect, really? If we are, first and foremost, competitive social beings, then the prospect of failure comes to define our lives. We are constantly comparing ourselves to others and worrying about the ramifications of every choice, action, or relationship. In turn, everyday life comes to feel so insecure and uncertain. As the Institute for Precarious Consciousness puts it, "Anxiety has spread . . . to the whole social field. All forms of intensity, self-expression, emotional connection, immediacy, and enjoyment are now laced with anxiety. It has become the linchpin of subordination."[2] Indeed, we will find that these pervasive, common, although privately experienced, anxieties are immensely powerful. They keep us living in competition, unable to imagine other social and political possibilities for ourselves, our communities, our future, and our world.

SELF-ENCLOSED INDIVIDUALISM

Living in competition turns us into certain kinds of people: specifically, what feminist theorist AnaLouise Keating calls self-enclosed individuals. **Self-enclosed individualism** is a form of "hyper-individualism" that tends to "focus exclusively on the human and define this human self very narrowly, in non-relational, boundaried, terms."[3] Keating uses the term *self-enclosed* to distinguish this idea of individualism from more positive concepts like personal agency, autonomy, and self-determination. Rather, she is keen to highlight the hard and fast-dividing lines between self/other and self/world that self-enclosed individualism draws. Keating explains,

> Self-enclosed individualism relies on a dichotomous framework that positions the individual in opposition to all other human and nonhuman beings. ("It's me against the world.") In this binary-oppositional structure, each individual is entirely separate from the external world.

> Self and society are mutually exclusive; to survive and thrive, each person must focus almost entirely on herself, evaluating all actions in egocentric terms: "What's in it for me?" "How can I succeed?" "How will this event, this situation, affect me?" "What can you do for me?" "What can I take from you?"[4]

Neoliberalism incites us to live as self-enclosed individuals, as competition necessarily pits us against our peers and the rest of the world. We thus move through the world with an "oppositional consciousness," where all things are potential threats to our own individual self. More specifically, neoliberalism asks us to be constantly calculating potential gains, losses, and risks, to be thinking about how this or that decision might or might not give us a competitive edge over the rest of the field. To ensure our success and survival, we must play to win. Indeed, according to neoliberalism, one is, first and foremost, a "firm," an "enterprise," the "CEO of oneself." The buck stops with you, so it is best, and even necessary, to cordon oneself off, severing potential connections that might not fit one's strategic plans.

Our anxieties stem from the ways that neoliberalism asks us to be self-enclosed individuals in charge of our own fates through competition. After all, individuals alone cannot control their fates in a global, complex, capitalist society, no matter how well they compete. I repeat: *Individuals alone cannot control their fates in a global, complex, capitalist society, no matter how well they compete.* As a result, self-enclosed individualism is impossible to achieve, yet neoliberalism insists we achieve it. No wonder we're so anxious. Our lives, our well-being, our success, and even our citizenship are defined by impossibility.

Just think about it: there are so many things that are out of our control. For example, we might work out religiously each and every day, always eat the most healthy foods we can find, and avoid risky lifestyle choices. However, all of these good choices and actions can't really ensure your health and well-being, much less your future success. No matter how hard we strive to be good, self-enclosed individuals responsible for bodies and health, our lives are necessarily connected to and dependent upon broader social systems and contexts. For example, just to be healthy, we need access to food, water, and environments that don't poison our bodies, but these are conditions that we can't possibly create, much less guarantee, on our own, as self-enclosed individuals. We are necessarily interdependent beings, vulnerable and connected to one another, as our lives are supported and made possible by a number of infrastructures (e.g., schools, roads and bridges, communication) that bring us into relation with one another. We need each other. We need social cooperation and a commitment to a common, collective good if we are all going to make it in this world.

Neoliberalism and its diffusion of competition throughout society make the infrastructures that undergird our lives profoundly unstable, while simultaneously diminishing our senses of interdependence and social connection. As we will see, living in competition paradoxically undercuts what enables our lives—that is, our social connections and infrastructures—while telling us to assume more and more responsibility through self-enclosed individualism, thereby squashing our capacities for coming together, trusting and caring for each other, and organizing for social change.

This book is written from the perspective that most all of us—regardless of our race, class, gender, sexuality, or citizenship status—are yearning for another world, one beyond self-enclosed individualism. Indeed, I imagine that all of us are capable of and, in fact, deeply yearning for social interconnection. We want strong, social infrastructures undergirding our lives. We want lives defined by mutuality, care, dignity, and security, not anxiety and competition. Thus, I imagine that, at some level, we are all suffering and suffocating, albeit in very different places, in very different ways, in very different voices. I imagine, too, that we may all want to resist and try to change the conditions of our lives, but doing so feels so precarious. After all, success, acceptance, and even survival now depend on living in competition.

In order to imagine and build a world beyond neoliberalism and self-enclosed individualism, we need relevant and effective intellectual resources for political intervention and social interconnection, and these are exactly what this book aims to provide. For it is only by getting a clear handle on the powers that shape our selves and the possibilities for social life that we can even begin to imagine—and start to build—the different worlds that we are all yearning for.

A CULTURAL STUDIES APPROACH

In recent decades, neoliberalism has become an important area of study across the humanities and social sciences. You may have encountered the concept in other classes or settings. Since the Great Recession of 2008, the term has increasingly found its way into popular discussions of the economy. For the most part, neoliberalism is understood as a set of political-economic policies that became dominant with the administrations of Ronald Reagan in the United States and Margaret Thatcher in the United Kingdom. These policies emphasized the rolling back of programs associated with social welfare and creating a new system of global capitalism in the wake of the winding down of the Cold War. However, in this book, we are going to approach neoliberalism from a cultural studies perspective. That means we are interested in how neoliberalism comes to matter in and shape folks' everyday lives and their sense of possibility. In other words, we are interested in neoliberal culture.

So, what do we mean by culture? **Culture** is a term that we toss around all the time but rarely stop to interrogate what exactly it means. Generally speaking, cultural studies understands culture in two interrelated ways via the foundational work of Raymond Williams.[5] On the one hand, culture refers to *a whole way of living*: that is, the shared worldviews, beliefs, values, rituals, traditions, and practices that bind folks together as a community or nation. Culture is what coheres individuals into a larger group, as sharing culture is sharing a way of life with others. Culture, in this sense of the term, is everywhere. It infuses all dimensions of our lives, providing a commonsensical, taken-for-granted ground for everyday living. On the other hand, culture can refer to the particular *representations and artifacts produced within a culture*. Here culture names specific texts and practices that embody the whole way of living of a group of people. Many people think of culture as those texts that have been deemed to reflect the highest accomplishments of a people (e.g., the ballet, the art that hangs in museums, Pulitzer Prize–winning novels). However, cultural studies is primarily interested in *popular culture:* those texts and practices that ordinary people engage with in the contexts of their daily lives.

As you have probably sensed by now, cultural studies is not merely interested in the study of culture. More importantly, it is invested in the study of *cultural power*. As cultural studies scholars, we want to learn about *how* culture—as a whole way of life and set of representations—structures our social worlds, our identities, relationships, and senses of possibility. Cultural power flows through our everyday lives in myriad ways—from the popular representations we see on our screens to the guiding beliefs and values that shape our institutions and give our lives form and meaning. It is cultural power that incites our practices of self, sets our relationships to others, and delineates the horizons of our lives. It is cultural power that produces the social conditions of possibility for both individual and collective life. It is cultural power that provides the blueprints for what can be thought, known, felt, cared about, fought for, and lived.

Crucially, cultural studies cares about cultural power because we are *interventionist* in our orientation toward intellectual work. This means that we are not interested in building knowledge of culture for its own sake, but rather in producing effective critical tools and resources for intervening in our everyday lives and changing the power structures that define them. Cultural studies theorist Lawrence Grossberg puts it this way:

> Cultural studies is always interested in how power infiltrates, contaminates, limits, and empowers the possibilities that people have to live their lives in dignified and secure ways. For if one wants to change the relations of power, if one wants to move people, even a little bit, one must begin from where people are, from where and how they actually live their lives.[6]

Cultural studies aims to account for how ordinary people struggle and survive—why things come to matter to folks, when and where they pin their hopes—in order to gain a clear and practical understanding of our social world and the possibilities for resistance and transformation embedded within it.

Ultimately, what distinguishes this interventionist, cultural power-focused approach from many others is its foundational belief in the *social constructedness* of our worlds and identities. In other words, from the perspective of cultural studies, there is nothing necessary or natural about neoliberalism, living in competition, and self-enclosed individualism. We find ourselves here, in neoliberal culture, because of a range of highly contingent forces and histories that have been constructed over time to serve specific aims and interests, most fundamentally, those of liberal (and now neoliberal) capitalism. By understanding how our world has been socially constructed, we can begin to dislodge the cultural powers of neoliberalism that make this world feel so inevitable, normal, and commonsensical.

In a culture composed of anxious, self-enclosed individuals, where market competition defines all of social life, we need now, more than ever, to see the social constructedness of our identities, worlds, and everyday lives. For neoliberalism's culture of living in competition is so entrenched that only a cultural studies perspective can produce the forms of knowledge we need to imagine and build new worlds. Indeed, a cultural studies perspective understands that possibilities of resistance and transformation are everywhere. As Grossberg puts it,

> power is never able to totalize itself. There are always fissures and fault lines that may become the active sites of change. Power never quite accomplishes everything it might like to everywhere, and there is always the possibility of changing the structures and organization of power.[7]

See, here's the thing: there's a gigantic paradox at the heart of neoliberal culture. On one hand, as we will see, neoliberalism presents itself as a totalizing situation where resistance and transformation seem impossible, as living in competition has come to define all aspects of our lives. On the other hand, though, neoliberalism's power over our lives is incredibly tenuous; for, as mentioned earlier, I am convinced that most of us are yearning for a vastly different world, one that is built upon and nurtures our interdependencies and shared vulnerabilities, not self-enclosed individualism and living in competition. Ultimately, this paradox of neoliberalism's totalizing yet tenuous status is what makes a cultural studies approach so important. Cultural studies, with its investments in cultural power and political intervention can expose the social constructedness of neoliberalism's all-consuming presence, while, simultaneously, helping us to identify those "fissures and fault lines" where resistance and transformation are in fact possible. In other words, once we start to see the constructedness of our world, we can begin to sense and imagine different possibilities in the course of living our lives. We can start to feel our own agency as historical actors who might just have some power to imagine and build worlds beyond neoliberalism.

SEEING OUR INTERCONNECTIONS, MAPPING OUR CONJUNCTURE

A cultural studies approach to neoliberalism enables what we might call an interconnectivist mode of critical work: a form of intellectual engagement that starts from and aims to clarify the radical **interconnectivity** that undergirds our lives as living beings.[8] Despite what living in competition and self-enclosed individualism would have us believe and feel, our lives are always already entwined with those of *everyone* else, as well as our environments. This is because we are all, in our own ways, living, breathing embodiments of broader histories, cultures, and politics. In other words, we share what cultural studies scholars call a **conjuncture**. According to Jeremy Gilbert, the conjuncture names "the specific ensemble of social, cultural and economic forces shaping possible political outcomes at a given moment."[9] We might think of the conjuncture as the social totality of forces and powers that define a particular milieu or moment. The conjuncture is the whole that is greater than the sum of the parts. While other disciplines tend to hone in on the parts, many cultural studies scholars take the social construction and transformation of the conjuncture as their primary object of study. If we want to *really* change our world and the conditions of possibility that define our lives, we need to be able to grasp our world in its totality. In other words, we need to be able to draw lines of connection between different processes, happenings, and peoples, and to locate specific feelings, events, and movements within the broader socially constructed contexts from which they emerge.

Indeed, in our global, rapidly moving, startlingly unequal society, it is more important than ever to see and study the conjuncture and the interconnections that define it. To intervene in the power relations that define our everyday lives, we need a clear-headed and practical view of our social world in all of its complexity. Even though this book's focus is contemporary U.S. neoliberal culture, my hope is that it will enable all readers to see threads between what initially might appear as disparate historical developments or social problems—to connect the dots in order to create transformative means toward different and, hopefully, much more egalitarian futures.

To see what I am getting at, let's consider just some of the defining features of our present neoliberal world:

- The richest among us accumulate wealth at a dizzying pace, while the vast majority lives with increasing material insecurity and danger.
- Money is allowed to flow freely across national borders, but people in search of safety and a better life are not.
- We all work harder and harder, but we are not gaining ground socially or economically.
- We are all very anxious and depressed, yet countless self-help guides and technologies promise to help us find health and happiness.
- Celebrities like Beyoncé signal racial progress and even black power, yet black and brown bodies are constantly harassed, incarcerated, and sometimes even killed by police.
- High-powered women like Facebook Chief Operating Officer Sheryl Sandberg promise that women can now "have it all"—a high-powered corporate career and a happy family life—while the vast majority of women struggle to make ends meet.
- There seem to be more and more opportunities to exercise free speech online, at the same time that laws like *Citizens United* and efforts to roll back voting rights work to drown out the voices of ordinary citizens.
- There are plenty of green products to purchase, yet these consumer choices mean little in the face of the environmental destruction wrecked by a fossil fuel economy and climate change.

How can we make sense of these many, and often contradictory, facets of our social world? How are these seemingly disparate developments in technology, everyday life, global economic policy, national politics, and social identity related to one another? What is the connection between Beyoncé and *Citizens United*? Between *Citizens United* and climate change? Between climate change and our own anxieties? Between our own anxieties and rising levels of income inequality? Put differently, how can we grasp the "big picture" of what's happening to ourselves, our communities, and the planet we all share? While there are many disciplines and scholars doing excellent and important work on the global economy, refugee crises, racial injustice, gender oppression, democracy, psychology, and the environment, these studies, on their own, are not able to articulate the interconnectedness of these issues, much less our interconnectedness as human beings. Only conjunctural analysis can do that.

I should note that, within academia, neoliberalism is a controversial term. Scholars continue to debate its usefulness. On one hand, for some, neoliberalism is a buzzword, a catchphrase; it is a term that is so often repeated and invoked that it has lost its meaning. According to these critiques, neoliberalism is presented as a scary monster that is everywhere and nowhere all at once. It has come to figure as shorthand for everything that is evil in our world, and as a result, it ends up teaching us very little about what specifically is wrong, how exactly we got here, and what actually can be done to change course. Thus, many scholars advocate not using the term at all. On the other hand, other scholars prefer not to use the term because they argue that it is misleading. For them, neoliberalism is simply an advanced form of liberal capitalism. There's nothing really new or *neo* here, so why overstate and confuse things with the prefix?

However, despite these critiques, I hang onto the term *neoliberalism*. My wager in doing so is that writing this book as a critical study of neoliberal culture gives us a way to map our current conjuncture. It allows us to hold together the "specific ensemble of social, cultural, and economic forces" at work in our world and, thus, to locate our lives in interrelation with those of others. Indeed, I have found during my work with students over the years that studying neoliberalism enables us to see our interconnectedness and the new ways of living that sensing our interconnectedness opens up. We all suffer when we're forced to live in competition as self-enclosed individuals. Studying the neoliberal conjuncture allows us to clearly identify the roots of our suffering, and to trace our connections with others who are also suffering, although often in variegated ways. In other words, when we map our conjuncture, we can see how our different lives are lived on common ground, which is a crucial step to creating a world beyond competition.

NEW STORIES FOR NEW WORLDS

As we will see in our mapping of the neoliberal conjuncture, competition's totalizing yet tenuous power over our everyday lives is rooted in what Keating calls "status-quo stories"—those stories that get told in popular culture, and that we often tell ourselves, which cement our relationship to our present conjuncture and our investment in the world as we currently know it. She explains:

> Generally spoken with great certainty, these and similar comments (commands, really) reflect unthinking affirmation of the existing reality and a stubborn, equally unthinking resistance to change. Because we believe that our status-quo stories represent accurate factual statements about ourselves, other people, and the world, we view them as permanent, unchanging facts. This belief in the status-quo's permanence becomes self-fulfilling: We do not try to make change because change is impossible to make. "It's always been that way," we tell ourselves, "so why waste our energy trying to change things?" "People are just like that—it's human nature, so plan accordingly and alter your expectations! There's no point in trying to change human nature!" Status-quo stories trap us in our current circumstances and conditions; they limit our imaginations because they prevent us from envisioning alternate possibilities.[10]

Status-quo stories double down on reality, making it seem like those socially constructed forces impinging on us are natural rather than historical, political, and subject to change. "Status-quo stories have a numbing effect," Keating writes. "When we organize our lives around such stories or in other ways use them as ethical roadmaps or guides, they prevent us from extending our imaginations and exploring additional possibilities."[11]

One of my students aptly described neoliberal culture as a "status-quo storytelling machine." To keep us living in competition, neoliberalism generates a host of status-quo stories about the naturalness and inevitability of self-enclosed individualism. Indeed, we might say that self-enclosed individualism operates as *the foundational* status-quo story of neoliberal culture, where competition has become synonymous with all of life. Self-enclosed individualism keeps us not only divided from one another, but also actively pitted against each other. We are stuck in an oppositional consciousness that refuses to acknowledge our social interconnections, even though, as our shared anxieties suggest, we've never had more in common than right now! No matter where we are or what we're doing, neoliberal culture encourages us to see each other through a competitive lens that makes the transformation of our social world, and ourselves, impossible. We become incapable of acknowledging how our fortunes and fates are entwined with those of others who are living very different realities. We become callous and hardened to the suffering of others. We see suffering and death everywhere, and while this might register as bad or wrong or upsetting, we nonetheless stay stuck within the horizons of our own self-enclosed bubbles.

The devastating powers of status-quo stories are clear in so many of the conversations we have on college campuses about power, privilege, and difference. In fact, I started teaching courses on neoliberal culture to help my students understand the broader histories and contexts that were impinging on these conversations and making them so fraught, and ultimately so unproductive. Time and time again, in open community forums and classroom discussions of systemic inequalities, I watched students voice painful personal experiences only to get nowhere. Indeed, when asked to consider various forms of privilege, many of my white, male students get defensive. The idea that they haven't earned their place through their own decisions and hard work, but rather benefited from inherited wealth and opportunity, means that they are not good people from the perspective of neoliberalism. Talking about issues of privilege threatens to diminish their sense of self and individual value, so they recoil from conversations that ask them to see their place within broader legacies of settler colonialism, patriarchy, and capitalism. Accordingly, they hold on tight to status-quo stories of self-enclosed individualism to protect themselves, doubling down on their privilege to secure their status in a competitive world.

However, it is important to see that status-quo stories of self-enclosed individualism also inform my students from historically oppressed and marginalized groups. These students suffer daily: they live in an environment that professes to celebrate "diversity," while, in the context of their own lives, they are reminded again and again just how much they don't belong or matter. Not surprisingly, they demand "safe spaces" and protection for themselves and their peers, and they often draw hard lines between allies and enemies. Here too though, we see neoliberal stories at work. What matters for my students, and rightly so, is the way that "microaggressions"—those daily, mundane experiences of discrimination that accumulate over time—diminish their own capacities for flourishing as self-enclosed individuals.

My point here is not to suggest that privileged students and marginalized students are *the same* because they are both invested in a version of self-enclosed individualism. Rather, my point is they share a situation; despite their different and unequal social positions, they have similar feelings—of defensiveness and a fear of failure—and status-quo stories *in common*. These commonalities do not imply evenness or equality, but rather interconnection, that is, a shared conjuncture. It is the recognition of this conjunctural interconnection that can thread our lives together and open up possibilities for more egalitarian futures. However, living in competition and the oppositional consciousness it demands obscure these commonalities and the interconnections that could bring students into new relations with one another. As a result, we stay caught up in the world as we know it. We stay stuck in competition, even though we all are yearning for different worlds.

We desperately need *new* stories, stories that offer us different pathways to each other. As Keating puts it, we need stories that help us move from "me" to "we" consciousness.[12] However, this book is not going to write these new stories for you. Rather, the goal of this book is to provide you with the resources for writing these new stories in and through your own lives.

THE WORK OF CRITIQUE

Ultimately, writing new stories will require a new sense of yourself and your world, as well as what is possible, and realizing this new sense will require, first and foremost, cultivating a deeply critical orientation toward the world as we currently know and experience it. This critical orientation dislodges the sense of inevitability of neoliberalism, self-enclosed individualism, and living in competition; it knows that things don't have to be this way and, thus, senses the possibilities for resistance and transformation that are everywhere.

It is so crucial to understand that this critical orientation is not simply about saying that aspects of neoliberal culture are "bad" or "wrong." Rather, the work of critique is about seeing the flows of power and ways of thinking that make the neoliberal conjuncture possible and hold it together. Critique is therefore a mode of knowing—a form of everyday intellectual work—that is aimed at exposing the myriad workings of power and its status-quo stories. As Michel Foucault explains, "A critique is not a matter of saying that things are not right as they are. It is a matter of pointing out on what kinds of assumptions, what kinds of familiar, unchallenged, unconsidered modes of thought the practices that we accept rest."[13]

To clarify Foucault's idea, let's think back to the student discussions of power and privilege discussed above. The work of critique is not simply about pointing out privilege, although this is, of course, vital work. The work of critique goes beyond pointing out what's wrong and seeks to unravel the socially constructed conjuncture in which these problems emerge and get negotiated. For only then can we step outside of the competitive, oppositional consciousness of neoliberal culture and begin to imagine a radically different future built on equality and shared security.

This work of dislodging the inevitability of our conjuncture and its status-quo stories is hard but vital intellectual work that requires not only critique of our social world, but also transformation of ourselves. Indeed, truly critical work is always profoundly disruptive of our own identities and knowledges. This work can be immensely painful, as it strips away the certainty and comfort provided by status-quo stories. This work can also be, and should be, immensely joyful and life-giving, as it enables us to free ourselves from the status-quo stories and devastating limitations they put on our lives, imaginations, and social relationships.

This mix of pain and joy at the heart of critical work comes from the way that critique asks us to "lose confidence" in our world. As feminist theorist Sara Ahmed writes,

> Losing confidence: it can be a feeling of something gradually going away from you, being eroded. You sense the erosion. You might stumble, hesitate, falter; things might gradually unravel so you end up holding onto the barest of threads. It might be an experience in the present

> that throws things up, throws you off balance. . . . When you lose confidence it can feel like you are losing yourself: like you have gone into hiding from yourself.¹⁴

Losing confidence in your world is thus a form of existential crisis—you are disoriented; your world is shattered. At the same time, losing confidence in status-quo stories means gaining confidence for resistance and transformation. We become bolder, less anxious, more optimistic, capable of social interconnection, political intervention, and acting on and from a place of commonality. This is real freedom.

Critique is ultimately about *unlearning* our world so that we might reconstruct it anew. Losing confidence in neoliberal culture means being able to say no to it in the conduct of our daily lives. In these capacities for resistance, we gain confidence that another world might actually be better, worth opening ourselves up to, worth fighting for. We begin to cultivate what Henry Giroux calls educated hope. **Educated hope** is not "a romanticized and empty" version of hope; rather, it is a form of hope enabled by critique that "taps into our deepest experiences and longing for a life of dignity with others, a life in which it becomes possible to imagine a future that does not mimic the present."¹⁵ With educated hope, our sense of who we are and of what might be possible shifts in profound ways. This is when those new worlds we are longing for open up.

WHAT'S TO COME

Each of the chapters that follow offer a variety of intellectual tools for mapping the neoliberal conjuncture. Taken together, they are designed to produce a holistic and thick understanding of neoliberalism and its myriad powers to shape our identities, sensibilities, social worlds, and political horizons. Having a thick understanding of neoliberalism means that you feel in your bones that there is nothing natural or inevitable about neoliberalism and its status-quo stories. It means that you understand that neoliberalism is the outcome of a range of contingent historical processes that have consequences across social, political, economic, and cultural fields. In other words, by the end of our journey, you'll know how our neoliberal conjuncture has been, and continues to be, constructed. You'll also, therefore, be able to sense the other worlds on the horizon that are just waiting to be constructed, so long as, together, we can develop the resources, capacities, and stories of interconnection for bringing them into being.

More specifically, the book is divided into two sections. The first section, titled "Critical Foundations," focuses on cultivating a broad, critical orientation toward neoliberal culture. The first chapter charts the rise of neoliberal hegemony through four historical phases. The goal is to illustrate exactly how competition came to be the driving cultural force in our everyday lives. As we will see, there is nothing natural or inevitable about neoliberalism. It was a political and class-based project to remake capitalism and liberal democracy that was conceived, organized for, and eventually won. In the second chapter, we delve into the world of neoliberal theory and its critical consequences. Here we'll explore exactly what neoliberal thinkers believe about the state, markets, and human actors, and what distinguishes neoliberalism from earlier schools of liberal thought. We'll also interrogate what I call the four *D*s—disposability, dispossession, disimagination, and de-democratization—which, taken together, enable us to clearly see and articulate what is so devastating about the rise of neoliberalism. The third chapter examines the cultural powers specific to neoliberalism. Neoliberalism advances through culture, specifically through the promotion of an enterprise culture that works to impose competition as a norm across all arenas of social life. In order to see and specify how neoliberalism works through culture, we take contemporary education as a case study and unpack the entangled cultural powers of neoliberal governmentality, affect, and ideology.

The second section is titled "Neoliberal Culture." In these chapters, we explore the worlds of neoliberal labor, affect, and politics respectively, tracing what happens when our everyday lives as workers, individuals, and citizens become organized around living in competition. The fourth chapter examines how neoliberalism turns everyday life into a "hustle," where all the contexts of daily life become animated by the demands of neoliberal labor. At stake here are the ways in which we are all hustling to get by, yet we stay radically divided from one another along lines of gender, race, and class thanks to the norm of self-enterprise. The next chapter hones in on what it feels like to inhabit enterprise culture by exploring neoliberal affect and the care of the self. As we already know, living in competition breeds widespread anxiety, not to mention depression and illness, making self-care an ongoing, pressing problem of everyday life. While neoliberal culture offers us plenty of tools for self-care that ultimately keep us stuck in our self-enclosed individualism, this chapter also considers how self-care might be a site for resistance and political intervention. The final chapter focuses on neoliberal politics, tracing what happens to citizenship and social action in our contemporary conjuncture. As we'll see, neoliberalism privatizes our political horizons by remaking democracy into a market competition for visibility and equality.

Throughout this mapping of the neoliberal conjuncture, we will engage in a mode of critical work that will, hopefully, enable you to *unlearn* neoliberalism and thus begin to write new stories about our conjuncture—including both our commonalities and differences—and the alternative worlds we are yearning for. Indeed, our critical work will only matter to the extent that it opens up our individual and collective horizons to a future beyond living in competition.

NOTES

1 Institute for Precarious Consciousness, "We Are All Very Anxious," *Plan C*, April 4, 2014, www.weareplanc.org/blog/we-are-all-very-anxious/

2 Institute for Precarious Consciousness, "We Are All Very Anxious."

3 AnaLouise Keating, *Transformation Now!: Toward a Post-Oppositional Politics of Change* (Champaign: University of Illinois Press, 2012), 171.

4 Keating, *Transformation Now!*, 171.

5 See Raymond Williams, *Keywords: A Vocabulary of Culture and Society Revised Edition* (Oxford: Oxford University Press, 1983), 87–93.

6 Lawrence Grossberg, "Cultural Studies: What's in a Name," in *Bringing It All Back Home: Essays on Cultural Studies* (Durham: Duke University Press, 1997), 257.

7 Grossberg, "Cultural Studies," 257.

8 See Keating, *Transformation Now!*, 175–182.

9 Jeremy Gilbert, www.radicalphilosophy.com/obituary/stuart-hall-1932–2014

10 Keating, *Transformation Now!*, 170.

11 Keating, *Transformation Now!*, 169.

12 Keating, *Transformation Now!*, 175.

13 Michel Foucault, interview by Didier Eribon, "Is it really important to think?" *Libération*, May 30–31, 1981.

14 Sara Ahmed, "Losing Confidence," *feministkilljoys*, March 1, 2016.

15 Henry A. Giroux, "Beyond Dystopian Visions in the Age of Neoliberal Authoritarianism," *Truthout*, Novermber 4, 2015, www.truth-out.org/opinion/item/33511-beyond-dystopian-visions-in-the-age-of-neoliberal-authoritarianism

Part I

Critical Foundations

1

A NEW HEGEMONY
THE RISE OF NEOLIBERALISM

CHAPTER OVERVIEW

At this point, you might have a sense of what neoliberalism is, but you're probably still fuzzy on the details. This chapter starts to clear things up by charting the making of our neoliberal conjuncture. By tracing the history and development of neoliberalism, we will learn how competition came to be the driving force in our everyday lives. Specifically, we will examine the rise of **neoliberal hegemony** in four phases.

Table 1.1 Four Phases of Neoliberalism

Phase I	1920–1950	*Theoretical innovation*
Phase II	1950–1980	*Organizing, institution building, and knowledge production*
Phase III	1980–2000	*Crisis management and policy implementation*
Phase IV	2000—Present	*Crisis ordinariness and precarity*

As we will see, neoliberalism is far from natural and necessary; rather, it represents a clear political project that was organized, struggled for, and won.

A NEW HEGEMONY

We begin our investigation with a historical account of the rise of neo-liberal hegemony. Hegemony is a concept developed by Italian Marx-ist Antonio Gramsci. Gramsci was keen to account for the definitive role that culture played in legitimizing and sustaining capitalism and its exploitation of the working classes. In our own context of extreme economic inequality, Gramsci's question is still pressing: How and why do ordinary working folks come to accept a system where wealth is produced by their collective labors and energies but appropriated individually by only a few at the top? The theory of hegemony sug-gests that the answer to this question is not simply a matter of direct exploitation and control by the capitalist class. Rather, hegemony pos-its that power is maintained through ongoing, ever-shifting cultural processes of winning *the consent* of the governed, that is, ordinary people like you and me.

In other words, if we want to really understand why and how phe-nomena like inequality and exploitation exist, we have to attend to the particular, contingent, and often contradictory ways in which culture gets mobilized to forward the interests and power of the ruling classes. According to Gramsci, there was not one ruling class, but rather *a historical bloc*: "a moving equilibrium" of class interests and values. Hegemony names a cultural struggle for moral, social, economic, and political leadership; in this struggle, a field—or assemblage—of prac-tices, discourses, values, and beliefs come to be dominant. While this field is powerful and firmly entrenched, it is also open to contestation. In other words, hegemonic power is always on the move; it has to keep winning our consent to survive, and sometimes it fails to do so.

Through the lens of hegemony, we can think about the rise of neo-liberalism as an ongoing political project—and class struggle—to shift society's political equilibrium and create a new dominant field. Specifically, we are going to trace the shift from liberal to neoliberal hegemony. This shift is represented in the two images below.

Previous versions of liberal hegemony imagined society to be divided into distinct public and private spheres. The public sphere was the purview of the state, and its role was to ensure the formal rights and freedoms of citizens through the rule of law. The private sphere included the economy and the domestic sphere of home and family.

For the most part, liberal hegemony was animated by a commitment to limited government, as the goal was to allow for as much freedom in trade, associations, and civil society as possible, while preserving social order and individual rights. Politics took shape largely around the line between public and private; more precisely, it was a struggle over where and how to draw the line. In other words, within the field of liberal hegemony, politics was a question of how to define the uses and limits of the state and its public function in a capitalist society. Of course, political parties often disagreed passionately about where and how to draw that line. As we'll see below, many advocated for laissez-faire capitalism, while others argued for a greater public role in ensuring the health, happiness, and rights of citizens. What's crucial though is that everyone agreed that there *was* a line to be drawn, and that there was a public function for the state.

As Figure 1.1 shows, neoliberal hegemony works to erase this line between public and private and to create an entire society—in fact, an entire world—based on private, market competition. In this way, neoliberalism represents a radical reinvention of liberalism and thus of the horizons of hegemonic struggle. Crucially, within neoliberalism, the state's function does not go away; rather, it is deconstructed and reconstructed toward the new end of expanding private markets. Consequently, contemporary politics take shape around questions of how best to promote competition. For the most part, politics on

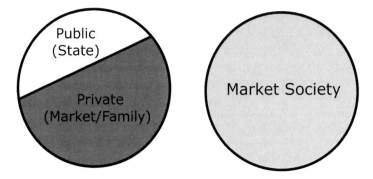

Figure 1.1 Liberal vs. Neoliberal Hegemony

both the left and right have been subsumed by neoliberal hegemony. For example, while neoliberalism made its debut in Western politics with the right-wing administrations of Ronald Reagan and Margaret Thatcher, leaders associated with the left have worked to further neoliberal hegemony in stunning ways. As we will explore in more depth below and in the coming chapters, both U.S. presidents Bill Clinton and Barack Obama have governed to create a privatized, market society. In other words, there is both a left and a right hegemonic horizon of neoliberalism. Thus, moving beyond neoliberalism will ultimately require a whole new field of politics.

It is important to see that the gradual shift from liberal to neoliberal hegemony was not inevitable or natural, nor was it easy. Rather, what we now call neoliberalism is the effect of a sustained hegemonic struggle over the course of the twentieth and twenty-first centuries to construct and maintain a new political equilibrium. Simply put, neoliberalism was, and continues to be, struggled over, fought for, and won.

In *Masters of the Universe: Hayek, Friedman, and the Birth of Neoliberal Politics,* Daniel Stedman Jones charts the history of the neoliberal project in three phases. The first phase saw the development of neoliberal ideas and philosophies in Europe during the years between World War I and World War II, as a relatively small group of economists (including most notably those from Austria, Germany, and France), wrestling with the rise of fascism, communism, and socialism, sought to envision a new liberal society that would protect individual liberties and free markets. The second phase was a period of institution building, knowledge production, and organizing that enabled neoliberalism to cultivate a powerful base in culture and politics, especially in the U.S. and United Kingdom. During this phase, neoliberalism developed into a "thought collective" and full-fledged political movement. In the third phase, neoliberal ideas migrated from the margins to the center of political life as they came to shape global trade and development discourse, as well as the politics of powerful Western democracies. As suggested by the theory of hegemony, none of these phases were neat and clean; each was shot through with struggle and contingency.

I am adding a fourth phase, which is the focus of this book. Here neoliberalism is not only a set of economic policies and political discourses, but also a deeply entrenched *sensibility* of who we are and can become and of what is possible to do, both individually and collectively. It is what Raymond Williams called "a structure of feeling." Thanks to a convergence of different social, economic, and cultural forces, which we will explore throughout the following chapters, competition has become fully embedded in our lifeworlds: it is our culture, our conjuncture, the air we breathe. More specifically, this fourth phase is characterized by widespread precarity, where crisis becomes ordinary, a constant feature of everyday life. As we will learn in coming chapters, we are prompted to confront the precarity neoliberalism brings to our lives with more neoliberalism, that is, with living in competition and self-enclosed individualism.

PHASE I: THEORETICAL INNOVATION

The Crisis of Liberalism and the Birth of the Social Welfare State

Neoliberalism emerged out of the crisis of liberalism that ultimately came to a head in the early twentieth century. It is crucial to understand that liberal hegemony was never a coherent, unified phenomenon. Rather, it developed around a central political antagonism. On one side were those who championed *individual liberty* (especially private property rights and free markets) above all else. They argued against government intervention in private life, especially in the market. On the other side, social reformers believed that government should be pursued for the *common good* and not just for individual liberties. In the decades leading up to the Great Depression, it became clear that the individual-liberty side, which had long been dominant, was inadequate for managing huge transformations in capitalism that were underway. These transformations included industrialization, urbanization, and internationalization, as well as the rise of large-scale corporate firms that squeezed smaller market actors. Huge gaps formed between the political-economic elite, the middle classes, and the poor. Simply put, liberalism was in crisis.

During this time of social, cultural, and economic upheaval, those espousing the common good gained political ground. Specifically, the misery and devastation of the Great Depression solidified the gains for social reformers, opening a new era where a new, common-good liberalism began to prevail. In the United States, President Franklin

Roosevelt's administration passed a comprehensive set of social policies designed to protect individuals from the unpredictable and often brutal operations of capitalism. These included the following:

Reforming banking: The Glass-Steagall Act of 1933 set up regulatory agencies to provide oversight to the stock markets and financial sector, while enforcing the separation of commercial banking and speculative investment. Simply put, banks couldn't gamble with your savings and future.

Strengthening labor: In 1935, the National Recovery Administration and the National Labor Relations Act were passed to recognize labor unions and the rights of workers to organize. At the same time, the administration spurred employment through the Public Works Administration, the Civil Works Administration, and the Works Progress Administration, while guaranteeing workers a dignified retirement with the Social Security Act of 1935.

Promoting housing: A range of programs, policies, and agencies were established, including the Federal Housing Administration and the U.S. Housing Authority, to encourage homeownership and provide housing to the poor and homeless.[1]

Taken together, these policies marked the birth of the so-called social welfare state, albeit one that was limited in scope and often highly exclusionary in practice. For example, a universal health care program was never realized. Many social groups, including African-Americans, migrant farm workers, and women, were prohibited by law from receiving federal benefits such as social security or unemployment.[2] Additionally, institutional racism plagued (as it still does) housing and banking institutions.

The Walter Lippmann Colloquium and the Birth of Neoliberalism

It is helpful to trace the emergence of our neoliberal conjuncture back to this moment where the common good was starting to win the day via the establishment of a limited and exclusionary social welfare state. For, despite the fact that these social welfare policies effectively "saved" capitalism from destroying itself, the individual-liberty side was deeply troubled. They feared that a new hegemony was on the rise, one that represented a threat to their core values of individual liberties, private property, and free markets. To the individual-liberty side, all of these social policies and demands smelled a lot like socialism, and they were determined to combat them with a new liberal hegemony of their own. So, in 1938, American author and political commentator Walter Lippmann organized a gathering of twenty-six leading liberal thinkers in Paris to discuss and debate the fate of **individual-liberty liberalism** in the current context. In addition to Lippman, key players included leading Austrian economists Friedrich Hayek and Ludwig von Mises, French intellectuals Louis Rougier and Jacques Rueff, and German economists Alexander Rüstow and Wilhelm Röpke.

The term *neoliberalism* was originally coined here at the Walter Lippmann Colloquium and referred to a new form of individual-liberty liberalism that was at once anti-common good *and* anti-laissez-faire. It is so important to see that this new form represented a key theoretical and political innovation. For, in previous versions of individual-liberty liberalism, laissez-faire was dogma: the only way to protect private property and market freedom from the state was to limit the powers of the state. Neoliberalism flipped the script by imagining an active, interventionist state actively working not in the interests of the common good, but in the interests of free markets.

While neoliberals agreed generally on the need for this "new" liberalism, they were not so united on what these new modes of state intervention on behalf of markets should look like. Some neoliberals (including Von Mises and Hayek) remained radically individual-liberty-oriented in their approach; for them, the state's only interventionist role should be to construct and enforce a robust legal framework for regulating and protecting private enterprise and market competition. However, others thought that the state also had a *social* role to play, particularly the German "ordoliberals," who were writing in the context of the social, political, and economic devastation borne of Nazism. While the former group prioritized economic growth at all costs, the latter believed the state must consider and work to mitigate potentially destructive market effects by constructing a social environment that would help to integrate people into the new market society. They advocated for the promotion of community and believed that political efforts to construct a market society needed to be more holistic and totalizing, targeting the social as a whole.[3]

These political tensions at the heart of neoliberal theory live on today and are embodied within recent political struggles and debates, for example, around health care reform. The Affordable Care Act, also known as Obamacare, represents an ordoliberal approach, where the government has an active role to play in creating a fully marketized society. Indeed, the Affordable Care Act (ACA) sought to extend coverage to all by *mandating* that everyone participate in a private health care and insurance market. The ACA also set up—that is, actively constructed—exchanges to facilitate market processes and competition. Those who opposed Obamacare did so on the grounds that government's role is not primarily social; it's simply to protect and police market competition. What's crucial to see here is that neoliberalism has come to define our political horizons, both left and right. Indeed, what was never on the table was a non-market, common-good approach (i.e., a socialized, single-payer system).

From its philosophical beginnings then, neoliberalism was far from a coherent thing. Rather than a consistent idea, we might say that neoliberalism represented a *new image of liberal political thought*—a new way to imagine, know, reason about, and thus govern society. In this way, the importance of Phase I cannot be underestimated. Even though ideas and politics were contained to a small group of political-economic elite, neoliberalism would not have been born without a space for critical theorizing and philosophical debate. Ironically however, while neoliberalism emerged out of radical critique of the existing hegemonic field, it seeks to systematically shut down these sorts of critical intellectual spaces for ordinary citizens, as we will see in coming chapters.

PHASE II: ORGANIZING, INSTITUTION BUILDING, AND KNOWLEDGE PRODUCTION

Embedded Liberalism

The impact of the Walter Lippmann Colloquium was limited due to World War II. However, soon after the war, Hayek took up the torch and established the Mont Pelerin Society (MPS) in 1947 to continue the work of dreaming up a new individual-liberty liberalism. At this point, neoliberalism was still swimming upstream, as the postwar era ushered in a new conjuncture that David Harvey calls **embedded liberalism**. Embedded liberalism was premised on a "class compromise" between the interests of workers and those of capitalists. In the name of peace, general prosperity, and global capitalism, a hegemonic consensus emerged "that the state should focus on full employment, economic growth, and the welfare of its citizens, and that state power should be freely deployed, alongside of or, if necessary, intervening in or even substituting for market processes to achieve these ends."[4] A central piece of the embedded liberal compromise was the Bretton Woods Accord, which attempted to stabilize the global economy by re-fixing currency rates to the gold standard. The idea was that national economies shouldn't be threatened by currency speculation in the financial markets. All this meant that an infrastructure emerged to protect citizens' economic and social security. To ensure the common good, capitalism must be embedded within "a web of social and political constraints."[5]

Neoliberalism developed largely as a coordinated political response to the hegemony of embedded liberalism. As Harvey explains, it was a project "to disembed capital from these constraints."[6] Indeed, the struggle for neoliberal hegemony waged a robust and successful class war on the "compromise" of embedded liberalism by developing, promoting, and implementing a new version of individual-liberty liberalism.

The Neoliberal Thought Collective

As the system of embedded liberalism was taking root and establishing its dominance in national and international affairs, neoliberals were working on the ground: creating think tanks, forging political alliances, and infiltrating universities. During this second phase, neoliberalism emerged as a "thought collective": a "multilevel, multiphase, multi-sector approach to the building of political capacity to incubate, critique, and promulgate ideas."[7] The **Neoliberal Thought Collective**, as Philip Mirowski coined it, was a vertically integrated network of organizations and people focused on radically shifting the hegemonic field through the production and dissemination of new knowledges and approaches aligned with their new individual-liberty liberalism.

Mirowski shows that the Neoliberal Thought Collective was structured as a "Russian Doll" as it was organized into different shells. At the center was the MPS, which operated as a private, members-only space where like-minded thinkers and political agents gathered to debate, prioritize, and organize. The MPS was funded in large part by affluent Americans and worked to nurture and direct relationships between different institutions and organizations associated with the neoliberal project. As Stedman Jones notes, at the intimate gatherings of the MPS, participants came to feel a part of a broader historical movement.

The Neoliberal Thought Collective developed around its center with different institutional layers providing protection and resources for its radical hegemonic project. Academic economic departments constituted a vital shell, as neoliberalism became dominant in a handful of important institutions, including the University of Chicago and George Mason University in the United States and the London School of Economics and St. Andrews in the United Kingdom. In addition to rooting itself in universities, neoliberalism also constructed a powerful cultural base via a bevy of charitable and philanthropic foundations dedicated to supporting neoliberal policies and approaches. These included the Volker Fund, the Earhart Foundation, the Relm Foundation, the Lilly Endowment, the John M. Olin Foundation, the Bradley Foundation, and the Foundation for Economic Education. Many of these foundations actively participated in the MPS, supporting their meetings and the activities of key figures.[8] More broadly, these organizations were able to promote and extend the neoliberal project under the rhetorical cover of charitable do-gooding, shaping the field of civic action by setting social priorities and investing in particular sorts of research and program development.[9] The final shells were think tanks such as the American Enterprise Institute and the Hoover Institute, which provided timely position papers and talking points for allied politicians and talking heads for media outlets. Crucially, this Russian Doll structure allowed the class origins and political agendas of neoliberalism to remain invisible, as neoliberalism found its way into the hegemonic field via seemingly neutral knowledges, programs, ideas, and prescriptions.

A New Historical Bloc

It is important to understand that the Neoliberal Thought Collective did not develop in a vacuum; rather, it was operating within, capitalizing on, and helping to construct particular historical dynamics at work in the postwar context. Put differently, this comprehensive and coordinated project of institution building and knowledge production took shape within broader political realignments and shifting cultural contexts. Ultimately, these historical conditions gave rise to opportunities that would eventually come to provide the Neoliberal Thought Collective with the political support needed to win consent for its new hegemony.

Particularly, in the postwar United States, a new conservative political scene emerged that united anti-communists, traditionalists (Christian, social conservatives), and neoliberals. What ultimately united these groups was their shared distaste for the cultures of embedded liberalism and the common-good sensibilities that defined the 1950s and 1960s. Anti-communists fought vigorously against anything that had a whiff of collectivism. Consequently, unions eventually went from being popular institutions for working people to allegedly dangerous organizations infiltrated by communists. Traditionalists, on the other hand, were motivated to oppose the rise of the counterculture and social movements for racial, gender, and sexual liberation. Concerned first and foremost with preserving traditional values and social order, this part of the bloc was deeply disturbed by demands for downward redistribution of resources and cultural power to women, people of color, and queer folk, as these demands promised to upset established social norms and roles. Finally, neoliberals were focused, of course, on dismantling the social welfare state, undoing the class compromise of embedded liberalism, and advancing their own global economic interests. All of these groups shared a belief that democracy, in one way or another, had gone too far. The antidote, conveniently provided by neoliberalism, was a return to the values of the free market. Strong alliances were actively forged between Christian ministries and free marketeers, while anti-communism provided a broad and flexible ideological umbrella for these organizing efforts.[10]

As we will soon see, this gelling of anti-communist, socially conservative, and neoliberal interests and values against embedded liberalism was immensely consequential, for it signaled the emergence of a new historical bloc that underwrote and facilitated the rise of neoliberal hegemony.

The Crisis of Embedded Liberalism and the Rise of Neoliberal Practice

At the same time that a new historical bloc was cementing against the social welfare state, the broader political-economic landscape was breeding widespread discontent with the status quo. While the postwar period initially was characterized by economic growth and prosperity, especially for the white working/middle classes, general economic downturn during the late 1960s and 1970s undermined optimism and spread disillusionment. Once again, liberalism was in crisis, and, thanks to the work of the Neoliberal Thought Collective, neoliberal ideas started to bubble up as a viable alternative to embedded liberalism. As Stedman Jones explains,

> The end of the Bretton Woods international monetary system, two oil price shocks in 1973 and 1979, the Vietnam War, the Watergate break-in at the Democratic Party headquarters in Washington, D.C., at the behest of senior figures of the Nixon administration and with the president's complicity in its cover-up, Britain's International Monetary Fund (IMF) loan of 1976, the virtual collapse of British and industrial relations, and the failure of the prices and incomes policies that were supposed to fight inflation in both countries all created a policy vacuum into which neoliberal ideas flowed.[11]

Specifically, Harvey traces the origins of neoliberal practice to the 1970s when neoliberal policy solutions were first experimented with in two very different contexts. First, there was the bloody U.S.-backed military coup in Chile. On September 11, 1973, the Central Intelligence Agency (CIA) partnered with the Chilean army to overthrow the democratically elected president Salvadore Allende, whose socialist agenda represented a major threat to U.S. political and economic interests in the country and region. The result of the coup was the brutal dictatorship of General Augusto Pinochet, whose regime was responsible for the countless deaths of people associated with the left, including activists, students, and unionists. When faced with rebuilding the country's economy, Pinochet turned to Chilean business elites who had supported him during the coup and their Chilean economist friends who had trained at the University of Chicago under Milton Friedman. Pinochet embarked on an aggressive, neoliberal-inspired restructuring of the Chilean economy, privatizing vital industries and state services and opening the country to foreign capital investment.

The second initial experiment with neoliberalism was what Harvey describes as the financial coup in New York City. The city was in major debt, and the banks decided that they were no longer going to roll the debt over. Instead, investors took financial control of the city and its budget and governed to ensure that their bondholders were paid. Consequently, the city had to cut expenditures by laying off workers and gutting social programs, including its public health services and education systems. City University of New York, for example, was tuition-free up until the financial coup. As Harvey explains,

> The 1970s was, if you like, a moment of revolutionary transformation of economies away from the embedded liberalism of the postwar period to neoliberalism, which was really set in motion in the 1970s and consolidated in the 1980s and 1990s.[12]

These two early examples are crucial to understanding the rise of neoliberal hegemony. Neoliberalism was not simply a new historical bloc; nor it was political dogma. Rather, neoliberalism emerged onto the political stage as a highly flexible set of ideas, prescriptions, and policies that could be applied in a time of uncertainty, when the field of action was suddenly opened for experimentation. In other words, neoliberalism is what Aihwa Ong calls a "mobile technology." According to Ong, neoliberalism is not "a fixed set of attributes with predetermined outcomes"; rather, it is "a logic of governing that migrates and is selectively taken up in diverse political contexts."[13] As a mobile technology, neoliberalism can be adapted to meet the demands and exigencies of any emergent situation. Thus, in practice, neoliberalism looks, and plays out, differently depending on where it's being implemented. This mobility is perhaps the defining feature of neoliberal hegemony, as this is what enables neoliberalism to be so expansive and resilient.

CRITICAL PRACTICE

- What do Phase I and II teach you about your own political commitments? Are you an individual-liberty liberal, a common-good liberal, both, or neither? Why?
- Draw a picture of the Neoliberal Thought Collective's "Russian Doll" structure. Now consider a particular political issue that we face (i.e., climate change, education, unemployment). How might the issue get shaped for public debate and action by the *networks* and *organization* of the thought collective?

PHASE III: CRISIS EXPLOITATION, POLICY IMPLEMENTATION, AND THE RISE OF A NEW HEGEMONY

Structural Adjustment

As represented in Figure 1.2, during the third phase of its historical development, neoliberalism migrated from the radical fringes to the mainstream center of politics through the ongoing exploitation of crisis.[14] As neoliberal public intellectual Milton Friedman put it in a famous essay:

> only a crisis—actual or perceived—produces real change. When that crisis occurs, the actions that are taken depend on the ideas that are lying around. That, I believe, is our basic function: to develop alternatives to existing policies, to keep them alive and available until the politically impossible becomes politically inevitable."[15]

As we saw above in Chile and New York, thanks to the Neoliberal Thought Collective, neoliberal ideas and advocates were "lying around," readily available. Naomi Klein calls neoliberalism's exploitation of crisis the **shock doctrine**. When a crisis emerges and everything is on the table, use uncertainty, devastation, and fear as an opportunity to enact radical political-economic change all at once. In other words, give folks what Friedman called "the shock treatment."

The Rise of Neoliberal Hegemony

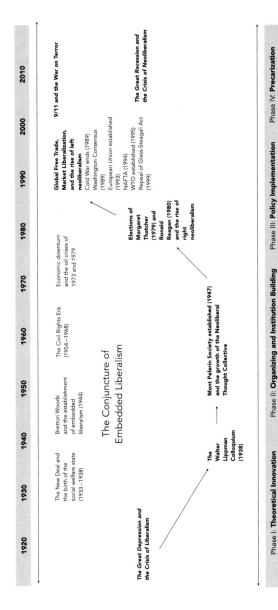

1920	1930	1940	1950	1960	1970	1980	1990	2000	2010

The New Deal and the birth of the social welfare state (1933–1938)

Bretton Woods and the establishment of embedded liberalism (1944)

The Civil Rights Era (1954–1968)

Economic downturn and the oil crises of 1973 and 1979

Global Free Trade, Market Liberalization, and the rise of left neoliberalism
Washington Consensus (1989)
European Union established (1993)
NAFTA (1994)
WTO established (1995)
Repeal of Glass-Steagall Act (1999)

9/11 and the War on Terror

Cold War ends (1989)

The Great Recession and the Crisis of Neoliberalism

The Conjuncture of Embedded Liberalism

The Great Depression and the Crisis of Liberalism

The Walter Lippman Colloquium (1938)

Mont Pelerin Society established (1947) and the growth of the Neoliberal Thought Collective

Elections of Margaret Thatcher (1979) and Ronald Reagan (1980) and the rise of right neoliberalism

Phase I: **Theoretical Innovation**   Phase II: **Organizing and Institution Building**   Phase III: **Policy Implementation**   Phase IV: **Precarization**

Figure 1.2 The Rise of Neoliberal Hegemony: A Timeline

As Klein explains, Friedman believed that "the speed, suddenness, and scope of the economic shifts would provoke psychological reactions in the public that 'facilitate the adjustment.'"[16]

The effects of the shock doctrine were felt most sharply, at least initially, outside of the West, as proponents of neoliberalism gradually infiltrated the World Bank and International Monetary Fund, global monetary institutions who were founded in the aftermath of the devastation of World War II to help stabilize and grow struggling economies through loans, technical expertise, and other development programs. If a country was in deep trouble, the International Monetary Fund (IMF) and World Bank were to provide resources to ward off the impending crisis. These institutions were important components of embedded liberalism and the Bretton Woods system, as they were imagined to be central ingredients in spreading capitalist democracy and creating a sustainable international peace. Importantly, these institutions never lived up to their mission, as they remained beholden politically to the most powerful nations and their own economic interests.

In the wake of decolonization and the winding down of the Cold War, the focus of the IMF and World Bank had turned to Latin and South America and Africa, as well as Eastern Europe. At the same time, neoliberal advocates, especially those associated with the Chicago School of Economics, had set up shop at the World Bank and IMF, working to realign the core logics, principles, and practices of development. In this way, neoliberalism shifted the terrain of global development policy away from modernization and stabilization to **structural adjustment**. This new approach to development, often referred to as "the Washington Consensus," demanded that, in return for desperately needed loans and other assistance from the World Bank or IMF, states must adopt and implement an aggressive free market agenda, rapidly structurally adjusting their economy in accordance with the principles of neoliberalism. Simply put, states could not pursue a common-good politics, much less an actual socialist agenda; in order to survive, they were forced to pursue an agenda aligned with the interests of global capitalists. Ultimately, as Klein explains, structural adjustment meant that the IMF and World Bank became administrators of shock and crisis rather than absorbers of shock and crisis.

Right Neoliberalism and Trickle-Down Economics

While the Washington Consensus was cohering and gaining ground within international institutions, neoliberalism arrived on the political stage of Western power centers with the elections of right-wing politicians Ronald Reagan in the United States (1980) and Margaret Thatcher in the United Kingdom (1979). Reagan and Thatcher rode into political power on the backs of a series of financial and social crises mentioned in the previous section. In a period of widespread distrust of government and economic downturn, Reagan and Thatcher offered up a new liberal vision based on rolling back the social welfare state and promoting individual responsibility and self-governance.

In his first inaugural address, Reagan famously proclaimed,

> In this present crisis, government is not the solution to our problem; government is the problem. From time to time we've been tempted to believe that society has become too complex to be managed by self-rule, that government by an elite group is superior to government for, by, and of the people. Well, if no one among us is capable of governing himself, then who among us has the capacity to govern someone else? All of us together, in and out of government, must bear the burden. The solutions we seek must be equitable, with no one group singled out to pay a higher price.

The crux of the argument was that if capital accumulation was freed from the state, its social obligations, and its governing elites, wealth would "trickle down" organically to those who worked hard and merited it.

In practice, these trickle-down theories of wealth and freedom demanded aggressive government action on behalf of private markets. Remember that the neoliberal state is not a laissez-faire state, but an interventionist state that works to actively promote and construct a free market society. Indeed, Reagan and Thatcher dramatically slashed taxes on the rich and cut social programs with the promise that this massive redistribution of income from public coffers to private ones would eventually result in greater prosperity for the average worker. Both also worked hard to break the power of organized labor, while reorienting the management of the economy away from the promotion of full employment for the citizenry, which demanded a large public works sector, to the much less social and much more technical control of inflation through monetary policies and institutions.

We cannot underestimate just how radical all of these policies were. They aimed to shred both the "web of social and political constraints" and the "class compromise" at the heart of embedded liberalism. In this way, the rise of **right neoliberalism** and trickle-down economics was also a practice of structural adjustment.

The Criminalization of Poverty and the Rise of the Neoliberal Police State

It is crucial to understand that consent for Reagan and Thatcher's radical new liberal hegemony was won in large part through the manufacturing of a social and cultural crisis: specifically, a crisis of crime. Although crime was down in the late 1970s, neoliberalism successfully articulated the need for a new liberalism rooted in individual liberty and responsibility to an alleged epidemic of black criminality. Pointing to poor, prominently black "ghetto communities," neoliberals argued that the welfare state had created an entrenched culture of poverty, violence, and crime. Rather than point to racist housing policies and white flight, the loss of manufacturing jobs due to globalization, and the widespread divestment both of these trends brought about, neoliberals argued simply that the common-good approach had failed. Instead of equality and uplift, the welfare state has generated subjects of entitlement and dependency. In other words, poor communities didn't need more resources like good jobs, well-supported schools, safe housing, or accessible health care; what they needed was discipline: good old-fashioned law and order. More policing. Harsher sentences. More prisons. Heightened social control. As they told the story, poor communities were filled with "thugs" and "welfare queens," people who had no interest in hard work, were incapable of self-government, and simply wanted to game the system. Wealth didn't deserve to trickle down to them.

Reagan, in fact, helped to invent the figure of "the welfare queen"; as early as 1964, he was circulating stories of black women abusing welfare, and these racialized and gendered narratives of welfare state dependency became central to his eventual presidential bids. It is important to see this campaign rhetoric was part of a broader political strategy pursued by the Republican party. In the wake of the Supreme Court decision *Brown vs U.S. Board of Education* and the passage of the Civil Rights and Voting Rights Acts, southern politicians abandoned the Democratic party in droves, as Republicans adopted a "Southern Strategy" for electoral success built on what Karen Fields and Barbara Fields call "racecraft."[17]

Racecraft refers to the ways in which race has been constructed to rationalize systems of economic exploitation. In other words, according to the concept of racecraft, race was never a biological reality, but a cultural phenomenon that was socially constructed to serve the broader political-economic ends of capitalism. For example, the *purpose* of slavery was not white supremacy; it was profit. White supremacy was the means of rationalizing the economic system that required large amounts of free labor in order to accumulate value. Similarly, the crisis of black criminality emerged as a rationale for neoliberalism's political-economic agenda of gutting social welfare programs and transferring huge amounts of wealth to corporations. Indeed, from the perspective of neoliberalism, it might seem to make more sense to simply dismantle welfare altogether; however, images of welfare queens perform key cultural work. These figures channel anger, displacing blame for global capitalism and the rise of the neoliberal hegemony onto black culture, thereby dividing working people by fueling racial resentments and obscuring shared economic conditions.[18]

Ultimately then, neoliberalism emerged as a successful political project in large part because it waged a class war through criminalizing a racialized poor. Through the racecraft of the crisis of crime, neoliberalism was able, in one fell swoop, to criminalize poverty and racialize the welfare state, thereby winning consent for its new liberalism even though the vast majority of white working- and middle-class folks were not poised to benefit from trickle-down economics and its dismantling of welfare-state policies that had actually worked to their benefit (and largely against poor folks of color) throughout the previous decades.

It is vital to see that, while the criminalization of black poverty rationalized the rolling back of the social welfare state, it simultaneously authorized the rapid expansion of a racialized police state. There is no clearer illustration of this neoliberal police state than the War on Drugs. Prior to neoliberalism, policing was predominantly the purview of state and local authorities. As Michelle Alexander details in

The New Jim Crow: Mass Incarceration in the Age of Colorblindness, in 1980, when Reagan ramped up the War on Drugs, local authorities were not necessarily sold on the idea; they were interested in more serious crimes than those associated with the circulation and use of illegal drugs, which had always been around and were actually on the decline. The federal government, however, created a system to incentivize *local* departments to prioritize the *national* War on Drugs. It provided much-needed resources in the form of money, bodies, training, and equipment (i.e., weapons), essentially bribing local agencies to engage in aggressive policing of poor communities in the name of rooting out illegal drugs. Alexander shows exactly how these practices and policies worked to turn thousands upon thousands of predominantly black and brown, non-violent drug users into demonized criminals. As the numbers consistently show, illegal drug use is just as prevalent in wealthier, white communities.[19] However, as we will learn in the following chapters, the fundamental purpose of the neoliberal police state is to manage the growing numbers of disposable people and populations created by trickle-down economics.[20]

Free Trade, Corporate Diversity, and the Rise of Left Neoliberalisms

Neoliberalism's hegemonic dominance began with right neoliberalism (a.k.a., the openly racist, anti-union administrations of Reagan and Thatcher). However, Democratic president Bill Clinton cemented neoliberalism as our new hegemonic frontier by creating a more progressive, left neoliberal political horizon.

Emboldened by the end of the Cold War and the expanding opportunities for global profiteering it opened up, elites of all political stripes got behind a wide-ranging agenda of free trade and market liberalization. Most notably, in 1994, Clinton signed the North American Free Trade Agreement (NAFTA), which resulted in millions of lost manufacturing jobs in the United States, as companies were incentivized to move operations south of the border, where workers and natural resources could be exploited and appropriated on the cheap. While post-Cold War free trade agreements promised greater prosperity through global competition, NAFTA was devastating, especially for workers and small farmers in both the Global North and South. Clinton also signed into law the repeal of the Glass-Steagall Act. As discussed above, this law was enacted in the wake of the Great Depression to protect consumers. Its repeal broke down the wall between investment and commercial banking, freeing up the financial industries to pioneer highly speculative forms of value production and economic exploitation, which ultimately led to the Great Recession of 2008.

However, despite the terrible consequences of market liberalization for a majority of people across the world, it is important to see that Clintonian neoliberalism represented a new, seemingly more progressive political horizon. This left version of neoliberalism was cosmopolitan and claimed to be inclusive, as it actively embraced certain forms of racial and cultural difference. Indeed, while Reagan and Thatcher had openly exploited discourses of black criminality, Clinton's neoliberalism was couched in more congenial rhetoric of a "third way": a middle path between the harsh policies of the Reagan and Thatcher and common-good approaches associated with the left. These seemingly more progressive policies mixed *social liberalism* with the *fiscal discipline* of structural adjustment.

On one hand, this period of aggressive market liberalization led to an embrace of market-oriented ideals diversity and inclusion. After all, competition in a global economy required workers who were sensitive to cultural, ethnic, and national differences. Workplaces needed to reflect the diversity of the world; they needed to be inclusive places lest they fail in the new economy. Universities and major corporations thus developed diversity programs, while an industry of diversity consultants and experts emerged. This embrace of diversity was also reflected in popular culture, as marketers and cultural producers sought to capitalize on these new discourses of social equality through niche marketing and the commodification of difference. Put a little differently, as we explore in Chapter 6, **left neoliberalism** represents a very different form of racecraft, whereby the progressive embrace of racial and cultural difference works to legitimate and garner consent for neoliberal hegemony and its new world order of global market liberalization.

However, at the same time that left neoliberal discourses of diversity and difference were proliferating, poor people, who are disporportionately people of color, were still being subjected to incredibly and increasingly harsh policies connected to ongoing, deeply racialized discourses of crisis and criminality. Indeed, while Reagan initiated a full-scale War on Drugs, it was the Clinton Administration who dramatically exacerbated its devastating consequences for poor communities with the passage of the Violent Crime Control and Law Enforcement Act of 1994. The largest crime bill in history, the Act rapidly expanded mass incarceration by extending policing operations and implementing harsh sentencing guidelines, while simultaneously eliminating public programs for inmates. As we will learn, we cannot separate neoliberalism's left, progressive face—its embrace of diversity, free trade, and global markets—from its right face—the punishing policies that have been, and continue to be, exacted on poor people, especially poor people of color. They are both part and parcel of neoliberal hegemony.

Resistance

It is crucial to note that the rise of neoliberal hegemony was met with resistance, especially when it came to global trade policy. Not everyone consented to the neoliberal hegemonic field, as its devastating effects were immediately felt throughout the world, especially in the Global South. On January 1, 1994, the day that NAFTA went into effect, the Zapatista Army of National Liberation (EZLN), comprised of indigenous rural folks who were poised to suffer even more than they already had under new global trade regimes, declared war on the Mexican neoliberal state. They occupied towns across Chiapas in hopes of fomenting democratic revolution against global capitalism. Although they fell short of revolution, the Zapatistas helped to inspire a wave of international resistance to neoliberal hegemony. In Western countries, for example, new political alliances began to develop between the labor and environmental movements, as neoliberalism's shock doctrine provided new common ground. After all, a large share of the "web of social and political constraints" neoliberalism set out to free itself from had to do with labor and environmental protections. These new alliances were in force in 1999 at the so-called Battle in Seattle, where tens of thousands of people gathered to protest the World Trade Organization, an international institution empowered to regulate global trade and enforce the interests of the global capitalist class. However, this burgeoning resistance, with its new alliances and new global common-good vision, was overrun by the mother of all crises: 9/11.

PHASE IV: CRISIS ORDINARINESS AND PRECARITY

9/11 and Perpetual War

We might say that the events of September 11, 2001, opened up an ongoing crisis, a permanent state of emergency and war, into which neoliberal interests and ideas could flow. The threat of another terrorist attack authorized a vast expansion of state power over all citizens (i.e., the Patriot Act and its unprecedented legalization of state surveillance), while providing a rationale for ongoing preventive war, as defending the homeland demanded aggressive state action and intervention. Consider, for example, the Iraq War, where fighting terror become an opportunity to structurally adjust Iraq, as well as U.S. government. On one hand, under U.S. occupation, the Iraqi state was auctioned off to global investors and firms. Similar to New York in the 1970s, financial agents wrote and implemented policy in their own interests, while local officials and organizations were prevented from caring for an Iraqi public devastated by war. In this way, the Iraqi people's shock therapy was arguably even harsher than previous experiments. At the same time, the Iraq War also allowed for further structural adjustment of the U.S. political economy. In the name of national security, the neoliberal state handed out massive contracts to private security companies like Halliburton to manage war and provide services to the troops. These companies make billions of dollars off public contracts, maintaining a privatized military force while simultaneously draining non-national security related budget lines, thereby helping to further starve public infrastructures and programs. Combatting the crisis of terrorism demanded financial austerity and shared sacrifice, both in terms of social resources and political rights. So, while the Iraq War is now largely discussed as a disastrous mistake and foreign policy failure, from the perspective of neoliberal hegemony, it actually accomplished a lot in terms of promoting private enterprise and market competition.[21] At the same time, it rapidly expanded the contours and powers of the neoliberal police state.

Crisis Ordinariness and the Generalization of Precarity

As suggested by this brief discussion of the Iraq War, the interminable crisis of the War on Terror has become a central process of furthering neoliberal hegemony and creating a global, privatized market society. This privatized, global society fueled by crisis is characterized by extreme violence, both at home and abroad—from secret drone strikes against alleged enemy combatants to militarized police forces increasingly empowered to turn on communities and citizens.

I want to suggest that this generalization of violence and crisis is entangled with the normalization of a crisis sensibility in our everyday lives. After decades of the Neoliberal Thought Collective and its exploitation of crises, the new individual-liberty hegemony has become deeply entrenched in our everyday experiences and sensibilities. We live in a world animated by what Lauren Berlant calls "crisis ordinariness."[22] Violence, both global and everyday, is increasingly unexceptional. Folks are insecure, broken, living on the brink, traumatized by life itself. It feels like, at any moment, something could go wrong, and often it does. People feel, and are, vulnerable, concerned about the smallest of failures or mistakes and their potential reverb.

Put differently, our neoliberal conjuncture is often associated with what many scholars call precarity. Generally speaking, precarity describes the dynamics of work and everyday life in the global neoliberal economy where the "web of social and political constraints" has been shredded beyond repair and, with it, fantasies of the good life and the myth of the American Dream. Unions, jobs-for-life, and the security and benefits these brought with them for at least some workers are gone. Workers today are constantly subject to threats such as downsizing, layoffs, and plant/branch closures. One's livelihood, and thus life, is constantly under threat.

It is important to point out that precarity is nothing new for so many marginalized, oppressed, and exploited populations who have long been forced to live their lives under constant and often far more intense forms of threat. We should thus be careful in how we understand the relationship between neoliberalism and precarity. Isabell Lorey argues that there are in fact three dimensions of the precarious. First is the precariousness of life itself. Regardless of how much we might try to fight it, we are dependent upon and vulnerable to others and the environments we inhabit. Precariousness thus refers to a shared existential condition of simply being alive and in relations of interdependence with others. However, it is crucial to see how this shared precariousness is segmented: some lives are deemed valuable and thus deserving of social protections, while others are regarded as less valuable and thus unworthy of safety and security. **Precarity**, the second dimension of precariousness, refers to the social, political, cultural, and economic processes by which society unequally distributes security and exposure to risk. For example, consider environmental racism. Research shows that poor, predominantly black populations are far more likely to be exposed to risks associated with pollution, toxic waste, and natural disasters. Deemed disposable, these communities are not considered worthy of social protection.[23]

While precarity is operative in most of modern historical contexts, **precarization** is specific to neoliberalism. Lorey developed the concept of precarization to capture the ways in which neoliberalism advances through the generalization of precarity; it works to distribute insecurity and risk across the entire social spectrum.[24] Now everyone is subject to precarity. Thus, precarity becomes a shared condition, although it still differentially distributed along lines of class, race, ability, gender, nationality, geography, and so forth. For example, in 2005 all residents of New Orleans were affected by Hurricane Katrina and the breach of the levees, which was owed in large part to the decline of public investment in our material infrastructures. Still, poor, black communities bore the brunt of the impact both before and after the storm thanks to longer histories and practices of racial exploitation and marginalization. Indeed, precarity looks and feels different depending on your social location and position. For middle- and upper-class folks lucky enough to have a familial safety net and social capital, precarity might figure primarily as a steady stream of anxiety and uncertainty about the future. For poor, working-class people who do not have access to privatized social protection like inherited wealth, precarity probably figures more prominently as a deeply material and economic threat to confront day in and day out.

Ultimately, the theory of precarization is meant to account for how neoliberalism governs us all through insecurity. By dismantling the institutions and infrastructures of the welfare state, neoliberalism brings increasing vulnerability and volatility, both material and affective, to more and more people's everyday lives, while actively inciting them to live in competition with friends, neighbors, and their social and natural environments. In this way, precarization ensnares us all in a vicious circle. Certainly, no one really wants to live with intensifying degrees of social and economic insecurity; however, the only viable response to precarity is to compete harder for seemingly scarce resources to guarantee your own security and fate, which only intensifies the bad feelings and unbearable realities of neoliberalism. After all, as discussed in the Introduction, the idea that we can manage, much less control, global and environmental risks on our own is quite absurd and bound to end in frustration, hopelessness, and failure. What is more, do we really want to live a life of denied social connection? Neoliberalism prompts us to set out into the world in competition, to strive to win and achieve security all on our own. However, these goals ultimately undercut what enables our lives—our social and material infrastructures, our health, and our relationships with others. They incite us to assume, impossibly, more and more responsibility for things we can't possibly be held responsible for. At the same time, they diminish our capacities for coming together, caring for ourselves and others, and organizing collectively by forcing us to live in competition.

Disaffected Consent and the Crisis of Neoliberalism

A new world has been won, and we are all suffering its consequences, as neoliberal precarization wages a class war on most all of us that extends into the depths of our subjectivities, affects, and capacities. As we will explore in the coming chapters, folks are incited by neoliberal culture to respond to precarization and its ongoing class war on all by turning inward and investing in individual dreams and private life projects. While right and left neoliberals fight over how to better marketize society, folks hustle through their days, working hard to put on a happy face, striving, above all, for resilience, to stay afloat, to keep competing.

While this all might sound incredibly depressing and hopeless, at this point, it is important to think back to the paradox of neoliberal culture discussed in the Introduction. As powerful as neoliberalism is, it is just as tenuous. See, what is unique about neoliberal hegemony is that it banks on what Jeremy Gilbert calls **disaffected consent**. Folks are deeply dissatisfied with the neoliberal status quo, yet they acquiesce nonetheless.[25] It's not like we actively, eagerly consent to this highly unequal, violent, and crisis-laden world. It's more like we don't sense a choice or an alternative, so we just keep on paddling along in our self-enclosed individualism, hoping against hope for some measure of security, certainty, and protection.

Mark Fisher calls this disaffection **capitalist realism**.[26] We can't imagine, much less act on, a reality other than the neoliberal status quo. We fully internalize Thatcher's insistence that "there is no alternative"—that capitalism is the only reality so we've reached the "end of history"—even though we are all anxious and angry with the way things are. But here's the thing: while precarization and crisis ordinariness might make us feel like we have everything to lose, we actually have very little to lose (except for our disaffected consent) and everything to gain.

As we explore in the Conclusion, our neoliberal conjuncture is in crisis. As we saw with previous hegemonies like laissez-faire and embedded liberalism, big fissures and fault lines are bound to emerge as political-economic realities shift and new political antagonisms develop. For example, think about the Great Recession of 2008 and its mass destruction. The neoliberal state bailed out large banks deemed "too big to fail," leaving individuals, families, and communities too small to matter to deal with the fallout on their own. Folks lost their livelihoods, their homes, and their futures. However, while disaffected consent allows neoliberal hegemony to keep churning, it is also clear that folks are primed for new stories and new worlds, as evidenced by the rise of the Tea Party, the Occupy movement, and the movement for black lives.

Our task is to develop critical resources for political intervention in this crisis—for writing new stories that will enable us to bring new, more interconnected and egalitarian worlds into being. Thus, in the following chapters, we explore not only the powers and workings of neoliberal hegemony, but also possibilities for transforming disaffected consent into collective social doing. However, before we can begin this vital work, we need to be clear on exactly what we are up against. While we now have a critical understanding of neoliberalism's history, we need to understand more precisely neoliberal thought.

CRITICAL PRACTICE

- How does the theory of hegemony ask us to understand the relationships between economic, cultural, social, and political forces? What does this theory contribute to our project of conjunctural, interconnectivist critique?
- What does our investigation of the rise of neoliberal hegemony teach us about how social transformation happens? How has this chapter confirmed and/or challenged your ideas about political struggle and change?
- What most surprised you in this history of neoliberalism's rise? What are the key historical and critical insights that you will take with you?
- What are your everyday experiences of precarity and precarization? How might these differ from those of others who don't occupy your social position?
- Does Gilbert's theory of disaffected consent hit home? If so, where and how do you experience this in your everyday life? How might the theory of disaffected consent help us to write new stories about our social world?

NOTES

1 Daniel Stedman Jones, *Masters of the Universe: Hayek, Friedman, and the Birth of Neoliberal Politics* (Princeton: Princeton University Press, 2012), 25–26.
2 Stedman Jones, *Masters of the Universe*, 25–26.
3 Pierre Dardot and Christian Laval, *The New Way of the World: On Neoliberal Society* (New York: Verso, 2014), 79.
4 David Harvey, *A Brief History of Neoliberalism* (Oxford: Oxford University Press, 2007), 10.
5 Harvey, *Neoliberalism*, 11.
6 Harvey, *Neoliberalism*, 11.
7 Philip Mirowski, *Never Let a Serious Crisis Go to Waste: How Neoliberalism Survived the Financial Meltdown* (New York: Verso, 2013), 43.
8 Stedman Jones, *Masters of the Universe*, 170.
9 Mirowski, *Never Let a Serious Crisis Go to Waste*, 44; Stedman Jones, *Masters of the Universe*, 169.
10 See Stedman Jones, *Masters of the Universe*, 134–179.
11 Stedman Jones, *Masters of the Universe*, 215.

12 Sasha Lilley, "On Neoliberalism: An Interview with David Harvey," http://mrzine. monthlyreview.org/2006/lilley190606p.html

13 Aihwa Ong, "Neoliberalism as a Mobile Technology," *Transactions of the Institute of British Geographers*, 32 (2007): 3–8. doi:10.1111/j.1475–5661.2007.00234.x

14 I am grateful to Aaron Donahue and Jordan Palmer for their work on the timeline.

15 Naomi Klein, *The Shock Doctrine: The Rise of Disaster Capitalism* (New York: Picador, 2007), 6.

16 Klein, *Shock Doctrine*, 7.

17 Karen E. Fields and Barbara J. Fields, *Racecraft: The Soul of Inequality in American Life* (New York: Verso, 2014).

18 See Patricia Ventura, *Neoliberal Culture: Living with American Neoliberalism* (New York: Routledge, 2016), 87–106.

19 See Michelle Alexander, *The New Jim Crow: Mass Incarceration in the Age of Colorblindness* (New York: The New Press, 2012), 59–96.

20 See Loic Wacquant, *Punishing the Poor: The Neoliberal Government of Social Insecurity* (Durham: Duke University Press, 2009).

21 See Ventura, *Neoliberal Culture*, 107–133; Klein, *The Shock Doctrine*.

22 Lauren Berlant, *Cruel Optimism* (Durham: Duke University Press, 2011).

23 Isabell Lorey, *State of Insecurity: Government of the Precarious* (New York: Verso, 2015), 10–15.

24 Lorey, *State of Insecurity*, 1–2, 10–15.

25 Jeremy Gilbert, "Disaffected Consent: That Post-Democratic Feeling," *Soundings* 60 (Summer 2015): 29–41(13)

26 Mark Fisher, *Capitalist Realism* (Winchester, UK: Zero Books, 2009).

2

NEOLIBERAL TRUTHS AND CONSEQUENCES
THE FOUR *D*s

CHAPTER OVERVIEW

The goal of this chapter is to help you get a firm handle on neoliberal thought—particularly how neoliberalism understands the market, the state, and the human, and the wide-ranging critical consequences of these theories and the truths they construct.

The first section explores neoliberal "truths," addressing the questions: What exactly do neoliberals believe? What philosophical ideas and concepts undergird and inspire neoliberal politics? What are neoliberalism's assumptions about people, markets, and society? It is important to take these questions seriously. Proponents of neoliberalism shouldn't be written off as evil conspirators out to wreck the world. Rather, we must confront their ideas and seek to understand how they think. Neoliberalism has become the water in which we swim. We may not agree with the policies or politics associated with the rise of neoliberal hegemony, but we are all neoliberal subjects, in a sense, trying to stay afloat in neoliberal seas. The only way we're going to be able to stop "dog-paddling" around and swim against the current is if we fully grasp the forms and movements of the waves we're up against.

In the second section, we'll turn our attention to the economic, political, and social consequences of neoliberal thought. More specifically, we'll consider what I call **the four Ds**:

- **Dispossession**: The accumulation of wealth through stealing vital resources from people.
- **Disimagination**: The destruction of our capacities for critique and radical thinking.
- **De-democratization**: The undoing of democratic ideals, institutions, and desires.
- **Disposability**: The relegation of individuals and populations to social death.

As we'll see, neoliberal truths can be very seductive, but the four Ds should give us great pause, as they throw into sharp relief what's at stake in the rise of neoliberal hegemony and the critical analysis of our conjuncture.

TRUTHS

As we saw in the previous chapter, neoliberalism emerged in its first phase as a *new image of liberal thought*, that is, a new way of imagining, knowing, and governing society. Put differently, neoliberalism constructed a new **social ontology**. Ontology refers to the philosophical study of being, existence, and relationality. Social ontology thus refers to the philosophical study of social being: to the conditions of society's existence and the relations that constitute it. To say that neoliberalism created a new social ontology is to say that it was a deeply theoretical and philosophical project, one that sought to radically reorient how we imagine and, thus, study society, including what we know about ourselves and others, how we think about politics and government, as well as the social fabric that threads our lives together. Specifically, neoliberal thinkers were keen to create a social ontology that would delegitimate and dismantle the social welfare state that emerged in the aftermath of the Great Depression. At the Walter Lippmann Colloquium and meetings for the Mont Pelerin Society, neoliberals worked to develop the contours for this new social ontology rooted in generalized competition and private enterprise.

Thanks to the rise of neoliberal hegemony over the course of the twentieth century, this new social ontology has become the unquestioned, taken-for-granted foundation for our social and political imaginations. In other words, **neoliberal social ontology** has become a **regime of truth**. According to Michel Foucault, every historical conjuncture is defined by a set of socially constructed "truths" that structures what we can know and how we therefore come to order society. Regimes of truth are so entrenched and powerful that they cannot be readily challenged or questioned. In other words, a regime of truth presents what is, in actuality, a socially constructed set of ideas to be the Truth. As Truth, these ideas seem natural and immobile; they seem to transcend history, culture, and politics, appearing as neutral and right. Foucault explains it this way:

> Truth isn't outside power. . . . Truth is a thing of this world; it is produced only by virtue of multiple forms of constraint. And it induces regular effects of power. Each society has its regime of truth, its 'general politics' of truth; that is, the types of discourse which it accepts and makes function as true.[1]

We can distill the neoliberal "general politics" of truth as follows:

- The individual's freedom to choose in the market is the highest, and in fact the only, form of freedom.
- Market competition is the best way to order and govern society.
- Individuals are personally responsible for their lives and outcomes, not the powerful structures that govern them.

In what follows, we will unpack neoliberalism's regime of truth by delving into the heart of its new social ontology, which is represented in Table 2.1. Specifically, we will consider neoliberalism's reconstruction of "truth" about the market, the state, and the individual.

Table 2.1 Liberal vs. Neoliberal Truths

Liberal Truths	Neoliberal Truths
Market	
Exists as a separate private sphere	Exists as a spontaneous order
Guided by an invisible hand	Acts as giant information processor
Operates according to the principle of exchange	Operates according to the norm of competition
Premised theoretically on equality among market actors	Premised theoretically on the inequality among market actors
State	
Exists as a separate public sphere	Is embedded in Empire and global market competition
Acts as a protector of society	Acts as a privatizing machine for corporations
Governs to ensure the rights of individual citizens	Governs to construct the conditions for competition
Human	
Humans are agents of knowledge and reason	Humans are ignorant
Humans are economic, social, and political beings	Humans are only economic beings
Individualism is premised on the possession of rights and property	Individualism is premised on speculation on one's human capital

THE MARKET: FROM INVISIBLE HAND TO INFORMATION PROCESSOR

Undergirding the neoliberal regime of truth is a new ontological understanding of the market. For neoliberals, the market is the omniscient and infallible basis of society, if, and this is key, it is actively constructed as such. Thus, for neoliberals, the market was no longer an "invisible hand" working naturally on its own, but it was *a social reality to be shaped and constructed* through the promotion of competition and private enterprise.[2]

Liberal political economist Adam Smith famously used the idea of the invisible hand to describe the workings and benefits of the market.

According to Smith, individuals pursuing their self-interest in the market would naturally result in a good and just society, so there was little need for state interference in the economy. The idea of the market as an invisible hand was used as a central justification for laissez-faire, individual-liberty liberalism discussed in the previous chapter. However, neoliberals think of the market differently: not as an invisible hand, but as a giant information processor whose knowledge vastly outpaces what the state or the individual could ever hope to know.[3]

Rather than viewing the market as a distinct private sphere operating according to natural laws, neoliberal social ontology views the market as the context for all of social life and thus as the medium of all social knowledge and truth. Here's how the information processor works. Private individual activities are vital input for the market. If we want a good society, we need to let the market determine what's good and useful based on all the "data" it processes. The implication here is that the market, as a giant information processor, always knows more and knows best.

This theory of the market as a giant information processor represents, first and foremost, a rejection of Keynesian economics. John Maynard Keynes, arguably the most influential economist of the twentieth century, believed that with the right information and the requisite technical expertise, educated public servants had the power to address society's ills. The architect of Bretton Woods and embedded liberalism, Keynes pioneered macroeconomic analysis (the study of the economy as a whole as opposed to the study of individual markets) and championed government intervention in and regulation of the economy. Neoliberals were deeply skeptical of Keynesianism and its utopian impulses toward what they called "social engineering." For example, neoliberal thinker Karl Popper explained,

> What I criticise under the name of Utopian engineering recommends the reconstruction of society as a whole, i.e. very sweeping changes whose practical consequences are hard to calculate, owing to our limited experiences. It claims to plan rationally for the whole of society, although we do not possess anything like the factual knowledge to make good such an ambitious claim. We cannot possess such knowledge since we have insufficient practical experience in this kind of planning, and knowledge of facts must be based upon experience.[4]

Keynesianism claimed to be able to direct society toward specific ends, such as full employment, through knowledge and management of the economy as a whole. Neoliberalism's theory of the market as a giant information processor instead insists that the market cannot be known, managed, or planned, but that it rather must be allowed to develop "freely" through private enterprise and competition. In contrast to Keynesian "utopian social engineering," neoliberals thought that economic policy must be responsive to specific outputs of the information processor and vigilantly attuned to the shifting needs of the market. The government of the market must therefore be shielded from democratic processes and common-good ideals and put in the hands of expert economists who are the only ones capable of constructing and regulating free market environments.[5] Indeed, one of the most striking features of neoliberal hegemony is the degree to which the government of the market has been removed from political consideration and democratic deliberation.

Spontaneous Order

Animating this vision of the market as a giant information processor is a deeper theory of society: the idea that the market provides a **spontaneous order**. Neoliberals argue that what holds society together is not a particular principle or core culture, but rather economic relations and activities themselves, that is, the market. Through the market, resources of all sorts get distributed organically, providing a spontaneous social order based on market truth and knowledge.[6] Accordingly, the market must not be tethered by a specific end (full employment) or directed toward a common purpose (social protection and security). Rather, it must be allowed to develop freely through competition and private enterprise.

For neoliberals, the market emerges through subjective processes. The market does not follow objective laws of nature; it is not readily predictable, much less controllable. Rather, it develops organically through the behaviors of situated individuals pursuing their own subjective ends. Crucially, these subjective processes can only be realized through the imposition of competition.[7] In neoliberalism, competition must be generalized as a social norm in order to produce the conditions for a spontaneous, market-driven order—that is, in order for the information processor to work.

In this way, neoliberalism breaks with earlier liberal political-economic thought. While competition certainly figured as a key component in earlier liberal theories, it was not the foundation of the invisible hand of the market. Smith's theories of the market were rooted in the general principle of exchange: markets worked efficiently and produced positive outcomes because actors were engaging in mutually beneficial exchanges of goods and services. Crucially, in the eyes of the invisible hand, actors were, theoretically at least, equal parties in the exchange process. However, in contrast to the principle of exchange, competition is not premised on equality between market actors. Rather, competition is premised on inequality. Inequality is baked into the system through the norm of competition as a necessary and even ideal consequence of the market's information processing. Equality is not something that should be guaranteed by the state or by a common principle. It is something that we must earn, or more precisely win, through competition.[8] Put a little differently, neoliberalism has us **competing for equality** in the market.

Let me try to illustrate the neoliberal idea of the market with an example. Consider social media crowdsourcing platforms like GoFundMe (See Figure 2.1). Here, individuals, families, and/or communities can seek funding for pressing problems like a medical emergency or a business venture by uploading their needs or ideas into the digital platform.

Figure 2.1 GoFundMe Webpage

According to neoliberal truth, requests with inherent market value will organically garner the funding they deserve, while those that don't earn support simply weren't meant to be, as they have no "market value" as determined by the information processor. The underlying logic here is that the information processor of the market is capable of sorting what is good, just, and valuable from what is not. Clearly, the spontaneous order of GoFundMe hinges on inequality. It automatically produces winners and losers.

CRITICAL PRACTICE

- It is important to consider the implications of the neoliberal theory of the market as an information processor capable of producing a spontaneous social order. Let's return to the example above. Are some people's medical emergencies worthy of being addressed, while others' are not? Are some people's dreams and visions inherently more valuable than those of others? In the spontaneous order of GoFundMe, what ultimately determines one's value? Do you think that this is a fair and just way to organize our social world? Why or why not?

THE STATE: FROM NATIONAL PROTECTOR TO PRIVATIZATION MACHINE

One of the most prominent misunderstandings of neoliberalism has do with the neoliberal state. Many popular accounts represent neoliberalism as rolling back state powers. This view is not unfounded. After all, neoliberalism is responsible for gutting social welfare programs and regulations designed to protect and support citizens. However, while the state might appear to be withering away, it is actually changing form from a protector of society and citizens to a protector of corporations and free markets.

At the heart of neoliberal social ontology is a new vision of and role for the state: one that governs aggressively and exhaustively for spontaneous market order. To be clear, even though individual liberty is still very much a linchpin of the neoliberal project, we are far from the laissez-faire orientation of early individual-liberty liberalism that argued for a limited public state function. What's new about neoliberalism is that, while it remains committed to individual liberty, it argues for a new and expanded state that is defined not by a public function, but rather by a private one. The idea of public function for the state represents an opening for socialism and collectivism; it suggests that there is a general will or common good that should be taken into account. Indeed, neoliberals, though especially right neoliberals, are often wary of words like *social* and *society*, and even the idea of democracy, as these all have the potential to open up space for more socialist thinking and activism. These anti-social commitments are perhaps best encapsulated in Margaret Thatcher's famous saying that, "there's no such thing as society. There are individual men and women and there are families. And no government can do anything except through people, and people must look after themselves first." As Thatcher's words suggest, the very concept of society implies something greater than individuals to be considered and cared for by the state. The neoliberal state only recognizes atomized private units of enterprise and competition: individuals, families, and firms.

Put differently, a vital part of realizing neoliberalism's spontaneous order involves reinventing the state function along private, market-driven lines; the neoliberal state's role is not to tend to society as a whole, much less to care for citizens, but to actively *construct* the conditions for private enterprise and competition.[9] There is an important paradox at work here: the free market relies on an aggressive, interventionist state that works vigilantly to protect and secure the "free" development and growth of the market. Thus, neoliberal spontaneous order is defined by two competing state tendencies: state enforcement of rule of law for the market and the insistence on market freedom from state regulation and democratic process.[10]

Privatization and Global Competition

More specifically, the neoliberal state seeks to construct a market society through an aggressive agenda of **privatization**, that is, through the privatizing of public goods, state functions, and social ends. Broadly speaking, privatization encompasses a range of interrelated processes including the following:

1. *The marketization of once publicly controlled resources.* For example, neoliberalism opens up vital resources like communication infrastructures and water supplies to market forces, making the management of these resources subject to the logics and demands of global economic competition.
2. *The deregulation of industries.* More aptly understood as the re-regulation of industries for the benefit of private corporations, deregulation rewrites government oversight and restrictions to promote competition and free markets instead of the public interest or general welfare.
3. *The economization of social welfare.* Neoliberalism insists that markets hold the key to addressing social issues and ills; therefore, initiatives to address problems like education and poverty should be executed according to market logics like efficiency and consumer choice. Public programs should be privatized, while non-profit organizations should think of themselves, quite ironically, as economic enterprises engaged in market competition.

Ultimately, all of this privatization is about shifting the function of the state from a public to a private one. While the earlier liberal state was charged with the security and health of the nation, the neoliberal state is charged with global competition. The neoliberal state governs and is governed as market player in the global economy, relinquishing social welfare provision in order to advance its position in the global economy.

By shifting its function from a national public to a global private one, the state embeds itself in a global market order that it has little to no control over. In other words, the neoliberal state not only disciplines its citizens through privatization, but it also disciplines itself by similar means. The state does not belong to or respond to the dreams, desires, and needs of citizens; it is beholden to its "shareholders." In other words, the state becomes more like a corporation that must be understood and governed as such. It cannot be directed toward common ends or public goods; it must stay ensnared, for better or worse, in global competition.[11]

As Michael Hardt and Antonio Negri argue, in this new global market order, the liberal state's power changes, as it operates according to a new principle of sovereignty that they call **Empire**.[12] What separates this Empire from earlier imperialist projects like colonialism is that it is not directed by a *state* acting to expand its territory and wealth, but rather by global finance. As Nick Dyer-Witheford and Greig de Peuter put it, "Empire is governance by global capitalism."[13] Its key institutions include powerful nation-states acting as global competitors, multinational corporations, international economic institutions (i.e., the World Trade Organization, the International Monetary Fund, stock exchanges), and the institutions of global governance (i.e., the United Nations and transnational non-governmental organizations). Empire works through these administrative networks of institutions and agencies to construct, police, and manage global competition.

Personal Responsibility

While Empire might seem like a big, abstract system that has little to do with us, it is important to see that we can't separate neoliberal global political economy from the feelings and possibilities that animate our everyday lives. After all, privatization of the state's function would be impossible if individuals like you and me didn't accept more and more **personal responsibility** for our fates and fortunes in the course of daily living. Just think about it. The dismantling of the social welfare state and the construction of a new state committed to global market competition requires us to take on more and more social responsibility for the conditions of our lives, from our health to our education to our safety and security. We must be trained *not* to desire or expect certain social protections or public infrastructures. We must learn to take care of ourselves with private resources provided by the market and its spontaneous order. Thus, neoliberalism works to construct not only private markets, but also a culture of personal responsibility, where *individuals* feel compelled to take on more *social* responsibility for their lives. This culture of personal responsibility is perhaps most evident in the explosion of self-help in recent decades (a phenomenon we explore in Chapter 5). Everywhere we turn, it seems, we are bombarded with advice for how to better manage our lives on our own.

Lisa Duggan argues that privatization and personal responsibility are the central linchpins of neoliberalism, explaining that "The valorized concepts of *privatization* and *personal responsibility* travel widely across the rhetorics of contemporary policy debates, joining economic goals with cultural values [emphasis in original]."[14] In other words, neoliberalism's *cultural* emphasis on personal responsibility is part and parcel of the broader *political-economic* agenda of privatization. With its connotations of independence and hard work, personal responsibility seems like a commonsense, positive cultural value that we should all strive to embody in our lives. However, while we all bear some personal responsibility for our lives, neoliberalism's promotion of a culture of personal responsibility is harsh and unrealistic. It suggests that, regardless of station or circumstance, we, as individuals, should be fully responsible for what happens to us, even those things that are out of our control (like Empire!). If something bad occurs, look inward, not outward, for answers or redress. This applies not only for ourselves, but also for others. In turn, we are supposed to laud those who accept personal responsibility and scorn those who supposedly can't or won't achieve it.

Duggan's crucial point is that the neoliberal culture of personal responsibility masks the devastating consequences of privatization in two key and interrelated ways. First, it muddies the redistributive aims of privatization and its transferring of wealth and power from the public to private sector. In the name of personal responsibility, citizens look to empower themselves by disassociating with the social welfare state and embracing the private market. Second, personal responsibility *simultaneously obscures and intensifies* existing inequalities. If the social ills that befall folks can be attributed simply to individual shortcomings, there is no need to acknowledge the existence of *histories* and *structures* like racism, capitalism, or patriarchy, much less address them through public policies and programs. According to neoliberal truth, social problems are individual-level problems that require individual-level solutions. In the end, this individual-level thinking about broader social problems works to harm everyone, but especially historically oppressed groups that do not have inherited wealth and social privilege to fall back on. So, while personal responsibility might seem like a neutral, uncontroversial cultural value, in the context of neoliberalism, it becomes a vehicle of intensified oppression that renders this intensified oppression invisible and even impossible to articulate.

Believing in the idea that we, and others, are personally responsible for what happens to us is a central status-quo story of neoliberal culture.

This story makes it feel commonsensical and natural to not rely on the state—or broader infrastructures and social systems—and to attribute our successes or failures to our own private and individual market choices—not the root structures that determine our social positions in the first place. We can see the power of this status-quo story in the everyday life of Brandon, a young African-American man who had big dreams and did everything he was supposed to in order to be successful in life. As Jennifer Silva documents in *Coming Up Short: Working-Class Adulthood in the Age of Uncertainty,* Brandon worked hard in high school and college, eventually earning a bachelor's degree in criminal justice in hopes of landing a job as a police officer. However, despite all his efforts, Brandon had been unable to secure his dream job and instead found himself working in retail, $80,000 in debt. Unable to move his life forward in a meaningful way, Brandon had gone back to school, taking on more student loans, only to still find himself stuck. Understandably, folks like Brandon feel betrayed and resentful. Education, employers, and the American Dream had all let Brandon down. And yet, and this is so crucial to see, Brandon and other working-class folks in Silva's study still readily and eagerly accept personal responsibility for their lives, including especially their perceived failures and disappointments. Brandon feels that he could have done things better; if he had made different choices along the way, he might have been successful.[15]

CRITICAL PRACTICE

- Where do you feel the culture of personal responsibility at work in your own life? Can you think of examples when, like Brandon, you've worked to accept personal responsibility for events or outcomes that were ultimately out of your control? What specific stories did you tell yourself? What were the larger conjunctural forces structuring the situation that you let off the hook?

- Can you recall times when you've judged others according to the status-quo story of personal responsibility? What stories did you tell yourself about others' lives? What broader structures got obscured in your stories?

Brandon's—as well as our own—stories of taking personal responsibility for our lives in the face of entrenched inequalities and precarization are not surprising. As we will explore below and in the coming chapters, in neoliberal culture, we are surrounded by media representations and technologies teaching us that this is exactly what we're supposed to do.

THE HUMAN: FROM POSSESSIVE TO SELF-APPRECIATING INDIVIDUALISM

Perhaps the most radical facet of neoliberal social ontology regards the idea of what it means to be human actor. While Enlightenment thought heralded human subjects (specifically though, white men) as agents of history, capable of shaping their own destinies and mastering their social worlds through science and reason, neoliberalism posits that humans must be understood as fundamentally *ignorant*. They cannot know what is good, just, or of value, as, for neoliberals, human activity is no more than input into the information processor, which is the ultimate site of truth. In other words, humans should not be encouraged to understand, much less critique or try to change, their society. Rather, they should be trained for competition in the market. For only via competition can individuals realize their freedom, which, for neoliberals, means realizing their place and purpose in the unfolding of spontaneous market order.

We can think of this shift from the Enlightenment subject of reason to the neoliberal subject of ignorance as a new theory of what it means to be a rational and self-interested actor. According to Hayek, "the individual is not an omniscient actor. He is possibly rational . . . but above all ignorant."[16] Put a little differently, within neoliberal theory, reason and self-interest are reduced to "a certain type of knowledge directly utilizable in the market."[17] As Dardot and Laval explain, "The market process thus supposedly resembles a scenario in which isolate ignoramuses, by interacting, gradually reveal to one another the opportunities that are going to improve their respective situations."[18] Self-interest and reason are not conscious processes of knowing the world, but rather the spontaneous, organic outputs of interacting with, and obeying the laws of, the market.

Undergirding this insistence on ignorant self-interest is the belief that humans are nothing more and nothing less than **human capital**. We are capital investments, financial instruments—always and everywhere economic actors, locked in competition with others for market resources and position. Indeed, neoliberal truth is animated by Social Darwinism. It's all about survival of the fittest in the market. As we will explore later in this chapter, this vision contrasts sharply with democratic ideals that insist upon seeing humans as social and political animals driven to community and collective governing. As human capital, we don't need to know or think about anything other than our own market actions. Indeed, in spontaneous market order, what is required of humans is not social knowledge—that is, conjunctural understanding and critique of society—but simply market knowledge for competition.

Neoliberal social ontology is thus premised on, and actively promotes, a sort of *structural* ignorance. Like inequality, widespread ignorance becomes an ideal social condition.[19] Thus, as we saw in Chapter 1, neoliberals have no problem with tactics like propaganda or blatant misinformation campaigns. Keeping individuals ignorant is what ultimately protects the market from common-good-oriented regulations.

Self-Appreciating Individualism

The neoliberal idea of the self as human capital signals a new version of liberal self-enclosed individualism. Earlier forms of liberal subjectivity were based on a *possessive* relationship to the self: individuality and freedom were imagined to be premised on the possession of private property and individual rights. In early liberalism, society was imagined to be organized into distinct social spheres. The state was the sphere of politics and governing; the market was the sphere of production and exchange; and the family was the sphere of domesticity. The first two were masculine spheres, where rational individuals acted in their self-interest, while the latter was an emotional space of care and consumption associated with femininity. Thus, in its incarnation, liberal individualism was clearly a white, masculine, and bourgeois ideology; women, slaves, peasants, and other non-propertied groups were excluded from dominant conceptions of individualism. They had little access to property, enjoyed few, if any, rights, and were assumed to be incapable of reason and rational self-interest. Simply put, these groups were assumed to be incapable of acting as individuals; instead, they were possessions.[20] Social movements had to fight hard to expand the cultural, political, and economic horizons of liberal individualism. It is also important to note that the rise of mass consumption in the twentieth century was a fraught historical development when it came to liberal ideologies of individualism. Indeed, consumer culture was linked to the feminized private sphere and often associated with irrationality, excess, and the erosion of good, liberal citizenship, despite its central role in the emergence of contemporary global capitalism.

Neoliberalism represents a shift within liberal ideals of individualism, as it sees people defined not by their possession of property and rights, but by their status as human capital. Neoliberal individuals are selves who think of and relate to themselves as an investment, that is, as subjects who are constantly working to *appreciate* the self and its value over time. Ultimately then, neoliberal individualism involves a different relationship to the self: instead of a possessive relationship, it demands a *speculative* relationship.[21] Neoliberal subjects must always be betting on an unknowable future, always weighing potential risks and rewards, always asking themselves: Will this action appreciate or depreciate my human capital? The self-appreciating individual thus lives in constant existential uncertainty and instability. Freedom and success are not guaranteed by one's status as a citizen; instead, they depend on making good choices and the right investments across all of the increasingly marketized contexts of everyday life.

Consequently, neoliberal individualism is not connected to the specific social spheres of the market or the state. The neoliberal subject is focused solely on self-appreciation in all arenas of their lives. In other words, **self-appreciating individualism** turns life into a boundless project of growth. As human capital, the self is something that can always be further developed, expanded, maximized, and optimized. There is no endpoint, no arrival time, only a never-ending process of speculation. Self-fulfillment is impossible because there is always potential for more self-appreciation.

As we will explore more fully in later chapters, the imperative to self-growth and actualization in the market represents another powerful, and seductive, status-quo story of neoliberalism.

CRITICAL PRACTICE

There is perhaps no clearer example of the neoliberal theory of the human than the celebrity of Kim Kardashian West. Kardashian West is a media empire. She is the star of the long-running reality program *Keeping Up With the Kardashians*. She has her own game, *Stardom: Hollywood*—where you can "Start a new life as an aspiring actor . . . and go from nobody to A-list celebrity"—and, as we see here, her own emoji, Kimoji. She has tens of millions of followers on Twitter and Instagram, and in 2015, she released a coffee table book titled *Selfish*, which featured some of her most revealing and beloved selfies.

Kardashian West appears in popular culture as a seemingly ever-expanding brand. Yet, despite the success of her empire, Kardashian West is perhaps one of the most controversial pop culture figures of the day. For many, she is imagined to embody the very worst of popular culture. Initially catapulting to fame on a sex tape and sustaining that fame through relentless self-promotion and self-commodification, she is lamented for being idolized not for her talent or contributions to society, but for the sheer fact of her media celebrity.

In his famous study of early and mid-twentieth century stardom, Richard Dyer argues that,

> "We're fascinated by stars because they enact ways of making sense of the experience of being a person in a particular kind of social production (capitalism), with its particular organization of life into public and private spheres. We love them because they represent how we think that experience is or how it would

---

be lovely to feel that it is. Stars represent typical ways of behaving, feeling and thinking in contemporary society, ways that have been socially, culturally, historically constructed."[22]

Figure 2.2 Kimojis

In this way, stars articulate the tensions inherent in individualism, "shoring up the notion of the individual but also at times registering the doubts and anxieties attendant on it."[23]

- How do neoliberal theories of human capital and self-appreciating individualism help to explain cultural fascination with Kardashian West? At the same time, how does Kardashian West's celebrity register "doubts and anxieties" associated with these neoliberal truths? Based on the above discussion of self-appreciating and possessive individualism, what role might gender, race, and sexuality play in the circulation of these doubts and anxieties?
- How do neoliberal truths of self-appreciating individualism inform your own everyday life and practices of identity? Where and how do you relate to yourself as human capital? What "doubts and anxieties," if any, do you harbor about these neoliberal truths?

CONSEQUENCES: THE FOUR *D*s

If you haven't already noticed, there's a contradiction at the heart of neoliberal social ontology: in the name of individual freedom and spontaneous order, neoliberalism constructs an aggressive and disciplinary state and a fundamentally unequal society. Through its diffusion of competition into all of arenas of social life, it *forces* us to be certain types of individuals, and to exercise certain forms of market-based freedoms exacted by competition. Neoliberals think of this process as enforcing a *highway code*. They don't care where you go, so long as you keep going, stay on the road, and obey the laws. But if we can't get off the highway, how free are we? When freedom is constricted and coerced, is it still freedom? And what happens to those who can't or won't stay on the highway and obey its code?

We can interrogate the social, political, and cultural consequences of neoliberal truths and their paradoxes through what I call the four *D*s: dispossession, disimagination, de-democratization, and disposability. Each of these names processes that result from the adoption, application, and internalization of neoliberal truths.

DISPOSSESSION

Dispossession is perhaps the central consequence of neoliberalism, and it affects nearly everyone, from the poor to the comfortably middle class. Neoliberalism leads to widespread **accumulation by dispossession**, as the neoliberal state facilitates a vast and ongoing redistribution of resources from public to private coffers. The idea is simple: wealth and power are accumulated by a few in the act of dispossessing—that is, stealing from—the population at large. Of course, our status-quo stories aren't wont to call it "stealing," given the fact that it's perfectly legal. While accumulation by dispossession has always been central to capitalism (e.g., think about the land that was stolen from indigenous peoples in American capitalism's early stages), David Harvey identifies four forms specific to neoliberalism.[24]

1. As discussed in the previous chapter: *the creation, management, and manipulation of crisis*. Recall the structural adjustment approach to global development that results in the devastation of already struggling countries, while enriching global capitalists.
2. *The privatization and commodification of public resources and goods*. Ultimately, privatization results in a transfer of wealth and power from the public sector, which is accountable to all citizens, to the private sector, which is accountable to shareholders and the demands of profit maximization.
3. Neoliberalism also generates wealth for global elites through *state redistributions*, which gut budgets for social welfare programs to make room for greater tax breaks for corporations and expanded military budgets required to wage perpetual war. It also revises the tax code to benefit the rich (e.g., lowering taxes on capital gains). This form of accumulation by dispossession often goes by the name austerity: the public must tighten its belt and sacrifice security to feed the global economy.
4. Finally, perhaps the most profound and complex form of accumulation by dispossession specific to neoliberalism is

financialization. Thanks to the deregulation of the banking and financial sectors, finance has come to play a heightened role in the economy and our everyday lives. Freed up to engage in risky, predatory lending practices in the pursuit of profit, the global financial system becomes a hotbed of accumulation by dispossession. For example, the Great Recession of 2008 was precipitated largely by an elaborate, highly sophisticated, and deeply unethical program of selling bad mortgages to homeowners, then bundling these mortgages as securities and re-selling them on financial markets as sound investments. The peddlers of these bad products actively targeted minority and working-class consumers, as well as public pension funds. They made a killing betting *against* them, making much of their money when folks started to default. Accordingly, banks, hedge funds, and wealthy investors positioned themselves to profit by creating widespread misfortune for working people. It is so important to understand that what happened with the mortgage crisis was not the result of a few bad apples. Rather, it was a product of neoliberalism and the rise of financialization. Andrew Ross argues that we live in a **creditocracy**, a financial system set up to keep everyone indebted to the financial industries—to keep people in debt. The golden rule of the creditocracy is that creditors must be made whole and that debtors must always keep repaying. We saw these rules at work in the aftermath of 2008. Banks were regarded as "too big to fail" and bailed out by taxpayers. They were made whole, while the victims of predatory lending and fraudulent ratings were, by and large, left personally responsible to pick up the pieces on their own, inevitably taking on more and more debt to survive.

While Harvey focuses on the redistribution of economic resources in his account of accumulation by dispossession, we can also think of dispossession as a cultural and political process. The next two *D*s address these dimensions, articulating more fully how neoliberalism's project to create a privatized, market society creates an impoverished, unfree social world sorely lacking in resources for critical thinking, social interconnection, and political transformation.

DISIMAGINATION

Recall that neoliberal theory regards humans as fundamentally igno-rant when it comes to understanding (let alone critiquing) the social totality—which, for neoliberals, is the spontaneous order of the mar-ket. Consequently, education and knowledge must be directed away from critical modes of knowing to focus on the process of training human capital, that is, entrepreneurial subjects who will follow "the highway code" and live their lives as self-appreciating individuals.

Neoliberal culture thus operates as a "disimagination machine." According to Giroux, **disimagination**

> refers to images . . . institutions, discourses, and other modes of representation, that undermine the capacity of individuals to bear witness to a different and critical sense of remembering, agency, eth-ics and collective resistance. The 'disimagination machine' is both a set of cultural apparatuses extending from schools and mainstream media to the new sites of screen culture, and a public pedagogy that functions primarily to undermine the ability of individuals to think critically, imagine the unimaginable, and engage in thoughtful and critical dialogue: put simply, to become critically informed citizens of the world.[25]

In other words, disimagination systematically stamps out the desire and capacity for radical thinking. Radical thinking here does not refer to the ideas of the extreme left or right, but rather to the etymologi-cal sense of the word: getting to the "root" of things (the Latin *radix* or *radic* means "root"). Indeed, radical thinking gets to the root of the problems we face so that we might confront them in ways that would be transformative and just. Without going to the root, we find ourselves thrashing around the surface of neoliberalism's tumultuous seas, unable to imagine, much less build, alternative worlds.

We can think of disimagination as the social consequence of self-enclosed individualism and its status-quo stories. We are "disimag-ined" when we look to ourselves for answers to social problems or when we deny our interconnections with others in order to stay focused on the growth of our own human capital in the market. Instead of reaching for other worlds, disimagination prompts us to turn inward, taking solace in self-appreciating individualism, which only intensifies the power of neoliberal truths.

Ultimately, disimagination is what reduces us to ignorant "input" for the information processor, pawns in the spontaneous order of the market. In this way, disimagination is a pernicious form of cultural discipline and social control; it strips us of an open future, of potentialities for creating different worlds. For when we are disimagined, we lose the utopian impulse—that sensibility that another, better world is possible—and thus stay stuck in capitalist realism. This book is, first and foremost, about countering neoliberalism's disimagination machine.

CRITICAL PRACTICE

We're covering a lot of ground very quickly in the chapter, so let's pause and see if you can start to pull things together through critical analysis of a specific example from popular media culture. As mentioned earlier and explored more fully in Chapter 5, self-help discourses are a central facet of neoliberal culture. Consider this "life lesson" from Oprah Winfrey who, throughout her long and highly successful career, has embodied and promoted neoliberal truths like personal responsibility and

Figure 2.3 Oprah's "Life Lesson"

self-appreciating individualism. In this short video, Oprah Winfrey shares her story with her media audiences:

> We're ready to move on to what I think is another power lesson that I started to get when I was a really young girl, having been raised by my grandmother and then at six years old being separated from my grandmother and being moved to Milwaukee and suddenly in a foreign environment for myself. I remember walking into that new space and recognizing that, in many ways, I was alone, which is a terrible feeling if you are six years old. But I have always had the deep understanding for myself that if anything was going to move forward in my life. . . . I was going to have be responsible for making that happen. And I know that to be true now, and can articulate it as: You are responsible for your life. And if you're sitting around waiting for somebody to save you, to fix you, to even help you, you are wasting your time, because only you have the power to take responsibility to move your life forward. . . . It does not matter where you come from. I have seen people come out of a desert, walk across the desert, being born in the most dire circumstances. It doesn't matter what your mama did, whether she did or had a Ph.D. or no D. What matters is now, this moment, and your willingness to see this moment for what it is. Accept it. Forgive the past. Take responsibility and move forward.[26]

- How is Oprah's "life lesson" indicative of neoliberal social ontology? Consider how this video reflects neoliberal truths of spontaneous market order, privatization and personal responsibility, and self-appreciating individualism.
- What is the relationship between Oprah's "life lesson" and disimagination? What does this example teach us about consequences of neoliberal social ontology and its regime of truth? More specifically, what does disimagination do to our capacities for critique, social interconnection, and political intervention?

DE-DEMOCRATIZATION

The next D is what political theorist Wendy Brown calls **de-democratization**. As we saw in the previous chapter, from the military coup in Chile to the financial coup in New York City, from structural adjustment programs to the economic devastation of 2008, neoliberalism undermines the power of public institutions by transferring governance and authority to the political-economic elite and the financial institutions of Empire. Simply put, neoliberalism is anti-democratic: as Brown shows, it slowly unravels democracy by promoting new forms of market order and rule.

The 2010 U.S. Supreme Court decision *Citizens United* exemplifies the process of de-democratization. However, this is not simply because it treats global corporations as individuals with First Amendment rights, thereby empowering them to flood national elections with money, but also because *it treats democracy itself as a free market* that must be "protected" from the public. "Perhaps what is most significant about the *Citizens United* decision, then, is not that corporations are rendered as persons," Brown explains,

> but that persons, let alone a people, do not appear as the foundation of democracy, and a distinctly public sphere of debate and discussion do not appear as democracy's vital venue. Instead, the decision presents speech as a capital right and political life and elections as marketplaces.[27]

Put differently, Brown is deeply concerned that neoliberalism is "hollowing out" the foundations of democracy, transforming institutions of and capacities for collective governing into processes and extensions of market competition and private enterprise.

Brown argues that democracy in its basic form—what she calls bare democracy—stands for a simple idea: the people rule. " 'Democracy,'" Brown writes, "signifies the aspiration that the people, and not something else, order and regulate their common life through ruling themselves together."[28] Bare democracy does not specify a particular social organization or institutional form; it names a set of promises: "the possibility that power will be wielded on behalf of the many, rather than the few, that all might be regarded as ends, rather than means, and that all may have a political voice."[29] It is important to note that these promises have long gone unrealized; historically democracy has been fully compatible with systemic class, racial, and gender exploitation and oppression. Whole populations have been denied voice and political participation, treated as merely a means to someone else's end (think about slavery!). What is crucial, though, is that the unfilled promise of democracy spurs critique, sparks political imagination, and nurtures our capacities for collective doing and resistance. Bare democracy holds out the idea that people *should* have the power to determine their lives in common, so there's always a better world on the horizon that is waiting to be won. Brown's argument is that neoliberalism undoes "the demos," the idea that people should rule, including the promises for social change and the spaces for enacting democracy and realizing its promises.

Neoliberalism insists that humans are incapable of ruling themselves, of ordering their world in common; instead, it insists that their capacities for democracy, like their capacities for radical thinking and critique, need to be replaced with the capacity for competition and enterprise. Indeed, according to neoliberal thought, humans are not social, political animals driven to democracy, community, and justice. Rather they are to be regarded and governed as self-appreciating human capitals, "rendered as entrepreneurial, no matter how small, impoverished, or without resources."[30]

DISPOSABILITY

By generalizing competition to all arenas of social life and hollowing out democratic institutions and processes, neoliberalism creates a world premised on fundamental inequality. Individuals and populations who are not able to successfully compete in the market are regarded as "disposable." Welcome to the underbelly of spontaneous order and the final D: what Henry Giroux calls the **biopolitics of disposability.**

As Foucault argued, the rise of liberalism hinged on a new relationship between the state and the physical life of citizens, that is, on **biopolitics**. While the king's power had been exemplified by the right to "make die or let live," the authority of the liberal state rested on the opposite power: the power "to make live or let die." Liberalism thus targeted life itself; it was concerned with regulating and normal-izing the population through studying human beings and their vital lives. The aim of this government of life and vitality was to shape citizens' conduct, guiding them to live in ways that were imagined to be productive and useful to the nation. Those who were deemed unfit or un-useful were relegated to the margins of social life. Unworthy of full citizenship, they were subject to precarity. For example, the eugenics movement was a prominent biopolitical project that aimed to optimize the white race and relegated non-white bodies to the vul-nerable social status of "bare life." These bodies could be imprisoned, experimented on, and let to die by the state.[31]

What distinguishes *neoliberal* biopolitics is the way in which they oblige citizens, through imposing competition, to take personal responsibility for their lives. Thus, the biopolitical power to "make live or let die" increasingly falls on the shoulders of individuals who are "free" to optimize themselves *for* and *within* the market. Those who cannot care for themselves and grow their human capital are dis-posable: they can be let to die.

Indeed, as we will explore, neoliberalism draws hard and fast cul-tural distinctions between people who have value by virtue of their ability to accept personal responsibility and contribute to spontaneous market order and those who do not—between the winners who we are to worship and losers who we are to shame. Unworthy of sympathy, much less social investment, losers are relegated to social death: they have no economic value, so they don't count as citizens. In this way, neoliberalism creates a sadistic culture of cruelty, where rich people, regardless of their actions, are exalted for their wealth, and poor peo-ple are scorned, and sometimes even locked up or killed, just for being sick or in need of a place to sleep.

We see the biopolitics of disposability at work when

- Poor folks can be shot by police without conscience or consequence
- Bombing campaigns and drone strikes kill people whose deaths are written off as "collateral damage."
- Individuals and families, forced to flee their homes due to war or other horrendous circumstances beyond their control, are turned away at borders or abandoned in refugee camps.

- Post-industrial communities no longer valuable to the state are allowed to carry on without basic resources like clean, safe drinking water.
- Poor youth are deemed unworthy of an education and other forms of social investment.
- Undocumented workers are exploited, threatened, and abused by employers, while often reviled by the broader public for allegedly taking good jobs away from hard-working, good people.

We must connect the dots between the neoliberal biopolitics of disposability and the neoliberal linchpins of privatization and personal responsibility: if there is no public function for the state, and folks are personally responsible for their outcomes, then it logically follows that those who can't contribute to the private market simply just don't matter as human beings. They have not competed successfully for their equality, so they have "earned" their unequal biopolitical status. Indeed, while neoliberalism speaks incessantly of individual, personal responsibility, it is, in fact, working to intensify social hierarchies, as not all individuals have the wealth and social capital to successfully compete in the market as human capital. Some folks are more readily disposable thanks to their social position (i.e., race, gender, class, citizenship). As Giroux explains, in neoliberalism

> entire populations marginalized by race and class are now considered redundant, an unnecessary burden on state coffers and consigned to fend for themselves. This new biopolitics is marked by deeply existential and material questions regarding who is going to die and who is going to live, and represents an insidious set of forces that have given up on the sanctity of human life for those populations rendered 'at risk' by global neoliberal economies.[32]

It is important to see that neoliberal precarization works to create growing masses of disposable people, as it governs for Empire and global competition, and not for the security and health of the people themselves. As suggested in the previous chapter, the neoliberal state responds to this situation of growing **disposability** not by expanding social welfare programs and public safety nets, but rather by criminalizing poverty and stepping up its efforts in the areas of policing and social control. As the neoliberal state offloads more and more responsibility for survival to self-governing individuals and families, it also operates a vast and bureaucratic police state to manage the social insecurity it produces.[33]

More specifically, neoliberalism constructs a **criminal industrial complex** to *capitalize* on the biopolitics of disposability. In the starkest terms, the underlying logics of the criminal industrial complex work like this. When poverty is a crime, it becomes easy to produce criminals, as we saw with the War on Drugs in the first chapter. Once criminalized, poor people can be easily denied basic rights, empathy, and dignity, as they have no standing as citizens in a world where citizenship hinges solely on human capital. They can thus be readily exploited and dispossessed. In other words, despite their disposable status, criminals can nonetheless be made to generate value for the market. For example, prison populations are offered up as cheap labor to companies, while, at the same time, they are forced to pay outrageous prices for basic goods and services essential to their own survival while incarcerated. In this sense, the contemporary criminal justice system is not simply a system of social control; it also a system of accumulation by dispossession. It is set up to nickel and dime poor people by transforming them into criminals who can be directly exploited by corporations and the state. As disgusting as this is, it should not be surprising; this is what gets authorized when the state governs for markets and not people.

This all might sound extreme and hard to believe for those of you who haven't had to deal with the neoliberal police state. However, for so many of us, the criminal industrial complex is a punishing, daily material reality. For example, consider the everyday life of Natividad, one of the people featured in Matt Taibbi's *The Divide: American Injustice in the Age of the Wealth Gap*. Natividad came to Los Angeles undocumented at age fifteen from Sinaloa, Mexico. Her husband was eventually deported, leaving her to care for their six children. Jobless and poor, her family was evicted from their apartment and forced to live in a small van, getting meals once a day through a meal service. Natividad tried for months to receive help from the L.A. Department of Children and Family Services to no avail. Finally, she was able to get her kids into a shelter and eventually into a halfway house. However, one morning, she was pulled over by police, and her car was taken due to the fact that she didn't have a legal driver's license. The state had recently banned undocumented immigrants from obtaining legal licenses; what is more, it also had passed a special rule for cars seized from undocumented immigrants: they would have to pay an enormous fee to get it back, which Natividad was unable to pay. Her car was taken from her, and she was given an expensive ticket, which she couldn't pay either, so she had to do community service.

Natividad was able to get another car a couple years later, only to be stopped at a checkpoint and lose it again. A year later, she was able to save up enough money for a third car and was stopped once again, though now she owed thousands of dollars to the state for past violations. This time, she went to court hoping to find relief; however, the judge showed no mercy, and Natividad was given 170 hours of community service to complete. For weeks, she slaved away—getting up before dawn, completing a full day's work of community service before completing another full day's of work for pay, all the while trying to get her kids to and from school. Today, Natividad only takes the bus. Even her kids, legal citizens who can get legal licenses, say they will never drive because of the way the state has punished their family so many times.

This aggressive and vast bureaucracy of criminalizing and exploiting the disposable poor is an oft overlooked feature of neoliberalism. The cruel irony in all of this is that everyone is potentially disposable under neoliberalism. As social infrastructures are shredded and people everywhere become subject to precarity, the "winning" status becomes harder to reach. Indeed, precarization means that a health crisis or sudden layoff could send someone who seems secure over the edge and into the land of disposability. Yet, in a world of competition, we are primed to let the biopolitics of disposability divide us.

TOWARD THE COMMON

At this point, big questions should be emerging for you. If people are disposable and readily dispossessed, do we still have the rights and protections associated with citizenship? If citizens are disimagined—unable to critique, reimagine, or change the conditions of our existence—are we still a democratic people? If our voices are no longer the foundation of democracy, does democracy even exist? I often wonder if neoliberalism has finally exhausted liberal versions of democracy, rooted in protecting private property and individual civil liberties. In other words, perhaps neoliberalism has sucked all of the life and promise out of the liberal social imagination by turning everyone's everyday lives into a cutthroat competition for survival and equality. We express this liberal democratic drainage in our disaffected consent.

Perhaps, then, it is time to experiment with and invent new social ontologies, new visions of living together, new ideas of democracy. The liberal/neoliberal political imagination is ultimately incredibly limiting, as it forces us to think in terms of public versus private, market versus state, the individual versus the collective. Instead of thinking through these deeply problematic liberal/neoliberal truths—that are readily compatible with inequality and precarity—let's start thinking about how we might move from a present of living in competition and self-enclosed individualism to a future of living in common. As we move forward in our critical work, let's consider how we might write new stories that take us away from the four Ds and toward alternative worlds built on social interconnection, real equality, shared security, and collective governing.

CRITICAL PRACTICE

- How do the four Ds help to clarify the stakes of our critical work and conjunctural analysis? What consequences of neoliberal social ontology and truth trouble you most, and why?
- While the biopolitics of disposability work to divide us from one another, drawing lines between winners and losers, might they also work to unite us? Disposability is what happens when freedom, citizenship, and equality become contingent on one's capacities for self-appreciation, competition, and personal responsibility, and when the state

becomes an agent of Empire, committed solely to global competition. What might become possible if we look across our different experiences of precarization to explore disposability as a common, shared reality that we would like to transform? How might doing so help us to nurture new visions of living in common and new capacities for collective caretaking, social interconnection, and political intervention?

NOTES

1 Michel Foucault, *Power/Knowledge: Selected Interviews and Other Writings* (New York: Harvester, 1980), 131.
2 See Pierre Dardot and Christian Laval, *The New Way of the World* (London: Verso, 2013), 301; Philip Mirowski, *Never Let a Serious Crisis Go to Waste* (London: Verso, 2014), 53–54.
3 Mirowski, *Never Let a Serious Crisis Go to Waste*, 54.
4 Quoted in Daniel Stedman Jones, *Masters of the Universe* (Princeton: Princeton University Press, 2012), 48.
5 Dardot and Laval, *The New Way of the World*, 302–303.
6 Dardot and Laval, *The New Way of the World*, 124–125.
7 Dardot and Laval, *The New Way of the World*, 106–107.
8 See Mirowski, *Never Let a Serious Crisis Go to Waste*, 63; Wendy Brown, *Undoing the Demos: Neoliberalism's Stealth Revolution* (New York: Zone Books, 2015), 38.
9 Dardot and Laval, *The New Way of the World*, 216.
10 Patricia Ventura, *Neoliberal Culture: Living with American Neoliberalism* (New York: Routledge, 2016), 44.
11 Dardot and Laval, *The New Way of the World*, 154–155.
12 Michael Hardt and Antonio Negri, *Empire* (Cambridge: Harvard University Press, 2000).
13 Nick Dyer-Witheford and Greig de Peuter, *Games of Empire: Global Capitalism and Video Games* (Minneapolis: University of Minnesota Press, 2009), xx.
14 Lisa Duggan, *Twilight of Equality: Neoliberalism, Cultural Politics, and the Attack on Democracy* (Boston: Beacon Press, 2002), 14.
15 Jennifer Silva, *Coming Up Short: Working-Class Adulthood in an Age of Uncertainty* (Oxford: Oxford University Press, 2013), 3–5.
16 Quoted in Dardot and Laval, *The New Way of the World*, 109.
17 Dardot and Laval, *The New Way of the World*, 110.
18 Dardot and Laval, *The New Way of the World*, 112.
19 See Mirowski, *Never Let a Serious Crisis Go to Waste*, 78–83.

20 See AnaLouise Keating, *Transformation Now!: Toward a Post-Oppositional Politics of Change* (Champaign: University of Illinois Press, 2012), 172; Duggan, *Twilight of Equality*, 5–6.

21 Michel Feher, "Self-Appreciation; or, the Aspirations of Human Capital," *Public Culture* 21.1 (2009): 34.

22 Richard Dyer, *Heavenly Bodies: Film Stars and Society* (London: Palgrave Macmillan, 1986), 17.

23 Dyer, *Heavenly Bodies*, 10.

24 David Harvey, *A Brief History of Neoliberalism* (Oxford: Oxford University Press, 2005), 160–165.

25 Henry Giroux, "The Politics of Disimagination and the Pathologies of Power," *Truthout*, February, 27, 2013.

26 *Oprah's Lifeclass*, "What Oprah Knows about Taking Responsibility for Your Life." Oprah Winfrey Network. Aired 10/20/2011. www.oprah.com/oprahs-lifeclass/what-oprah-knows-about-taking-responsibility-for-your-life-video

27 Wendy Brown, "Booked #3: What Exactly is Neoliberalism?" (interview with Timothy Shenk), *Dissent Magazine*, April 2, 2015.

28 Brown, *Undoing the Demos*, 202.

29 Brown, *Undoing the Demos*, 202–203.

30 Brown, *Undoing the Demos*, 65.

31 Nikolas Rose, *The Politics of Life Itself* (Princeton: Princeton University Press, 2007), 52–64.

32 Henry Giroux, "Reading Hurricane Katrina: Race, Class, and the Biopolitics of Disposability," *College Literature* 33.3 (2006): 171.

33 See Loic Wacquant, *Punishing the Poor: The Neoliberal Government of Social Insecurity* (Durham: Duke University Press, 2009).

3

THE CULTURAL POWERS OF NEOLIBERALISM

A CASE STUDY

CHAPTER OVERVIEW

Now that we know something about neoliberalism's history and its theories of society, we can turn our attention to the questions at the heart of cultural studies. Why do we accept and internalize neoliberal social ontology and its status-quo stories? How do we come to tolerate, and even embrace, the four *D*s? How does neoliberalism construct our social worlds, identities, and senses of possibility? To answer these questions, we must sharpen our critical perspective to focus on *how we become* neoliberal subjects. Getting to the root of neoliberalism requires understanding its history and social ontology but also wrestling with its specific cultural powers to shape the contours of our individual and collective lives.

In this chapter, then, we are going to examine how neoliberalism works to construct our institutions, practices, values, beliefs, and everyday lives—in other words, our culture—through a case study: contemporary

K–12 education. Specifically, we'll adopt three conceptual tools from cultural studies to explore three modes of neoliberal cultural power:

- First, we'll focus on the power of **governmentality** and the ways in which neoliberalism operates as an order of political reason. As we'll see, a central policy initiative of the Obama Administration, Race to the Top, works to impose a norm of competition that determines how we think about—and thus what we do about—education.
- Next, we'll concentrate on neoliberal **affect** by exploring how young people actually experience neoliberal education. Neoliberalism is not only embedded in institutions and policies; it is also a "structure of feeling" that impinges on our very sense of the world and of what is possible to do and who it is possible to become.
- Finally, we'll tackle the power of neoliberal **ideology**. Through an analysis of *Waiting for Superman,* a documentary about problems that plague public education and the promises of the charter school movement, we'll explore how neoliberalism works through the ideologies of meritocracy and "the freedom to choose" to garner our spontaneous, albeit disaffected, consent.

As we'll see, these different modes of cultural power cannot be separated from one another. They work together at different registers to construct neoliberal subjects. The examples of neoliberal education discussed below—Race to the Top, student experience, and *Waiting for Superman*—help to crystallize the entangled cultural dimensions of neoliberalism. They also cut to the heart of student lives and work, as well as the stakes of neoliberalism for democratic citizenship and equality.

CULTURAL POWER AND NEOLIBERALISM

We can't map our neoliberal conjuncture without understanding the specific cultural powers that shape our lives for competition. As we saw in previous chapters, culture is the central front in neoliberalism's political-economic project to construct a market society. Neoliberalism works to diffuse market logic into all social spheres of life by creating a culture of personal responsibility. By this means, neoliberalism aims to construct an **enterprise culture** via "the generalization of an 'enterprise form' to *all* forms of conduct—to the conduct of organizations hitherto seen as being non-economic, to the conduct of government and to the conduct of individuals themselves."[1] We might think of enterprise as the fundamental form of neoliberal society; it is the model for all of social life, even those facets that were previously regarded as separate from the market, such as education. Certainly, culture has long been an instrument of power and a site of struggle. But within neoliberalism, culture and enterprise become intertwined to constitute the dominant medium of state and market power.

Put another way, neoliberalism hinges on cultural (re)regulation. To realize spontaneous market order, neoliberalism must create a culture premised on ideals, beliefs, practices, and values connected to competition and private enterprise. As Stuart Hall argued of Thatcher's neoliberal agenda, it aimed "*both* to de-regulate the economy in relation to the state, and to re-regulate morality in relation to the market."[2] Ongoing privatization is carried out through the ongoing re-regulation of how we think and live and what we come to value as good and just. "Economics is the method, but the aim is to change the soul," Thatcher proclaimed; as we will see, culture is where individual "souls" are actively reconfigured as human capital and society's "soul" is remade for enterprise and competition. Indeed, as Hall explains,

> If culture, in fact, regulates our social practices at every turn, then those who need or wish to influence what is done in the world or how things are done will need—to put it crudely—to somehow get hold of 'culture', to shape and regulate it in some way or to some degree.[3]

And what better way to "get hold of 'culture'" than education!

EDUCATION IN CRISIS

In *Class War: The Privatization of Childhood,* Megan Erickson argues childhood is no longer a playful time to be protected from the hardships of adult life. Instead, it has become a deeply privatized experience, transformed into an extension of cutthroat competition and social positioning. For rich families, children figure as important "investments" in relation to which families expect a return; accordingly, they pour enormous time and resources into cultivation and development. At the same time, middle- and working-class families find themselves desperate to give their own children a leg up on their peers. Where resources are unequally distributed and opportunities are scarce, childhood becomes overrun by the demands of competition, converted into a vital time to prepare for a future career. Parents, as well as school boards, communities, and states, must in effect compete for a "good education" to ensure a future for their children.

The privatization of childhood is owed generally to neoliberalism and the enormous shifts in education brought about over the past 30 years. Where the post-World War II era of embedded liberalism authorized an unprecedented expansion of public education, the goal of preparing all students to participate in democratic life moved to the center of educational theory and practice; with it, so did the idea that all citizens, including the working classes and other marginalized social groups, should have access to a form of education that had previously been reserved for the elite. This surge in democratic thinking around public education emerged within the Cold War context, when policymakers were keen to demonstrate the promises of liberal, capitalist society and its superiority to communist regimes when it came to intellectual freedom and equality.[4]

However, in response to the social democratic movements for civil rights and gender justice and the economic downturn that defined the 1960s and 1970s, neoliberal arguments began to circulate that the country was experiencing an "excess of democracy." While young people were resisting dominant culture and demanding the expansion of equality and rights, America was falling behind. The only way to turn the ship around was to remake the education system. In other words, America's "excess of democracy" demanded the de-democratization of education.

Consequently, public education became a pressing "crisis" to be solved through privatization. According to neoliberal truth, education should no longer be thought of as a public good, but rather a business whose product are students. The idea of public education as a collective project indispensable to democracy was dissolved and replaced by a new regime of truth. As Lester Spence writes, contemporary education "reduces our political imagination to the point where it is difficult for us to even imagine a form of education that isn't solely about increasing one's preparedness for a *job*."[5] The education system is perhaps the key facet of neoliberalism's disimagination machine; today educational institutions, classrooms, and curricula increasingly become the sites where young people learn the ways of enterprise culture, as well as their place in this competitive world as self-appreciating subjects.

NEOLIBERAL GOVERNMENTALITY

In order to theorize the cultural powers of neoliberalism, many critical scholars turn to the highly influential lectures and writings of Michel Foucault on governmentality. Late in his career, Foucault focused on the development of liberalism and its practices of government. Foucault's research showed how the twinned rise of capitalism and democracy demanded the invention of a new form of state power that he labeled governmentality. Without ordained monarchies, how would state power operate, and how would it garner legitimacy? How could the protection of individual rights and promotion of market freedoms be reconciled with the maintenance of social order? **Governmentality** emerged as a way to address these fundamental problems of rule in an open capitalist society where people are supposedly free.

In contrast to earlier modes of state power, governmentality is a form of soft power. It doesn't directly oppress. Instead, governmentality seeks to guide people's conduct "at a distance"—through culture. It works through the "freedom" of individuals by delineating social norms and appropriate forms of behavior—rules of the road—that we internalize and apply to our own lives.[6] Thus, governmentality is not easy to see. In contrast to the sovereign power of a king or queen, for example, its power can only be identified through stepping back and critiquing cultural ideas and practices of freedom and citizenship, as well as the various social institutions that shape our conduct.

With the concept of governmentality, Foucault tried to capture the ways in which the liberal state sought to govern not through brute force, but rather through the development of expert knowledges and their application to our lifeworlds. In other words, governmentality exercises biopolitical power by getting us to live according to particular regimes of knowledge. The power of governmentality is thus largely technical and practical; it works to shape individual bodies and behaviors. In this way, governmentality does not refer to the institutions of government so much as the activity of shaping the conduct of social and cultural institutions and their subjects. Governmentality aims to structure the field of social action and possibility.[7]

At the center of any regime of governmentality is political reason: a mode of reasoning about how best to conduct social conduct and shape the social field of action and possibility. Governmentality provides a framework for thinking about and addressing specific social problems, as well as for governing individual and collective life more broadly. As political reason, governmentality is immensely powerful. It determines how we can think about governing and what we can know and do collectively.

Neoliberal Reason and Government Through Competition

The rise of neoliberalism can be seen as representing a shift in governmentality and political reason: the neoliberal state is no longer invested in creating policies to secure the population and shaping conducts for democratic citizenship. Rather, it is invested in constructing a society ripe for global capitalist investment and accumulation and shaping conducts for enterprise. Neoliberalism is, as Wendy Brown puts it, "an order of normative reason" that "disseminates the model of the market to all domains and activities— even where money is not at issue—and configures human beings exhaustively as market actors, always, only, and everywhere as *homo oeconomicus*."[8] Recall from the previous two chapters that neoliberalism is radically *constructivist* in its orientation toward governing (as opposed to laissez-faire). It is an aggressive governmentality, one that is determined to construct the necessary institutional environments for expanded competition. Brown describes **neoliberal governmentality** as "termitelike": "a reality principle remaking institutions and human beings everywhere it settles, nestles, and gains affirmation . . . it's mode of reason boring in capillary fashion into the trunks and branches" of everything including ourselves.[9]

Here is what this "order of normative reason" looks like in the field of education:

- Education matters primarily for the health of the market, not the health of democracy.
- Education is a private market, not a public good.
- Parents and individual families are "consumers" of education, not citizens.

- Students are human capitals, not curious thinkers.
- Teachers are human capitals in the business of producing human capitals.

Neoliberal reason was especially apparent in President Obama's approach to public education. For example, on July 25, 2009, President Obama and his Secretary of Education Arne Duncan announced their signature initiative, Race to the Top, a federally sponsored competition between states designed to spur innovation and reform in K–12 public education. The prize was a share of $4.35 billion that had been allocated as part of the American Recovery and Reinvestment Act and would be distributed to "winners" across three rounds of competition. Here's what President Obama had to say at the program's rollout:

> America will not succeed in the 21st century unless we do a far better job of educating our sons and daughters. . . . In an economy where knowledge is the most valuable commodity a person and a country have to offer, the best jobs will go to the best educated—whether they live in the United States or India or China. In a world where countries that out-educate us today will out-compete us tomorrow, the future belongs to the nation that best educates its people. Period.
>
> Because improving education is central to rebuilding our economy, we set aside over $4 billion in the Recovery Act to promote improvements in schools. This is one of the largest investments in education reform in American history. And rather than divvying it up and handing it out, we are letting states and school districts compete for it. That's how we can incentivize excellence and spur reform and launch a race to the top in America's public schools.
>
> That race starts today. I'm issuing a challenge to our nation's governors, to school boards and principals and teachers, to businesses and non-for-profits, to parents and students: if you set and enforce rigorous and challenging standards and assessments; if you put outstanding teachers at the front of the classroom; if you turn around failing schools—your state can win a Race to the Top grant that will not only help students outcompete workers around the world, but let them fulfill their God-given potential.

> This competition will not be based on politics or ideology or the preferences of a particular interest group. Instead, it will be based on a simple principle—whether a state is ready to do what works. We will use the best evidence available to determine whether a state can meet a few key benchmarks for reform—and states that outperform the rest will be rewarded with a grant. Not every state will win and not every school district will be happy with the results. But America's children, America's economy, and America itself will be better for it.

Race to the Top throws neoliberal governmentality into sharp relief. Following President Obama, the goal of education is global competition. The United States is an "enterprise" that must not get out-competed by India or China; it must seek to improve its market position in the global economy by creating a skilled workforce that will attract corporate investment. In this scenario, students are first and foremost human capital; nurturing their capacities to outcompete their peers is tantamount to helping them realize their "God-given potential." Thus, the only education they need is what is imagined to prepare them for enterprising participation in the market.

Importantly though, competition is not only what we are striving for (the ends of education); it is also how we are going to get there (the means of education). Following the logic of Race to the Top, the way to excellence in education (and thus to global superiority) is to promote competition between states, schools, school districts, even teachers, parents, and children. Rather than distribute $4.35 billion to the schools that need it most (i.e., those located in poor urban or rural communities where there is little income from property taxes), Obama *constructs* a competition, a "race to the top," that "not every school district will be happy with," but will supposedly make America, its children, the economy, and the nation better in the long run.

Race to the Top shows how neoliberal governmentality works to shape institutions and conducts, bringing them into alignment with broader political aims through *imposing* the norm of competition. For example, Secretary Duncan called the initiative a "once in a lifetime chance to change our schools": for, in order to win the race and its multi-million dollar prize, states had to be ready to articulate and implement an "ambitious yet achievable" reform agenda.[10] Race to the Top was thus constructed to shape the field of action in very particular ways. States submitted proposals to the administration that were evaluated via a "scorecard," earning points for key priorities established by the rules and norms of the competition. Specifically, competitive proposals earned points for adopting international standards and techniques for enhancing scores in math and language arts. Points were also awarded for emphasis on STEM. In other words, applicants were "incentivized" to adopt specific educational philosophies, approaches, policies, and curricula especially when it came to turning around underperforming schools.

It is important to point out that, by and large, the arts and humanities are not included in the dominant formula for neoliberal reform. Once the centerpiece of democratic citizenship, liberal arts education is often regarded today as superfluous from the perspective neoliberal reason. It simply doesn't promise a strong return on investment (ROI), the key metric of neoliberal reason. Indeed, it is not surprising that music and other arts programs are most often the first to be cut as public school districts and administrators wrestle with declining revenue and tightened budgets in an increasingly competitive and scarce environment.

Good Governance

The Obama approach to education sounds a lot like the Washington Consensus's structural adjustment programs discussed in Chapter 1, right? To receive much-needed aid, schools have to radically transform their system, bringing it in line with the interests of global capitalism. Indeed, Race to the Top demanded fundamental political-economic change in exchange for funding. Specifically, if states wanted to have a shot at "victory," they had to be ready to change their systems for recruiting, hiring, firing, and evaluating teachers. In other words, applicants had to find ways around teacher unions and tenure job security in the name of creating a more competitive system, where underperforming human capital could be readily let go. According to the National Council on Teacher Quality, a think tank devoted to education reform,

> Human capital reform will be challenging and contentious and, to date, states have been unwilling to take it on in a comprehensive manner. It will require break the mold initiatives and iron political will on the part of states to undertake a human capital reform agenda—and, accordingly, the Department has assigned the big points and promised the big money for this tough work.[11]

In this way, Race to the Top represented a targeted attack on one of the largest remaining public unions. Recall that breaking the power of unions is central to the rise of neoliberal hegemony. Ultimately, Race to the Top is part of this wider effort to "structurally adjust" public education through the economization of schools, teachers, and learning.

Crucially, this structural adjustment agenda cannot be readily challenged, as it is has come to operate under the banner of **good governance**, another key feature of neoliberal governmentality. Good governance emphasizes standards, best practices, and benchmarking that, together, work in powerful ways to structure the field of action through the norm of competition, ensuring that education stay within the parameters of neoliberal reason. For example, *Benchmarking for Success: Ensuring U.S. Students Receive a World-Class Education* is a report that was prepared by the National Governors Association, the Council of Chief State School Officers, and Achieve, Inc. (a non-profit organization focused on education reform) that lays out a "roadmap" for reform. Specifically, it offers "Five Steps Toward Building Globally Competitive Education Systems":

Action 1: Upgrade state standards by adopting a common core of internationally benchmarked standards in math and language arts for grades K–12 to ensure that students are equipped with the necessary knowledge and skills to be globally competitive.

Action 2: Leverage states' collective influence to ensure that textbooks, digital media, curricula, and assessments are aligned to internationally benchmarked standards and draw on lessons from high-performing nations and states.

Action 3: Revise state policies for recruiting, preparing, developing, and supporting teachers and school leaders to reflect the human capital practices of top-performing nations and states around the world.

Action 4: Hold schools and systems accountable through monitoring, interventions, and support to ensure consistently high performance, drawing upon international best practices.

Action 5: Measure state-level education performance globally by examining student achievement and attainment in an international context to ensure that, over time, students are receiving the education they need to compete in the 21st century economy.[12]

The plan promises to achieve competition through "best practices." The idea is that good education will come via good governance and the ongoing evaluation, measurement, accountability, and assessment of benchmarked standards. Similarly, as Obama made clear in his rollout, Race to the Top depended on "a few key benchmarks" and "the best evidence" to determine the winners. In turn, the winners served as models of good governance for other schools and districts, accelerating reform and innovation, while weeding out losing approaches.

This is not to say that we have nothing to gain by paying attention to what works in particular contexts. However, it is important to note what happens to the vital social infrastructure of public education when it is remade according to neoliberal reason and the norm of competition—that is, when good governance replaces democracy. On one hand, it shifts power over education from local communities and public entities to political-economic elite and technical experts. In the name of good governance, unelected and unaccountable corporate elites like Bill Gates (a driving force behind education reform and Common Core standards), as well as textbooks companies (poised to make a killing off of the development of international standards), are invited into the reform process as key partners, experts, technicians, and stakeholders.[13] In this way, good governance translates a hijacking of vital public institutions by private interests into a congenial and innovative "public–private partnership." As Brown explains,

> Neoliberal governance facilitates a more open-handed and effective fusion of political and economic power, one that largely eliminates the scandal of corruption as it erases differences in goals and governance between states and capital, indeed, as the best practices circulating between them perform this erasure.[14]

What is more, good governance reduces public education, and public life more broadly, to "problem solving and program implementation, a casting that brackets or eliminates politics, conflict, and deliberation about common values or ends."[15] Education is no longer a moral, ethical, or political issue; it is a *technical* one to be solved by economized approaches and market enterprise. Just like Thatcher proclaimed, the soul of education has been remade by the method of economics. Democratic control of schools gets lost as good governance decouples governing education from serious and collective deliberation over what it means, and what it should mean, to educate. In this way, good governance is also a process of disimagination. It promotes structural ignorance and an inability to critique, much less transform, the roots of our problems.

In conclusion, the power of neoliberal governmentality is to guide the practices, knowledges, and conducts of institutions, thereby shaping the field of social action and possibility. As we have seen, neoliberal reason works to set the ends, means, content, and future of education. Through good governance, competition comes to operate as neoliberalism's "reality principle" by constructing and disciplining how we think and what we do about education—from what we get to learn, to how we learn, to why it all matters in the first place.

You might be thinking that neoliberal governmentality doesn't really sound all that bad. After all, we do live in a global economy, and we do need jobs. Isn't the good governance of Race to the Top just bringing everyone together toward the goal of improving education? Aren't innovation and enterprise good in this case? After all, reform is desperately needed. Are we really trading democracy for competition? Let's keep these questions in mind as we explore other modes of neoliberal power.

NEOLIBERAL AFFECT: PRIVATIZED RISK AND PERFORMANCE ANXIETY

Neoliberalism is more than new form of political reason; it is also what Raymond Williams called a "structure of feeling."[16] With the concept of structure of feeling, Williams was trying to theorize a register of cultural power that accounted for how the mundane feelings that make up everyday life get structured by broader historical forces.

Williams was keen to consider how our social sensibilities of agency and social relation get shaped by the conjuncture in which we live. In other words, who, and with whom, can we become? How and why do things come to matter to us? To what people, ideas, and life projects do we hitch our wagons?

Answering these questions about our **structures of feeling** requires attending to the realm of affect. **Affect** should not be confused with emotion, although it is certainly related. We might think of emotion as a hardening of affect into something tangible, something that we can name or identify. Affect itself, though, is simply the *potential* to be moved by something, to come into relationship with someone or something, to become something or to become undone by something. Simply put, affect is "a body's *capacity* to affect and be affected."[17] Affect shapes our sense of possibility and our orientation toward our social world. As such, it is a powerful social and cultural force. Affect is what won't let us get out of bed in the morning when we are depressed. It is what moves us excitedly into a new relationship or softly out of an old one. It is what opens up to and/or shuts down specific encounters, experiences, and social possibilities. Affect cannot be easily separated from governmentality; after all, government aims to contain and channel affect by working to bring our practices and sensibilities of freedom into alignment with specific political ends.

The rise of neoliberal governmentality in education structures the everyday lives and sensibilities of young people by subjecting them to the norm of competition. For example, Julie has been making straight *A*s since sixth grade. She takes AP classes, runs cross-country, holds internships, and participates in charitable activities, all in hopes of molding herself into the perfect college candidate. Hair thinning from stress, Julie regularly skips lunches; for not a moment should be wasted on something that isn't going to enhance her chances of getting accepted to a top university. Julie is just one of the young people featured in Alexandra Robbins' book, *The Overachievers,* which documents the ordinary worlds of students attending an elite private school. Robbins is deeply troubled by what she calls the "overachiever culture" in which Julie lives. "Overachiever culture is disturbing not because it exists but because it has become a way of life," she writes. "Nation-wide, the relentless pursuit of perceived perfectionism has spiraled into a perpetual cycle of increasing intensity and narrowing ideals."[18]

Julie spends high school engulfed in an atmosphere of competition that is largely self-imposed. Indeed, she knows that, in pouring all of her energies into getting into college, she is sacrificing social relationships and her own health. For example, when reflecting on her determination to earn a higher score on her SAT, Julie laments, "I've put so much time into those stupid tests; this is how sick I am. Think of all that I could have been doing instead. Every time I look at that book, a little bit of me dies."[19] Yet, when Julie successfully raised her score, she felt proud and accomplished; the sacrifice had paid off. In a journal entry written shortly after receiving her new and improved SAT scores, Julie lauds her efforts: "I could thank the SAT gods for the birthday present, but the truth is, I did it all on my own. There was no luck involved. I spent more time with that wretched red 10 Real SAT book than any smart girl should."[20] Crucially, Julie seems to know that these scores aren't a good measure of her worth and potential, but they still mean a lot to her. "I hated how I was only described in numbers and letters and no words," she wrote in her journal.

> Why couldn't colleges just take my word that I was a really good runner and just as smart as anyone who got a 1500 on their SATs? I don't know what happened, but something clicked. Now I have the numbers to go along with my life.[21]

Eventually, after weeks of worrying whether she had made the right decision, Julie was accepted early decision to a top liberal arts college. However, shortly after the good news arrived, Julie started to lose interest in her life, especially cross-country:

> I no longer have to view my classmates as obstacle to run over so that I can get to a good place. I'm going to a good place. But without being an athlete I don't know who I am. I don't know what I like to do. I feel so lost.[22]

The race was over for now, and Julie had won, though without the race she felt "so lost." Julie wrote,

> For as long as I can remember, I have had two after-school activities every day followed by a long night of homework. Occasionally I would take breaks to eat dinner or call a friend, but for the most part I was

> plugging away every day. During this time I had tons of problems—
> with friends, with acne, with depression—but mostly I just pushed
> these issues aside because I was too busy. Just like my room, I may
> look organized and put together on the surface, but under my bed and
> in my closet where I hide junk, my life is a mess.[23]

Winning didn't make the problems go away; "neither her 1520 SAT score nor acceptance to a prestigious college had fixed her unhappiness and insecurity."[24] Julie found herself with no real friends and no community.

Neoliberal subjects like Julie embody the norm of competition in their everyday lives, as neoliberalism comes to shape her very sense of what is possible. Specifically, neoliberalism keeps Julie moving through her world as a self-enclosed individual. Incited by competition, she trades her health and social connection for the individual payoffs of high performance (an improved test score, acceptance to an elite school). While Julie *knows* that she is more than a number and that her overachieving lifestyle is detrimental to her health, she nonetheless soldiers on, propelled by a powerful sense that if she works really hard, she will achieve her goals. As a result, Julie shuns relationships in order stay focused on competition.

Ultimately, weighing on Julie's affects are broader social realities connected to the rise of neoliberal governmentality. Specifically, in order to grasp Julie's affective life, we need to understand the **privatization of risk**. As discussed in the previous chapter, personal responsibility is the cultural linchpin of neoliberalism. This is because the privatization of public goods, services, and infrastructures ultimately demands that individuals and families take on more social responsibility for their health, security, and futures. Individuals come to bear more and more risk, effectively becoming their own insurance agencies in a world where work and a livable future are far from a sure thing. While earlier regimes of liberal governmentality distributed risk across governments and corporations, neoliberalism works to condense risk onto individuals. Social protections have been shredded, so it's up to individuals to protect themselves and their own interests. Resources are scarce; nothing is guaranteed; focusing on self-appreciation is the only way forward.

Simply put, neoliberal governmentality works through self-governmentality. To succeed (and not become disposable), individuals, including young people like Julie, feel they must construct their own vigilant regimes of government rooted in neoliberal reason so as to guarantee their social position and mitigate any risks that might lead to failure. As we'll see in the next chapters, these self-regulated regimes extend the demands of competition and performance into all crevices of our lives. Everyday life becomes a narrow, intensely focused project of self-appreciation. As Julie's life suggests, this situation breeds constant performance anxiety. Even though she's working (too) hard and performing at high levels, she is always anxious, worried that she has made the wrong decision or a poor investment of time and energy. As Robbins notes, "When teenagers inevitably look at themselves through the prism of our overachiever culture, they often come to the conclusion that no matter how much they achieve, it will never be enough. And the pressure steadily mounts."[25] And, as we have seen, this performance anxiety makes her sick.

I should point out that Robbin's book was brought to my attention by one of my students who worked on research for this book. Ironically, she was forced to read it in high school as a cautionary tale, that is, as an example of what not to do, of who not to be. However, instead of working positively to assuage the pressures and stresses of competition, the book and its stories only reaffirmed her own sensibilities of what she needed to do to excel. Indeed, my summer research assistant described having her own performance anxieties intensified by reading about overachievers like Julie. If they could do it, so should she. For Julie and my students, even when they know better, something from deep inside spurs them onward toward competition. This is the cultural power of affect and our structures of feeling.

You might ask: Why we should care about Julie (or my research assistants for that matter). She's privileged and perhaps an extreme example. However, as Robbins argues,

> The intensifying pressures to succeed and the drive of overachiever culture have consequences that reach far beyond the damaged psyches of teenage college applicants, though that effect alone should be enough for us to take notice. Overachiever culture affects not only overachievers and the college application process, but also the U.S. education system as a whole, non-overachieving students, the booming college counseling and test-prep industries, the tendency to cheat and use

cutthroat tactics to get ahead, the way parents raise children, and campus drug culture. It contributes directly to young adults' paralyzing fear of failure. It has diminished leisure time for all ages. It is believed to be a major factor in the 114 percent spike in suicide rates among fifteen-to-nineteen-year-olds between 1980 and 2002.[26]

In other words, overachiever culture is symptomatic of the broader neoliberal conjuncture and the ways in which personal responsibility, competition, and the privatization of risk work to engender structures of feeling that systematically shut down possibilities for living in common. Julie's ordinary affects help us to see how self-appreciating individualism is structured, imposed, and lived and how young people's subjective capacities for health, interconnection, love, community, equality, and democratic life get diminished by enterprise culture. This is what disimagination looks and feels like in everyday life.

CRITICAL PRACTICE

- How does the privatization of risk come to shape your everyday life as a student? Do you experience performance anxiety like Julie, or does this structure of feeling register in other ways for you?

NEOLIBERAL IDEOLOGY: MERITOCRACY AND THE FREEDOM TO CHOOSE

As Julie's life suggests and we explore more fully in later chapters, neoliberalism registers devastating effects on our bodies, affects, and social relationships. The evidence is clear: living in competition breeds depression and anxiety, even for privileged young people like Julie. The question thus emerges: Why do people stay attached to living in competition? What makes neoliberal governmentality seem like a good and just system? The answer is neoliberal ideology.

Most basically, we can think of an **ideology** as a dominant worldview: a set of beliefs that undergirds how we interpret and make sense the world. French philosopher Louis Althusser understood ideology as the *imaginary* relationships we have to our *material* realities. In other words, *ideologies imagine what's happening to us for us*, most often in ways that support the status quo and current systems of power. Ideology is what makes history, culture, and power seem natural and normal, and thus good and true. It is those commonsensical, unquestioned, unarticulated assumptions that condition our knowledge and values. Simply put, ideology is "what you think *before* you think or act—what thinking and action silently take for granted."[27]

It is important to see that ideology is more than a sort of false consciousness that we can simply snap out of. For, as Althusser explains, ideology *interpellates* us, hailing us into a specific world of meaning, value, and power, thereby constituting us as subjects. Althusser gives the example of an encounter with police. Say you're walking down the street, and an officer yells, "Hey you!" You automatically turn around, simply assuming you're the "you" being called. In turning around, you've actually become the "you" being called, despite the fact the officer's call was a generic one and not necessarily addressed to you. In other words, in turning around, you've become a subject to the law; you've been successfully interpellated by the power of the state. That's the cultural power of ideology: it creates a *subject position* for us to occupy, and from which to view the world, that we readily accept without question or thinking. Through the process of interpellation, ideology constructs our subjectivity, making our world appear natural and normal, while erasing power, history, and social constructedness. Ideology and interpellation are what garner our spontaneous, albeit disaffected, consent for neoliberal hegemony.

While neoliberalism works through long-standing liberal ideologies of personal responsibility and individual freedom, it does so in particular ways. Indeed, neoliberalism is sustained and expanded through two specific ideologies: meritocracy and the freedom to choose. **Meritocracy** is the seductive and driving ideological force of neoliberalism that says we should live a world where the people are rewarded in life based on individual merit. In other words, if you work really hard, good things will certainly come your way, or at least they should. We might think of meritocracy as the warm and fuzzy face of neoliberal governmentality. It makes neoliberalism's harsh world of competition appear good and just. After all, who doesn't believe that hard work and effort should be rewarded? That's just commonsense.

While meritocracy has long been a central ideology connected to the American dream, in neoliberalism, meritocracy becomes the life-blood of neoliberal governmentality. Indeed, Julie is disaffected with neoliberal culture but nonetheless propelled by what Jo Littler calls that "meritocratic feeling,"[28] a deep-seated belief that if you work really hard, your efforts will be rewarded with success. She cannot, and should not, depend on anything or anyone but herself and her own hard work. In popular culture, the ideology of meritocracy circulates relentlessly. For example, competition reality shows like *The Voice* and *So You Think You Can Dance* interpellate audiences by the ideol-ogy of meritocracy, as they are routinely positioned to root for those individuals who have overcome obstacles—for example, a parent's death or childhood poverty—through their own dedication. These are the contestants that pull at our heartstrings, spontaneously earning our affection and respect. Of course, the implication is that those who have not worked hard and taken personal responsibility in the face of hardship are not so deserving of emotional and social investment.

The ideology of meritocracy goes hand in hand with neoliberal-ism's other driving ideology: the freedom to choose. If one is going to make it on their own—through their own hard work and initiative—they must be free to make their own choices. While meritocracy makes competition feel good and right, the freedom to choose makes the impossibilities of personal responsibility and privatized risk feel, paradoxically, empowering. As we have already seen, competition and personal responsibility are not, in actuality, our "choice," strictly speaking; rather, they are imposed on us by neoliberal governmen-tality. In a sense, we are forced to choose competition, or else we are rendered disposable. However, the ideology of free choice obscures and naturalizes this process, and as a result, our beliefs about choice, agency, and freedom get aligned with neoliberal reason. We come to feel empowered by the very things that are oppressing us. Indeed, the freedom to choose *imagines for us* that free markets and privatiza-tion represent commonsense solutions to the social problems we face, such as education. At the same time, the freedom to choose produces self-enclosed individualism, mobilizing neoliberal subjects against public or collective forms of action. For within neoliberal ideology, the highest, and in fact, the only valuable form of freedom is market choice. Our own freedoms are thus always and necessarily in competition with the freedoms of others, which makes thinking more collectively about a vital social infrastructure like education exceedingly difficult.

Neoliberal Ideology and *Waiting for Superman*

Waiting for Superman is a potent example of neoliberal ideologies at work in contemporary education discourse. The documentary follows the individual struggles of working- and middle-class families to secure their children a good education amidst a broken public education system. The film opens with a voiceover by its director, David Guggenheim, explaining the situation at hand:

> In 1999 I made a documentary about public school teachers and I spent an entire school year watching them dedicate their lives to children. These teachers embodied a hope and carried with them a promise that the idea of public school could work. Ten years later, it was time to choose a school for my own children and then reality set in. My feelings about public education didn't matter as much as my fear of sending them to a failing school. So every morning, betraying the ideals I thought I lived by, I drive past three public schools as I take my kids to a private school. But I'm lucky. I have a choice. Other families pin their hopes to a bouncing ball, a hand pulling a card from a box, or a computer that generates numbers in random sequence. Because when there's a great public school, there aren't enough spaces. So we do what's fair—we place our children, and their future, in the hands of luck.

As the film argues, public schools are failing under-advantaged kids who have big dreams and much to contribute to society. Parents and their children know this all too well and are desperate for more options, as kids' futures hinge on finding an alternative to their local public schools. However, rather than being able to freely choose what school their children will attend, unlike the more privileged director, these underprivileged families are at the mercy of the luck of the draw. Their childrens' futures are contingent on random selection, as there are only so many spots available in the good schools that promise to nurture childrens' potential. Certainly, given the sorry state of so many public schools and their increasingly standardized approaches outlined above, it is easy to understand why parents are desperate for more options. However, charter schools, which are the film's solution to the problem of public education, are part and parcel of the project to structurally adjust public education.

Waiting for Superman features the voices of parents and children, as well as reformers in the charter school movement. Documenting their typically maddening experiences with the public education system, the film explores what it sees as the cause of the crisis in public education: state bureaucracy and teachers' unions. The film ends with most families losing out on opportunities for their children and a bittersweet celebration of the few whose numbers are called. Like the reality TV shows mentioned previously, *Waiting for Superman* tugs forcibly at the heartstrings, generating sympathy for the families, especially the children, and admiration for the reformers who are fighting for better schools and more choices; most notably, it generates frustration, even rage, at a public school system that is shown to squash the dreams and futures of many young people in order to protect bad teachers. We're left with a clear message: families need more choices (a.k.a. more charter schools), so they can do right by their kids whose futures shouldn't be left in the hands of fate, much less the state and unions.

In this way, *Waiting for Superman* interpellates us through the ideologies of meritocracy and the freedom to choose, translating neoliberal "truths and consequences" into a commonsensical world of villains, victims, and heroes. The arch villain, not surprisingly, is the social welfare state, which, in *Waiting for Superman*, is represented by the public education system and teachers' unions. As the film makes clear, public education is to blame for public education's failure, not capitalism, markets, or the unequal distribution of wealth and power. *Waiting for Superman* parrots Ronald Reagan's famous line—"Government is not the solution to our problem. Government is the problem."—when it proclaims that, "For generations, experts tend to blame failing schools on failing neighborhoods. But reformers have begun to believe the opposite—that the problems of failing neighborhoods might be blamed on failing schools."

According to the film, the public school system is both inefficient and immoral. On one hand, the state is too big and bureaucratic to be effective. Guggenheim breaks it down for his audience, telling us,

> The federal government passes laws and sends money to the states, but the states fund schools too, and set their own often conflicting standards. And there are more than 14000 autonomous school boards. Making school governance a tangled mess of conflicting regulations and mixed agendas. . . . The things we've done to help our schools work better have become the things that prevent them from working.

"You've got local school boards, people from the state departments of education, federal department of education, district superintendents and their huge staffs," explains *Newsweek* editor and author Jonathan Alter. "This whole collection of people, which is sometimes called the blob, has been an impediment to reform. No individual is necessarily to blame, but collectively, they are the goliath of the system." To make matters worse, this blob of bureaucracy is costly; the film reports that, while education spending per student has doubled, outcomes have "flatlined."

The public education system is not only inefficient in this depiction; it is also immoral, as teachers' unions and tenure practices are alleged to protect bad teachers. In fact, teachers' unions are positioned as the most entrenched problem facing public education. According

Figure 3.1 Waiting for Superman Trailer

to Guggenheim, "the other thing reformers and experts will tell you, often under their breath, is that their biggest obstacle to real reform is a contract with teachers' unions, which ties their hands." Alter elaborates, explaining how unions served an important purpose in the past, as women dominated the profession but were not well paid due to their gender. However, unions have outlived their noble political purpose of promoting equality and transformed into, as Alter puts it, "a menace and impediment to national reform." Accordingly, the film represents teachers as the "welfare queens" of public education—lazy, entitled, and often just leeching off the system, when, in fact, teachers' unions and tenure are what institutionally protect teachers' power to advocate for their students, families, communities, and schools within the increasingly defunded, competitive field of neoliberal public education. Thus, the real heroes of *Waiting for Superman* are the leaders from the charter school movement who are seeking out ways to defy the entrenched powers of state bureaucracies and teachers' unions in order to implement real reform in public education. Unbound by the rules and contracts weighing down traditional public schools, these educational entrepreneurs are making things happen and finding ways to deliver results with limited resources that help children achieve their dreams.

Waiting for Superman's world is one where meritocracy and the freedom to choose are painfully absent thanks to a bureaucratic and immoral public education system that blocks every effort of reform, while dashing the hopes and dreams of students. The film fosters our identification with the filmmaker, the reformers, as well as the kids and their parents, while mobilizing viewer antipathy toward teachers, especially unions. Parents and children, as well as the real entrepreneurs, are demoralized; their hard work is not being rewarded by this blatantly un-meritocratic system. The only commonsense solution is to break the power of the unions and empower the innovative and entrepreneurial reformers who, unlike teachers' unions that only seem to care about teachers, appear to really care about children's futures.

In all of these ways, *Waiting for Superman* interpellates us as neoliberal subjects. We leave the film yearning for a meritocracy: a world where good governance—the best ideas, practices, and people—might prevail. We need a system with more choice, more competition, and more entrepreneurs and enterprise. The fates and fortunes of under-privileged children should not be in the hands of the state and unions, but unleashed to the spontaneous order of market society. Of course, as ideology, this appears as good and natural commonsense. However, meritocracy and the freedom to choose are anything but benign worldviews. These ideologies are the cultural backbone of enterprise culture, the medium by which we come to accept a world of worthy individuals and disposable populations, of de-democratization, disimagination, and fundamental inequality.

Right and Left Neoliberalism

Waiting for Superman presents itself as progressive social activism. It aims to transform public education, making our social world more just and equitable. However, as we have seen, despite its progressiveness, the film is perfectly in step with neoliberal governmentality and enterprise culture. As such, it makes clear that neoliberalism's cultural powers are not politically monolithic, and that's part of what makes critiquing neoliberal conjuncture so tricky.

Recall from the previous chapters that most policymakers view the world through the lens of neoliberal social ontology. Thus, what is at question in education is how best to construct a competitive education system. There are different ways to answer this question. Hence, as we have seen, there are different versions of neoliberalism that circulate, some on the right and others on the left. To grasp these distinctions, think of a racing track, where starting blocks are staggered to ensure a fair competition. Right versions of neoliberalism insist that the market is inherently meritocratic, so there's no need to stagger the start; the conditions of market choice automatically mete out just rewards, sorting the deserving from the undeserving. Left versions of neoliberalism, however, suggest that there's work to be done to ready the track: as long as disparities between people based on race or gender continue to exist, the starting blocks aren't staggered fairly, and the competition has been corrupted. Accordingly, the state has a role to play in ensuring meritocracy by fighting discrimination and inequity. Some racers have to cover more ground due to circumstances beyond their control, while others have an easier path to victory, which is not a true meritocracy. Crucially though, *no one*, not even left neoliberals, want everyone to win the race by ensuring equal outcomes. Indeed, both sides want a more perfect competition, where the cream of the crop can rise to the top regardless of their station in life. Simply put, left neoliberalism seeks to actively construct a more competitive market for historically marginalized groups, while right neoliberalism focuses on promoting competition without regard to such marginalization. What distinguishes left neoliberalism, then, is its emphasis on social justice and remediating the hurts of the past. However, the goal is not a truly egalitarian society, but just a "fairer" meritocracy.

Indeed, the real tragedy depicted in *Waiting for Superman* is that the students will not have their fair shot at winning the race. Their futures are in the hands of the state, not free market competition, which is the ultimate site of social truth and justice. *Waiting for Superman* is a powerful example of left neoliberalism, or what Randall Lahann and Emilie Mitescu Reagan call progressive neoliberalism:

> [W]e define progressive neoliberalism as a shared belief in five assumptions about the nature of public education and education reform: (1) public education, as it is currently constituted, reinforces social inequities by failing to provide an excellent education to all students; (2) public education can benefit from deregulating market reforms that reward the most efficient service providers, encourage innovation, and bridge the private and public spheres; (3), public education can benefit from the logic, technology, and strategy of business; (4), the market cannot be trusted to rectify inequity by itself, and instead positive action is required to offset historical disparities; and (5) public education is an arena for social activism in which actors can work both within and against the system for equitable ends.[29]

As an example of progressive, left neoliberalism, *Waiting for Superman* helps to crystallize neoliberalism's ideological promises: through creating a free, truly competitive system, we can realize an equitable society of self-appreciating human capitals. This utopian promise cycles throughout popular and political culture, and as a result, the idea that life is, or at least should be, a fair "race to the top" among personally responsible, freely choosing actors seems natural and good. However, meritocracy implies that some of us are losers. Indeed, let's not forget that neoliberalism is premised on this fundamental inequality, drawing lines between "worthy victims," like the families in *Waiting for Superman*, and disposable populations and institutions who are just getting what they deserve. Is this the world we really want to inhabit? Is equality ultimately just about equitable opportunities for competition?

COUNTER-CONDUCT AND COMMON REASON

I hope that this case study of contemporary education has revealed two important features of the neoliberal conjuncture: (1) the "termitelike" cultural powers by which neoliberalism constructs our social infrastructures, identities, and senses of possibilities; and (2) the extent to which this enterprise culture of living in competition breeds disaffected consent. Our education system has been thoroughly infiltrated by neoliberal governmentality, and pretty much everyone agrees that our schools desperately need changing. However, neoliberal structures of feeling and dominant ideologies keep us stuck within the horizons of neoliberal reason.

So, here's the million-dollar question: How can we begin to think about critiquing and resisting neoliberal governmentality, and thereby transform the conditions of our individual and collective lives? I want to suggest that the answers are at once profoundly simple and complicated. Because neoliberalism advances through cultural power and our own subjectivities, the way we conduct our daily lives and our relationships with others becomes a crucial site of resistance and transformation. Instead of chugging along in our disaffected consent, we can refuse to conduct ourselves as private, self-appreciating enterprises, and we can refuse to relate to others via competition and the oppositional consciousness that it demands. This is what Pierre Dardot and Christian Laval call **counter-conduct**.[30] Simply put, we can start small, right now, in our daily lives, by acting counter to neoliberal reason. We can develop new practices of freedom for ourselves based on alternative ethical considerations. Of course, this is a tall order, as the performance anxiety created by privatized risk is immensely powerful. In enterprise culture, we certainly feel like we have a lot to lose by engaging in counter-conduct, but do we really? What exactly are we afraid of losing? What might happen if we refused to be governed by enterprise culture?

CRITICAL PRACTICE

- Where are some places in your everyday life that you might begin experimenting with counter-conduct? What values and beliefs would guide these new forms of conduct? How might these counter practices of freedom change your sense of social possibility and the horizons of your social world and relationships?

Crucially, experiments with counter-conduct in the context of our daily lives at once require and inspire us to think carefully and systematically about what kind of world we want to live in. To undertake this critical work, we must understand that cultural power in itself is not necessarily a bad thing. After all, culture is what binds us together. It provides our shared foundations for living in common. I want to suggest that it is not enough to critique and resist neoliberal culture and its insistence on living in competition. We also have to be able to imagine different social infrastructures and cultural powers that might be capable of holding new worlds together. Put differently, through counter-conduct, we can begin to develop *counter-reason*. As we know, neoliberal reason is rooted in the imposition of competition and sustained by the ideologies of meritocracy and the freedom to choose. We need to develop new theories of political reason by asking good, critical questions. What do we want our individual and collective lives to feel like? Do we want our lives to be defined by performance anxiety, privatized risk, and precarity? What alternative affects, structures of feeling, and senses of possibility do we want to animate our everydays? What governmentality and political reason do we want to structure our individual and collective lives, our fields of social action and possibility?

As a counter-reason, I often think about **common reason**, a mode of political reason that would start not from a place of self-enclosed individualism, competition, and private enterprise, but from a place of real equality, interdependency, and shared vulnerability. It's well worth asking what kind of world might a political reason rooted in commonality and social interconnection open up and help us to construct.

CRITICAL PRACTICE

To conclude our case study, let's consider more specifically what common reason might do in the context of education. This chapter has focused on education because it is a shared site where disaffected consent is pronounced, and people are, by and large, in agreement that fundamental change is required. How might common reason transform how we think about, and thus what we do about, education? Here's an activity to help us think through the question at hand.

As we have already seen with Race to the Top, the Obama Administration's approach to education has been guided by neoliberal reason and the imposition of competition. Consider another powerful example that perhaps hits even closer to home for many of you. In 2015, the Obama White House unveiled a College Scorecard, an online platform that makes "reliable data on every institution of higher education" accessible to the general public. Specifically, users are able to find out "how much each school's graduates earn, how much debt they graduate with, and what percentage of a school's students can pay back their loans, which will help all of us see which schools do the best job of preparing America for success."

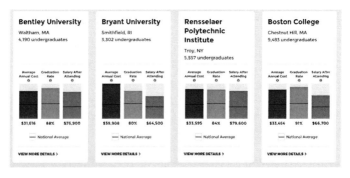

Figure 3.2 The College Scorecard

The College Scorecard is neoliberal reason in its purist form. If college students are first and foremost human capital, valued primarily for their contribution to the global economy, then it follows that colleges should be ranked by the economic outcomes of their graduates. These are "key benchmarks" and "best evidence," since, after all, from the perspective of neoliberal reason, college is simply an investment in a future career. The College Scorecard is an individual's tool to assess their options in the "market" of contemporary higher education and to determine what school offers the best ROI. Much like Race to the Top, the College Scorecard is designed to promote a competition between colleges of all sorts. Policymakers have even talked about making access to federal loans and aid contingent on such economic metrics and rankings.

Now let's think against neoliberal reason through common reason:

- What would a college education guided by common reason look like? What sorts of values and policies would govern this educational system? What would its aims and goals be?
- If we were going to construct a method for communicating what colleges have to offer their students from the perspective of common reason, what would this system look like? Would you keep the "scorecard" format? What attributes of educational experience would be highlighted, and why?

This concludes section one. Now that we've established some vital critical foundations for approaching neoliberalism and unlearning its status-quo stories, it's time to delve more deeply into neoliberal culture.

NOTES

1 Graham Burchell, "Liberal Government and Technique of the Self," in *Foucault and Political Reason*, eds. Andrew Barry, Thomas Osbourne, and Nikolas Rose (Chicago: University of Chicago Press, 1996), 28–29.

2 Stuart Hall, "The Centrality of Culture: Notes on the Cultural Revolutions of Our Time," in *Media and Cultural Regulation*, ed. Kenneth Thompson (London: Sage, 1997), 231.

3 Hall, "The Centrality of Culture," 232.

4 See Wendy Brown, *Undoing the Demos: Neoliberalism's Stealth Revolution* (New York: Zone Books, 2015), 177–200.

5 Lester Spence, *Knocking the Hustle: Against the Neoliberal Turn in Black Politics* (New York: Punctum Books, 2015), 4.

6 See Michel Foucault, "Governmentality," in *The Essential Foucault*, eds. Paul Rabinow and Nikolas Rose (New York: The New Press, 1994), 229–245; Mitchell Dean, *Governmentality: Power and Rule in Modern Society* (London: Sage, 2009); Nikolas Rose, *Powers of Freedom: Reframing Political Thought* (Cambridge: Cambridge University Press, 2006).

7 Pierre Dardot and Christian Laval, *The New Way of the World: On Neoliberal Society* (London: Verso, 2013), 4.

8 Brown, *Undoing the Demos*, 31.

9 Brown, *Undoing the Demos*, 35–36.

10 See "A Race to the Top Scorecard," *The National Council on Teacher Quality*, www.nctq.org/dmsView/Race_to_the_Top_Scorecard_NCTQ_Report

11 "A Race to the Top Scorecard," 3, www.nctq.org/dmsView/Race_to_the_Top_Scorecard_NCTQ_Report

12 "Benchmarking for Success: Ensuring U.S. Students Receive a World-Class Education," Report by the National Governors Association, the Council of Chief State School Officers, and Achieve, Inc. www.corestandards.org/assets/0812BENCHMARKING.pdf

13 See Nicole Aschoff, *New Prophets of Capital* (London: Verso, 2015), 107–143.

14 Brown, *Undoing the Demos*, 150

15 Brown, *Undoing the Demos*, 127.

16 Raymond Williams, *Marxism and Literature* (Oxford: Oxford University Press, 1977), 128–135.

17 See "An Inventory of Shimmers," in *The Affect Theory Reader*, eds. Melissa Gregg and Gregory J. Seigworth (Durham: Duke University Press, 2010), 1–4.

18 Alexandra Robbins, *The Overachievers: The Secret Lives of Driven Kids* (New York: Hyperion, 2006), 17.

19 Robbins, *The Overachievers*, 54.

20 Robbins, *The Overachievers*, 105.

21 Robbins, *The Overachievers*, 106.

22 Robbins, *The Overachievers*, 208.

23 Robbins, *The Overachievers*, 207–208.

24 Robbins, *The Overachievers*, 268.

25 Robbins, *The Overachievers*, 17.

26 Robbins, *The Overachievers*, 15.

27 Jeffrey Nealon and Susan Searls Giroux, *The Theory Toolbox: Critical Concepts for the Arts, Humanities, and Social Sciences* (Plymouth: Rowman and Littlefield, 2012), 99.

28 Jo Littler, "Meritocracy as Plutocracy: The Marketising of 'Equality' Within Neo-liberalism," *New Formations: A Journal of Culture/Theory/Politics* 80–81: 52–72. doi:10.3898/NewF.80/81.03.2013

29 Randall Lahann and Emilie Mitescu Reagan, "Teach for America and the Politics of Progressive neoliberalism," *Teacher Education Quarterly* 38 (2011): 13.

30 Dardot and Laval, *The New Way of the World*, 319.

Part II

Neoliberal Culture

4

THE HUSTLE

SELF-ENTERPRISE AND NEOLIBERAL LABOR

CHAPTER OVERVIEW

In Part I, we worked to develop a thick understanding of neoliberalism by examining its historical development; its regimes of truth and their consequences; and its cultural powers to shape our social worlds, identities, and possibilities. Now we are ready to delve more fully into Phase IV with a look at everyday life in neoliberalism's enterprise culture.

This chapter explores the neoliberal world of labor, where precarity and global competition have everybody hustling to get by. As we will see, the *hustle* represents a new ideal of labor, one in which earlier ideas of labor rooted in class are replaced with neoliberal ideas of labor rooted in human capital and **self-enterprise**.

Specifically, we trace how the hustle takes over the entirety of our lives. For, when market competition is generalized across the social field, all dimensions of life become defined by self-enterprise and the appreciation of our human capital. As we will see, we must hustle not only for a paycheck, but also to care for each other in an increasingly insecure and unstable world. In addition to exploring these work and care hustles, we will also consider the ways in which the neoliberal state forces us to hustle through its operation of aggressive systems of accumulation by dispossession built to capitalize on our shared precarity and disposability.

Throughout our investigation of these work, care, and state hustles, we will find how much we have in common, but also how different our relationships to, and sensibilities of, neoliberal labor are. In other words, the hustle connects us to one another, but in the course of our everyday lives, we tend to experience the hustle as a form of social disconnection. Ultimately, if we want to be able to imagine and build a world beyond neoliberalism, we have to find ways to hustle together across those lines of class, race, and gender that continue to divide us.

THE HUSTLE

Here's what we already know. Neoliberalism aims to construct a market society by dismantling the limited social welfare protections that emerged in the mid-twentieth century and imposing competition across all dimensions of social life. Central to this project is the promotion of an enterprise culture. According to neoliberal social ontology, society should be understood as "an enterprise made up of enterprises," that is, an amalgamation of autonomous, private individuals, families, communities, and firms competing in the market.[1] Humans are self-appreciating individuals. As we explore throughout this chapter, the implication of this is that the entirety of our lives come to be defined by the demands of neoliberal labor.

In other words, everyday life in enterprise culture is a hustle. In his book *Knocking the Hustle: Against the Neoliberal Turn in Black Politics,* Lester Spence suggests that one way to think about the rise of neoliberalism is in terms of the changing meaning of the word *hustle*:

> Whereas in the late sixties and early seventies the hustler was someone who consistently sought to get over, the person who tried to do as little work as possible in order to make ends meet, with the 'hustled' being the people who were victimized by these individuals ('He hustled me'), the hustler is now someone who consistently works.[2]

Nowadays, everyone is a hustler, as neoliberal precarization has folks working longer and harder in all arenas of life, just to make ends meet.

As Spence argues, this new idea of the hustle is connected to the rise of human capital discourse. As human capital, our lives are to be lived as a project of economic growth. Regardless of whether one is actually at work or not, they must always be looking to grow and develop their capacities for competition in the market. Consequently, lines between everyday life and the market blur, as the myriad contexts of daily living become opportunities to invest in and augment one's self and its capital. This blurring of self, everyday life, and the market across all contexts of social life is why Wendy Brown argues that neoliberalism creates a world where we are always and everywhere *homo oeconomicus*.[3] In other words, when reduced to self-appreciating individuals, our lives become all about labor, specifically the labor of producing and growing our human capital. We live in what many contemporary Marxist scholars call a social factory, where everything we are and everything we do is subsumed by capital, that is, processes of value production and exploitation.

While the discourse of human capital might not sound all that bad in theory, we have to remember that, in neoliberalism, we're all potentially disposable: we exist and matter only insofar that we are deemed worthy of investment by the state or a corporate firm. We don't matter as citizens, only as potential value to the market.[4] I firmly believe that most of us wouldn't consider neoliberalism's reduction of human beings to human capital good or just. And, certainly, most of us don't want the entirety of our lives to be overrun by the demands of labor, economic survival, and competition. So, how exactly did we come to hustle, and why do we accept a life of hustling? These are the questions at the heart of this chapter.

The Self as Enterprise

Melissa Dawn Simkins is a self-branding expert who promises to help her clients "brand a beautiful life," just as she has. "Life in Corporate America was great," Simkins explains on her website. "The thought of entrepreneurship came but didn't stick." It wasn't until tragedy struck that Simkins discovered her true passion for helping others to

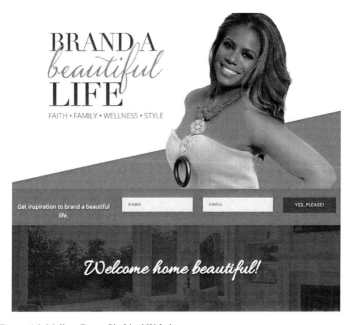

Figure 4.1 Melissa Dawn Simkins' Website

brand themselves. "Although I had a great career, it didn't matter," Simkins writes. "In my deepest pain, I was reunited with a higher purpose . . . to take my passions, knowledge, experience and expertise to serve the world." Leaving behind "a great title and cushy benefits" with "no contacts, contracts, or clients," Simkins set out to "turn her passion for people into profit" by branding herself.

Now a highly successful industry expert, Simkins markets her personal branding program to company leaders and individual entrepreneurs, promising to help them "unleash the power of your personal brand." Simkins also markets her own personal self-brand as a model for other women to create "the life you dream." Specifically, her model encourages women to see "Faith, Family, Wellness, Style" as crucial facets of the self-brand. For carefully tending to these personal sites is a means to nurture, enhance, clarify, and cohere the self and its purpose. In Simkins' model, personal branding is the path to realizing one's true potential.

In so many ways, Simkins epitomizes the hustle, as she actively transforms the entirety of her life and her relationships (with God, family, her body, and soul) into a context for cultivating and developing her human capital. More specifically, Simkins epitomizes the neoliberal ideal of self-enterprise. Simkins is an "entrepreneur of the self." She does not need security and protection from an employer or a state. She is actively empowered by the privatization of risk, as she finds beauty, happiness, and success by applying an entrepreneurial spirit to all of life's endeavors.

However, despite Simkins' individual empowerment, self-enterprise is not as much a choice as it is "a new subjective norm."[5] In other words, while the discourse of self-enterprise might enable us to feel like we're in the driver's seat of our lives, in actuality, this discourse is what keeps us following the neoliberal highway code. Once again, we find that there is thus a gigantic contradiction at the heart of neoliberal culture. What we are supposed to experience as freedom—the ability to live one's life as an enterprise—is not really freedom at all. That's the power of neoliberal governmentality: our freedom to compete is the medium of social control. As we are going to find out, neoliberal labor exists on a continuum, where we are at once "free" and "forced" to hustle to different degrees, depending on our social position in market society.

For example, in her book, *Be Creative,* Angela McRobbie describes how young, working- and middle-class women from a range of cultural and racial backgrounds actively embrace self-enterprise in their quests to land work in the creative and cultural industries. Specifically, they embrace the *command* to "be creative." For McRobbie's students, this command is experienced as a press to self-expression and self-actualization. As Simkins' rhetoric suggests, this command to be creative is "encouraging rather than coercive." It is "an invitation to discover one's own capabilities, to embark on a voyage of self-discovery."[6] Put a little differently, while neoliberal governmentality and the norms of competition are highly disciplinary, the subject of self-enterprise translates market discipline into personal freedom. The imperative to be creative compels subjects to willingly and "freely" take on risks (i.e., debt, uncertainty) in the name of self-empowerment. This risk-taking is equated with personal freedom and responsibility which, as McRobbie notes, helps to obscure, and even negate, the material threats of neoliberal precarization. In this way, the command to "be creative" helps to dismantle the social welfare state, as it provides a "template for being middle class and learning to live without welfare protection and social security."[7] Through discourses of creativity, subjects of enterprise are incited and excited to live precarious lives premised solely on their own initiative and entrepreneurial creativity. They are prompted to desire a social world untethered from public infrastructures and more collective forms of social doing.

It is so important to point out just how empowering and promising this creative command *feels* for McRobbie's working-class students. A creative career promises them individual fulfillment and gender freedom, as well as an imagined path to middle-class belonging, all things that their parents did not necessarily have access to. However, while self-enterprise presents itself as a potentially empowering project of self-making and citizenship, it represents one of neoliberalism's primary status-quo stories: namely, that self-enterprise is the only way to freedom and equality. But as we will see, self-enterprise actually perpetuates the exact opposite: social control and inequality. It keeps us stuck in the disimagination machine, unable to envision alternative possibilities.

Divided We Hustle

The goal of this chapter is to critique the status-quo story of the self as enterprise by unpacking the logics of the hustle, the interconnected forms of exploitation this logic sustains, and its consequences for our individual and collective lives. More specifically, we examine how the status-quo story of the self as an enterprise cuts deep into our capacities for commonality and collective doing in two interrelated ways.

The first way that the norm of self-enterprise shuts down our capacities for commonality is through **de-proletarianization**. The status-quo story of self-enterprise invites workers to think of themselves not as a class—that is, workers with experiences, positions, and problems in common—but as private, highly individualized enterprises locked in competition with each other. We are out to achieve the American Dream for ourselves, to best our peers, and to realize our own potential as human capital. Indeed, thanks to discourses of human capital, we, as workers, are no longer interpellated as a class (the proletariat), that is, as a collective bargaining unit, much less a historical force in a struggle between capital and labor as Marx had elaborated. Rather, we are addressed as enterprises unto ourselves: self-enclosed, individualized agents freely pursuing our ends in the market. Consequently, workers come to see themselves not as workers exchanging their labor for a wage, but rather as empowered individuals where the very idea of labor as class and exploitation disappears into the project appreciating human capital. In this way, the norm of self-enterprise de-proletarianizes workers. Workers no longer appear alienated and exploited like Marx had suggested, as de-proletarianization means "abolishing any sense of alienation and even *distance* between individuals and the enterprises employing them."[8] As we saw above with McRobbie's students, when interpellated as entrepreneurs of the self, workers are invited to imagine themselves as part of a meritocratic classless society. Here, social mobility and status are the product of individual ingenuity, creativity, and innovation, not the material realities of class and worker exploitation. Rather than banding together around our common experiences of rising insecurity and inequality, human capital guides workers to meet the precarity with self-enterprise, that is, to take personal responsibility for their lives through engaging in heightened competition. After all, a world where all workers are potentially disposable requires us to work to maintain our competitive edge over others and prove ourselves worthy of investment. We must be constantly working to grow, manage, optimize, and enhance our own human capital.

The second way that the status-quo story of the self as an enterprise diminishes our capacities for commonality is through its connection to the **biopolitics of disposability**. The norm of self-enterprise also works to divide workers according to their perceived economic value and capacities to hustle "freely." Indeed, while some hustles (for example, Simkins') are heralded as empowering and liberating, other hustles are deeply oppressive. Put another way, being able to self-brand oneself into a job represents success in enterprise culture. But what happens to those who can't successfully self-enterprise like Simkins? What happens to those whom competition renders disposable? As we know, in neoliberal culture, failure to successfully enterprise the self is attributed not to broader systems like capitalism, racism, or patriarchy, but rather to individuals and individuals alone. People who don't, can't, or won't conform to the norm of self-enterprise are considered disposable and thus subject to harsh and aggressive regimes of social control. All in all, the message is clear: as Britney Spears puts it, "you better work, bitch."

In so many ways, the discourses surrounding the rise of the so-called gig economy epitomize these new ideas of labor rooted in self-enterprise, including the promises of de-proletarianization and the cruelties of disposability. In the gig economy, stable jobs with security and benefits are replaced with a series of short-term, contract-based gigs and side-gigs. Supposedly, in being unleashed from the confines and drudgery of traditional employment, gig workers are the true entrepreneurs. Creative and risk-taking, they are empowered to chart their own dreams and destinies. Traditionally, musicians epitomized

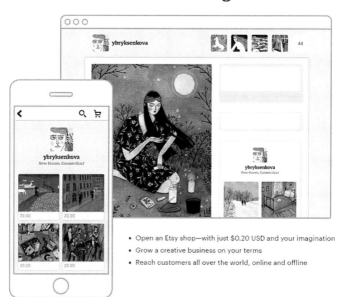

Sell creative goods

- Open an Etsy shop—with just $0.20 USD and your imagination
- Grow a creative business on your terms
- Reach customers all over the world, online and offline

Figure 4.2 Etsy's Website

the gig worker, as they hopped from gig to gig to pursue their creative passions. In recent years however, digital technologies and platforms have rapidly expanded the gig economy. Consequently, folks' creative energies for living become potential resources to be capitalized on and valorized through gig work.

For example, Etsy (see Figure 4.2) is an online marketplace where "creative entrepreneurs" can sell their unique goods (e.g., handmade jewelry, vintage home decor). Etsy provides an accessible platform for enterprising individuals to set up shop and start capitalizing on their creative energies and talents. The site's mission is "to reimagine commerce in ways that build a more fulfilling and lasting world." Similarly, companies like Airbnb and Uber allow anyone (with a home/apartment or a car and a good driving record) to become an enterprise unto themselves. This digitally fueled gig economy is often referred to as a "sharing economy" poised to realize a market utopia of small entrepreneurs—a spontaneous order of autonomous and free actors providing goods and services through the most efficient and socially beneficial means. However, while gigs, side-gigs, and digitized marketplaces promise creativity, flexibility, and freedom, they offer little in the way of protection, benefits, and security, as workers, not the state or the employer, must assume all of the risk and uncertainty of doing business.

In a way, enterprise culture and the hustle invite us—and require us—to be gig workers. However, not all gigs are created equal. For example, let's hold celebrated gigs like owning an Etsy store or driving for Uber together with the horrific murder of Eric Garner by New York City police on July 17, 2014. Garner's death was attributed to the police officers' putting Garner in a chokehold and compressing his chest, aggressive actions that his health could not sustain. When initially approached by the police officers, Garner was working a gig: he was acting as an entrepreneur, selling loose cigarettes on the street. Ultimately, Garner lost his life because his self-enterprise—his "hustle"—was criminalized; therefore, a lethal state response was "justified." As the devastating circumstances surrounding Garner's death make clear, enterprise culture is built on *shared precarity* (we are all hustling), but also on *expanded, retrenched inequality* (the hustle divides us). The subjective norm of self-enterprise creates stark divisions between those who are fit to hustle "freely" and those who are ultimately disposable.

The Three Hustles

In the remaining sections, we trace how the hustle—the norm of self-enterprise and its consequences of de-proletarianization and disposability—come to define the totality of our lives. Specifically, we explore "work hustles" (how folks hustle for pay); "care hustles" (how folks hustle to sustain and reproduce their social world); and "state hustles" (how folks are forced to hustle by the neoliberal state). Crucially, these hustles work simultaneously, though in different ways, to keep us divided from one another, even though we are all hustling, all of the time. I insist that our critical understanding of the neoliberal culture remains radically incomplete if we cannot see the connection between work, care, and state hustles. In other words, we must come to see, and feel, that we are all living in the social factory; we just may be working in different buildings, on very different sorts of projects. Ultimately, the cultural politics of the hustle have profound implications for our future, diminishing our capacities for class and worker solidarity, as well as for collective caretaking and social interconnection, at the very moment when we've never had more in common, and more to gain from, as Spence puts, "knocking the hustle."

WORK HUSTLES

For most people, work sucks. It's defined by excruciating hours, declining pay and benefits, tedious yet demanding tasks, and insecurity and uncertainty. So, why don't more folks demand better working conditions, better job security, and better pay? Why don't more people support and organize themselves into labor unions? Why don't we all recognize and act on our shared experiences of precarization? To answer these questions, we have to take a trip through the neoliberal world of work.

Post-Fordism

It is crucial to understand that the rise of enterprise culture and the hustle is connected to deeper shifts in capitalism ushered in by the advancement of neoliberal hegemony. As we learned in Chapter 1, these shifts are not the result of natural developments in capitalism, but of hegemonic struggle. In constructing a world of global competition, where capital is free to flow across geographic and institutional borders with fewer and fewer restraints, neoliberalism has created new global systems of profit-making and worker exploitation.

More specifically, the neoliberal world of work is what many scholars describe as a "post-Fordist" economy that is very different from the world of industrial capitalism. Fordism refers to Henry Ford's industrial-capitalist approach to manufacturing automobiles. In this system, accumulation is organized around the mass production and consumption of goods. Companies manufacture commodities like cars in high volumes and sell them at prices workers can afford. From the perspective of capitalism, the most important unit of this process is the commodity. Profits are reaped from selling goods to households at prices that exceed the costs of production (i.e., workers' wages, materials). In its heyday, this system aligned with Keynesian macro-economics, which strove to maintain a balance, albeit one tilted toward capital, between the interests of workers (mostly male and white) and the interests of owners (mostly male and white). Thus, the Fordist world of work was not some utopia. It excluded many women and minorities, and, in fact, even actively relied on their oppression and exploitation.

Post-Fordism, on the other hand, emerges in tandem with neoliberalism. Here's how the story goes: in a world of economic competition, countries cannot be tied down by that "web of social and political constraints" established by embedded liberalism. Rather, corporations have to be free (that is, permitted by government re-regulations) to lower wages and benefits, to lay off workers, and to shift operations overseas for competitive purposes. Above all, competition requires more "flexible" processes of capital accumulation. What David Harvey calls flexible accumulation ultimately means that companies don't have to rely on mass production and consumption to make money. Instead, they can shift their focus to manufacturing batches of goods with cheap labor and little environmental regulation in the Global South; these goods are then marketed to specific consumer groups in the Global North at exorbitantly marked-up prices.

Consequently, a new international division of labor has emerged, as many manufacturing plants have migrated to developing countries for cheap labor, while post-industrial nations transform themselves into service/communication/knowledge-based economies. For example, think of a technology company like Apple. Many of the jobs in post-industrial economies of the Global North are in product design and development as well as in retail and sales. However, the phones, laptops, and tablets that are conceptualized and sold to consumers are primarily manufactured by workers in the Global South under often horrendous conditions—long hours, terrible pay, unsafe facilities, and poor living conditions. Apple famously came under public scrutiny in 2013 when it was revealed that eighteen workers had committed suicide at one of its plants; the company's response was to put up safety nets to prevent future acts.

All told then, flexible accumulation might help corporations compete, but it also means heightened and often brutal exploitation of workers around the world. In this context, corporations hold the threat of disposability over communities, forcing a "race to the bottom" when it comes to salaries, worker protections, and tax breaks for large businesses. In other words, communities must compete for jobs by offering up riper conditions for worker and resource exploitation.

It is important to note briefly that, in post-Fordism, since the manufacturing of commodities becomes so cheap and flexible, individual commodities cease to be the primary site of value production. Instead, in contemporary global capitalism fueled by financialization, large, multinational firms are now primarily in the business of selling themselves and their brand through the strategic construction and communication of cultural meanings and values. For what matters most now for a company's bottom line is how they are positioned within and viewed by the global financial networks and markets of Empire.

Immaterial Labor

The transition to post-Fordism, flexible accumulation, and branding means significant changes in the everyday worlds of workers, particularly when it comes to the sorts of jobs that are available and the forms of labor these jobs demand. In Fordist capitalism, the leading form of labor was manufacturing. In post-Fordist capitalism, the leading form of labor is what Marxist scholars call **immaterial labor**. Nick Dyer-Witheford and Greig de Peuter explain that immaterial labor "is not primarily about making a material object, like the work that

Table 4.1 Immaterial Labors

Immaterial Labor	Examples
Developing technology and managing information systems	Tech industry, data management
Communication and social relations	Public relations, project management, human relations
Servicing consumers and clients	Customer service work, jobs in distribution and transportation
Generating cultural content, emotions, and feelings	Advertising and marketing, sales, creative work

makes a car roll off an assembly line or extracts coal from a mine"; instead, it refers to "less-tangible symbolic and social dimensions" of production.[9] Simply put, immaterial labor produces knowledge, information, meaning, symbols, and affects. As Table 4.1 suggests, immaterial labor is central to a range of different jobs common today in post-industrial countries like the United States.

The workplaces of post-Fordism are very different from those of Fordism, as immaterial labor is a form of all-consuming labor where the lines between self and employer, labor and leisure, office and home, fade away. The neoliberal world of work reaches deeply into the nooks and crannies of worker lives and subjectivities as the primary site of worker exploitation and value extraction is no longer workers' activity on a production line, but their own affective and cognitive capacities.

For example, many available jobs these days are in the service industry. These jobs require selling products, lifestyles, and experiences, and thus hinge on what sociologist Arlie Hochschild calls "deep acting" and "feeling games."[10] Regardless of what's happening, workers must perform for their customers. Put on a smile. Hold back anger. The customer is always right. Indeed, when you work for a company, you're required to calibrate your attitude (not to mention your appearance) to fit your employer's brand and economic interests. In these jobs, the site of exploitation thus encompasses workers' affects and emotions. Work requires what scholars call affective or emotional labor, as it is your job to produce particular feelings and experiences for your customers and/ or clients. This shift in labor is often discussed—and lamented—as a feminization of work, as emotional and affective labor are associated with labors of femininity and care work.

While affective and emotional labor are central to many forms of service work, cognitive labor is central to many other jobs in the knowledge and information industries. For example, companies like Google provide comfy places to nap and gyms for blowing of steam, all in hopes of better exploiting the creativity and imagination of their workforce. Indeed, big technology firms are often celebrated for constructing fun, elaborate campuses, designed to keep employees at work all the time. Instead of capitalizing on workers' affective performances and the feelings, these companies seek primarily to exhaust workers' cognitive capacities.[11]

In addition to its all-consuming nature, work in the post-Fordist economy is characterized by intense individual competition. Thanks to the power and organizing efforts of unions, the manufacturing jobs associated with Fordism were often secure jobs with rising incomes and good benefits. Generally speaking, they afforded working-class people (primarily white men) middle-class lives—the American Dream of a self-reliant, nuclear family. However, flexible accumulation demands flexible workers, that is, individuals who can live with high degrees of insecurity and change and are willing to work more and more for less and less. Instead of expecting to find stable, full-time employment (the goal of Keynesianism), today's workforce must be trained to expect insecurity and to compete for work.

Good vs. Bad Jobs

So here's the funny thing about the neoliberal world of flexible accumulation and immaterial labor. Work sucks for everyone, but as Spence explains, powerful cultural distinctions exist between good and bad jobs. On one hand, some gigs pay a high salary and come with perks and benefits; moreover, they provide their workers with access to powerful social networks and forms of cultural capital. These are good jobs. They support a comfortable lifestyle, and they supply the necessary social connections so that workers can often find other good jobs if and when their time comes to have to "flexibly" adapt to a new position. On the other hand, there are bad jobs that rarely offer a living wage; thus, often, workers must have more than one bad job just to get by. These jobs pay low wages and provide few perks and benefits. These are dead-end jobs with little opportunity for advancement—much less fun, autonomy, creativity, self-actualization, and self-enterprise. Of course, everyone is desperate to land a good job, but the jobs most readily available are bad jobs.

In a culture of personal responsibility, generalized competition, and rampant inequality, these distinctions between good and bad jobs translate easily into distinctions between good and bad workers. We often assume those with good jobs must have earned, and thus deserve, them. Those with bad jobs must be losers who didn't successfully compete. Therefore, there appears to be no reason to address broader structures of work and systems of exploitation; people are getting precisely what they deserve in the spontaneous order of the market. But here's the thing: everyone is hustling, working on overdrive for the benefit of global corporations and markets. The distinctions between good and bad jobs, and good and bad workers, prevent us from seeing our commonalities and the shared structures of exploitation that delineate our working lives within neoliberal capitalism.

Karen Ho's ethnography of work on Wall Street, arguably the epitome of a good job, is revealing. Those who land jobs on Wall Street are heralded as the cream of the crop in their field. They are recruited from elite universities and have much more social capital than most. Yet, they are intensely exploited as they enter what Ho describes as a "workplace of rampant insecurity, intense hard work, and exorbitant pay for performance compensation."[12] Ho recalls her own experience of a training program to become a Wall Street analyst:

> I was initially surprised about how candid Wall Streeters were in recognizing and laughing about the exploitation of analysts (and many associates) until I realized that regularly working over 100 hours per week for years was not only normative, but widely accepted, even touted as a positive attraction of the investment banking workplace.[13]

Wall Street workers embrace precarity and disposability, working pretty much 24/7 not only to earn performance-based perks and compensation, but for the sake of the hustle. For it's this intense, all-consuming nature of their hustle that makes them good, self-enterprising workers and augments their human capital. As Ho explains, "For investment bankers, the labor of most nine-to-five workers, the honest (but plodding) day's work from which my informants regularly distinguish themselves, is understood as complacent and stagnantly routine."[14] From the warped perspective of Wall Street labor, a job that does not consume your life is a bad job—it connotes a lack of self-enterprise.[15]

Meanwhile, in the shadow of Wall Street, everyone is hustling, but one's sense and experience of the hustle depends on one's social position. Recall people like Brandon (who we read about in Chapter 2): instead of being empowered by the exciting, highly valued hustle of global finance, folks like Brandon hustle at far less glamorous jobs in the service industry in order to take personal responsibility for their lives and decisions. Brandon is smart; he works hard, and he hangs on the idea that one day he will land what, for him, represents a good job: a nine-to-five occupation that provides some measure of self-fulfillment and security. As such, his work hustle is more about making ends meet as he continues to search for that elusive path to the good life.

CRITICAL PRACTICE

- How does our quick trip through the rise of post-Fordism help you make sense of your everyday life as a worker? What forms of labor do you/have you performed at work? Do you feel exploited? When and where do you feel exploitation most acutely?
- What is your idea of a good job and a bad job? Ultimately, what distinguishes good and bad jobs in your imagination? What are the critical implications of these distinctions when it comes to how you think about work, your future, and your connection to other workers?
- How would common reason (discussed in the conclusion of the previous chapter) invite us to respond to the neoliberal world of work? How might we begin to draw lines of connection between our different experiences of post-Fordism, neoliberal precarity, and Empire?

The Labors of Self-Enterprise

In this new world of work defined by ever-diverging good and bad jobs, workers must not only give more of their lives to their employers. They must also work outside of their workplace to develop human capital in hopes of landing a good job. We can think of these ancillary forms of immaterial labor performed outside of the realm of paid work as the **labors of self-enterprise**. Perhaps the most obvious and pervasive labor of self-enterprise is self-branding. As we saw with Simkins, self-branding involves the active and purposeful cultivation of a coherent and lucrative self-image. According to Ernest Sternberg, this demand is relatively new. Since the rise of industrial capitalism, there have been three distinct ways of talking about work. In romantic labor, work was connected to inner virtue and goodness of character. Modernist labor, on the other hand, was scientific and quantitative. In the infamous workplaces designed by William Taylor, work was understood in terms of measurable outputs. Workers were not imagined to be valued for their inner worth or work ethic, but for their material, observable productivity. More recently, we see the rise of phantasmagoric labor where "workers labor to produce personae consonant with the dictates of their particular jobs."[16]

In other words, the contemporary workplace, defined by insecurity and the threat of disposability, demands that workers think of themselves as brands and thus work to always present themselves as valuable commodities and sound investments. Just like a company that works to create meaning and value for itself and its products, workers must develop and manage their own branded personae for their audience of potential employers and consumers. As media theorist Alison Hearn suggests,

> Just as we accept the loading up of goods with evocative emotions and meanings by advertisers, we understand that we, ourselves, must also consciously self-present. We load ourselves up with meaningfulness; we work hard at issues of self-image in an effort to constitute ourselves as 'significant' iconic-workers.[17]

It is crucial to understand, however, that only certain worker-selves are brandable, as what performances and personas are imagined to have value in the first place are intimately bound up with broader cultural codes, discourses, and social hierarchies. Self-branding requires the commodification of the self, and self-commodification requires access to distinct forms of social, cultural, bodily, and economic capital. As Hearn explains, "Self-branding involves the self-conscious construction of a meta-narrative and meta-image of self through the use of cultural meanings and images drawn from the narrative and visual codes of the mainstream culture industries";[18] in other words, branding yourself in a way that aligns with popular images, identities, and ideologies. Thus, not everyone is capable of crafting a consumable, competitive image; not everyone's body or self-presentation is readily legible as human capital.

While these processes of self-commodification might seem to diminish one's authenticity and individuality, in the contexts of everyday precarious life, discourses of self-branding promise agency and empowerment in an insecure world where the threat of disposability looms large. The ultimate goal of self-branding is the cultivation and presentation of a self who signifies youthfulness, the potential for growth and change, and the ability to "let go of the past."[19] As Dardot and Laval note, within neoliberal culture, self-mastery "no longer consists in leading one's life in a linear, rigid and conformist way, but in proving oneself capable of flexibility, of entrepreneurship."[20] For, in the new world of work, one cannot be viewed as stagnant, stubborn, or too attached to a particular position or role, as these qualities are now associated with welfare and its alleged "culture of dependency." Rather, workers must prove themselves to be flexible and personally responsible—to stay relevant and competitive. Through crafting a unique, yet recognizable self-brand from the popular codes of what's fashionable, youthful, and hip at the moment, one demonstrates their entrepreneurial spirit and commitment to a life of constant personal growth, flexibility, and self-reinvention, that is, to a life of self-appreciation of one's human capital.

Self-Enterprise on Reality TV

As many critical media scholars like Hearn have shown, reality television is one cultural site that reflects and participates in the neoliberal world of self-enterprise, where the demands of neoliberal labor are represented and negotiated by "real" people. Competition shows like *The Apprentice*, *Survivor*, and *The Bachelor*, for example, actively construct all-consuming, phantasmagoric work environments, where contestants—eager to hustle for free in exchange for a chance to win a competition (as well as grow their own brand and media celebrity)—offer up the totality of their lives for exploitation by the media industries. Viewers, in turn, watch these contestants engage in various forms of immaterial labor with the aim of besting their peers and avoiding disposability on the show.

Laurie Ouellette's analysis of *America's Next Top Model* (*ANTM*) is a useful example. *ANTM* is a talent competition where aspiring young models, often from underprivileged backgrounds, are taught the in-and-outs of the modeling industry through a series of challenges that test their capacities for flexibility, adaptability, self-branding, and hard work. "Games like *ANTM* teach contestants (and, vicariously, TV viewers) to envision themselves as human capital, so that the line between playing a role for television, navigating the conditions of work, and creating oneself as a marketable product is inextricably blurred," explains Ouellette.[21] Reality TV thus becomes an extension of neoliberal governmentality, as viewers watch contestants learn to adopt the techniques of immaterial labor and to internalize the demands of flexible work and the norm of competitive self-enterprise. Audiences are encouraged to identify with and pull for those characters who seem deserving and to relish the demise of those contestants who do not. Indeed, so many reality shows position viewers as judges, inviting us, with the help of the program's official experts, to evaluate the contestant-worker's merit and their performance of self-enterprise.

While competition shows like *ANTM* narrate and normalize the all-consuming and competitive nature of immaterial labor, makeover programs circulate more specific and practical strategies for navigating the precarious workplace. As a popular genre that circulates across media culture—from the proliferation of YouTube make-up videos to reality television programs like *What Not to Wear* (*WNTW*)—makeover programming engages viewers in the work of strategic self-fashioning: "remaking one's body, personality, and image in a calculated way to bring about personal advantage in a competitive marketplace."[22] On shows like *WNTW*,

> shopping ceases to be a recreational venue for escaping the drudgery of work (as in the leisure-time activity of "going to the mall") or fulfilling oneself through symbolic commodities, and becomes instead a route to carefully building an image that is salable in the marketplace of work.[23]

However, the stakes of the makeover are larger than one's marketability for a specific job. Brenda Weber suggests that we live in "Makeover Nation" where one's citizenship hinges on the capacities for self-transformation, that is, for clearing the slate and starting anew. Makeover media put on display the "before" and "after" self, tracing a journey from a "failed or imperiled selfhood . . . stalled and stagnated" to new, more empowered and authentic self who has earned citizenship in Makeover Nation. "Such is the power of transformation that makeovers empower subjects to voice wondrous statements of jubilation and reward ('I can do anything now!' 'I'm going straight to the top!')," Weber explains.[24]

Ultimately, the makeover is about fashioning oneself as flexible, self-appreciating, and worthy of investment. In this way, the labors of self-enterprise are a tenuous means of counteracting the threat of disposability. A made-over appearance or new self-brand can enhance the self-enterprise in an insecure, flexible economy. The hope is that presenting a self who is not "stalled or stagnated" but ready to work, grow, and realize their potential within the cultural norms of enterprise culture will allow workers to find a good job in the uncertain world of flexible work and bad jobs. However, as we already know, individuals cannot actually guarantee their own success no matter how much they work to grow their human capital.

Ultimately, the labors of self-enterprise prompt workers to become more fully engaged in competition. Accordingly, neoliberal workers don't look to their shared class horizons, despite common experiences of precarization and insecurity. Instead, the labors of self-enterprise engender de-proletarianization and a process of disimagination, whereby the only working-world that is felt to matter is a self-enclosed one of growing human capital.

CRITICAL PRACTICE

- How would you makeover yourself and construct a self-brand? What are the dominant cultural codes and norms that would inform these practices of self-fashioning? Why do you imagine that these codes and norms have value? In other words, why do you think they will sell? What resources do you need to fashion and maintain your brand? Can you envision self-brands that would not sell? What makes them lacking in value?
- Based on your responses to the above questions, what is the connection between self-branding and social inequality? How does self-branding work to perpetuate the norm of self-enterprise and its critical consequences of de-proletarianization and the biopolitics of disposability?

CARE HUSTLES

Neoliberalism's enterprise culture not only forces us to hustle to get paid. It also turns social reproduction—that is, the work of caring for and sustaining ourselves and each other—into a hustle. It is so crucial to understand that capitalism and the world of paid labor depend on the often invisible world of usually unpaid reproductive labor. After all, someone has to take care of the workers who produce the value and profit. Simply put, children need to be raised; food needs to be bought, prepared, and consumed; homes need to be cleaned and maintained. Ideally, within liberal capitalism, the care work associated with social reproduction happens in the private sphere of family and is undertaken by women.

As Nancy Fraser argues, neoliberalism creates an acute *crisis of care and social reproduction*, as precarization demands that *everyone* engages in longer and harder work hustles, leaving little time and resources left to actually sustain, replenish, and reproduce workers.[25] In order to deal with this scarcity in the realm of social reproduction, care itself becomes a hustle. For the most part, care hustles fall on the shoulders of women, who continue to be regarded as the keepers of the home and naturalized as caretakers. It is important to point out that poorer families and single-headed households have long had to contend with capitalism's crisis of care. However, precarization generalizes this crisis across the population. No wonder there's so much talk these days about the problem of work–life balance! Of course, if you're wealthy, dealing with the crisis of care can be handled by outsourcing the labor of social reproduction to paid caretakers. However, most folks don't have the means for this solution. Instead, women just hustle harder, taking responsibility for their families through self-enterprise.

Postfeminism and the Gender Division of Labor

While post-Fordism demands new forms of work on the self, it also relies on old divisions of labor: most notably, the *gender division of labor* that is endemic to liberal capitalism. In the heyday of Fordist capitalism, for example, men were positioned as the primary paid workers, while women were regarded as the keepers of the domestic realm and as primary consumers of all the new products being produced. Women—specifically white, middle-class women—were not imagined to participate in paid labor. Rather, their roles were consumption and domesticity: tending to the private sphere of home and family. The second-wave women's movement was largely about challenging this gender division of labor at the heart of liberal capitalism.[26]

This image of domestic stability and gender division represented a powerful cultural norm that circulated throughout popular culture, for example, on television programs like *Leave It to Beaver* (though, this idealized gender norm was far from reality for most families). Such representations of white, happy, self-enclosed households articulated embedded liberalism's promise of the good life enabled by the family wage. Crucially, these representations of family happiness and gender division stood in sharp contrast to poor families, especially African-American families, who did not conform to the nuclear ideal of a single male breadwinner and dependent female caretaker.

However, the neoliberal transition to flexible accumulation and immaterial labor has both unsettled and intensified the gender division of labor, as well as its racial and class politics. Nowadays, the family headed by a single, male breadwinner is an increasingly impossible model to follow for more and more families. Consequently, rather than adopting a purely domestic role, women are now actively encouraged into the world of paid, flexible work. Increasingly, all women, not just poor women, become responsible for contributing to the family wage, but they also continue to shoulder primary responsibility for the domestic realm as "natural" caretakers.

In the neoliberal world of work, then, new gender ideologies and cultural ideals circulate. Specifically, women are interpellated by what feminist media scholars have theorized as postfeminist discourses. **Postfeminism** is a sensibility that suggests that the goals of feminism have been achieved and that women are now free to make a life of their own.[27] To work or not to work: they have the freedom to choose. Supposedly, you can even "have it all," a high-powered, fulfilling career and a happy family life, so long as you hustle and make good choices. In this way, postfeminism represents a gendered version of neoliberal self-enterprise. Young women are widely heralded as "can do girls," full of capacity, potential, and human capital.[28] However, the women remain responsible for the bulk of care labor such that most can't actually participate in the flexible economy on par with men. As we know, immaterial labor demands long and unpredictable hours at odds with the ongoing demands of raising children. And while unions have been decimated and the neoliberal state is evermore loathe to provide public supports like child care, there is little recourse for women seeking greater equality and workers' rights.

As Angela McRobbie suggests, postfeminism is profoundly para-doxical in this sense, as it doubly entangles subjects in supposedly gender-neutral values of self-enterprise and highly gendered norms of traditional motherhood and domesticity. On the one hand, in post-feminist ideology, liberal feminist ideals of equality become embed-ded as commonsense: of course, women are equal to men and should participate in paid labor and public life. On the other hand, women are subjected to conservative gender discourses that retrench the gen-der division of labor and reinscribe women's responsibility for social reproduction.[29]

Mamapreneurialism

While postfeminist ideologies entangle female subjects in the competing demands of self-enterprise and family care, ongoing precarization and the crisis of care also mean that women must hustle to maintain and reproduce their families. Within neoliberalism, the private sphere of the family—once imagined to be a space of care shielded from the whims of the market—becomes the primary site for dealing with the day-to-day challenges of living in competition. Thus, neoliberalism intensifies women's care work as they are increasingly asked to deal with the fall-out of neoliberal governmentality, including shrinking public supports, underfunded schools, and insecurity in the workplace. Indeed, neoliberalism dramatically extends women's work: as the state steps back from providing infrastructures for social protection and security, it is women who pick up the slack, for example, by volunteering in schools and churches, caring for aging parents or other extended family members, and picking up side-gigs to augment the family's bottom line. In this way, neoliberalism makes the traditional work of caring for the family increasingly fraught and difficult. In a precarious world where resources are scarce and competition is fierce, mothers must work harder and harder just to ensure their family's survival.

All this means that, in addition to working a "first" shift of paid labor alongside a "second" (and often "third") shift of unpaid caring labor, women also must find ways to secure the family in a precarious world. Indeed, enterprise culture requires women to become mamapreneurial, that is, to see themselves as the CEOs of the home and to take personal responsibility for their families' social security, protection, and reproduction. In this way, mamapreneurialism promises to patch up the structural crisis of care by inciting individual mothers to enterprise themselves and their families.[30]

For example, consider Jenny's story. Jenny is a working-class, Christian-conservative, stay-at-home mother of three, whose family was devastated by the Great Recession of 2008. When her husband lost his job in the oil industry, the family was forced to sell their home at a loss, give up their family vehicle, and move back to Jenny's home-town. In the face of these massive losses, Jenny took it upon herself to hustle the family back to economic security. While her husband struggled to find steady work, Jenny become a mamapreneur. She started couponing and established two home-based marketing busi-nesses, first with Thirty One, a Christian company that sells totes, can-dles, and other lifestyle products, and then with Get Life, a company that sells health and beauty supplies, most notably, fat-trimming body wraps. Jenny was determined to provide economic security for her family through market enterprise, explaining to us that she hoped her sales work would one day be so successful that her husband would not actually have to worry anymore about finding a job. Consequently, Jenny dedicated all of her spare time to realizing this goal for her family, turning her friendships and social networks into a platform for her own self- and family enterprise.[31]

Ultimately, as the mamapreneurial CEOs of the domestic realm, mothers are responsible not only for warding off neoliberal threats to the family, but also for ensuring that the family enterprise is happy and autonomous despite precarization. It is so important to understand that, for Jenny, the maintenance of a self-enclosed, nuclear family serves as the primary compensation for a life of insecurity and uncertainty. For a happy, self-reliant family continues to signal the good life, even though many of the social infrastructures that made it possible have gone away.

Importantly, this happy family ideal that women work hard to maintain is also about distinguishing one's own family from those that are not able to achieve a good life through self-enterprise. For example, Jenny felt deeply empowered by Get Life and credited the company for her family's recovered happiness. Additionally, Jenny explained proudly how Get Life has empowered two friends to "get off welfare." Being dependent on the state is a sign that one's family is unhappy, as they cannot achieve happiness on their own through self-enterprise.[32] Put differently, mamapreneurialism guides women to disconnect their family situation from those of others, especially from those who are most devastated by neoliberal precarity. Of course, *all* mothers are working hard to care for their families, but the mamapreneurial hustle refuses the commonalities of the care hustle, enacting a cultural process of de-proletarianization in the highly gendered and increasingly crisis-laden world of social reproduction.

STATE HUSTLES

The final set of hustles we are going to explore are different from the work and care hustles discussed above. In these latter hustles, individuals and families are allegedly "free" to hustle, that is, to self-enterprise and take personal responsibility in the market.

In stark contrast, state hustles represent institutionalized forms of hustling where people are directly forced into highly exploitative, state-sponsored labor. In these hustles, the neoliberal state and private corporations work together to capitalize on the biopolitics of disposability and our shared precarity. Thus, these institutionalized hustles are closer to the traditional sense of the word described by Spence—hustling as "getting hustled"—as ordinary people, especially the poorest and most vulnerable, are offered up as a disposable means to corporate profit. As disturbing as they are, state hustles should not really surprise us. After all, neoliberal governmentality is no longer aimed at securing and protecting population, but rather promoting the private interests of global capitalism and Empire.

From Welfare to Workfare

The first state hustle that we will consider is being on welfare. Welfare reform is perhaps the centerpiece, both culturally and political-economically speaking, of neoliberalism and its dismantling of the social welfare state. It used to be that welfare programs constituted a vital part of our social reproduction infrastructures, supplementing the unpaid labor of individual women caring for their families in the private sphere of the home. A form of collective caretaking, they provided a bare minimum of protection for poor families, especially women and children. It is important to understand that folks on welfare have long been made to stand in contrast to the private autonomous nuclear family discussed above; indeed, there is nothing specifically neoliberal about Jenny's investment in creating a happy, self-reliant family and distinguishing her own family from those who are on welfare. However, what *is* new about neoliberal welfare is that these programs are no longer about providing social protection and safety to poor families; instead, they are about forcing poor people to hustle for corporations. Today welfare is workfare.

As Patricia Ventura examines in *Neoliberal Culture: Living with American Neoliberalism*, the face of social welfare has changed dramatically since the first federal cash-assistance program, Aid to Families with Dependent Children, was established in 1935. Then, it was the figure of a helpless white widow in need of protection and support for her family that grounded discourses of social welfare. Today, as we know, welfare discourses are rooted firmly in the image of the black "welfare queen" who supposedly is out to game the system. Here's the history of this shift in broad strokes, according to Ventura. Early nineteenth-century welfare programs were designed to help the "worthy poor" only and thus imposed strict "moral character" provisions on recipients. While these provisions were challenged and reformed, they were nonetheless conveniently relied on throughout the early twentieth century to disqualify African-American women from receiving support. Public assistance was reserved for white women, so that they wouldn't have to work for a living, thereby abandoning their children and domestic duties. In sharp contrast, black women were not associated with the virtues of motherhood and therefore were regarded as better suited for working outside of their own homes, so they were denied benefits and forced into precarious, unprotected, low-wage work often as domestic servants in other folks' homes. The civil rights movement, however, helped to challenge state discrimination around welfare eligibility and who should qualify for social protection, enabling more black women in need to receive benefits. Around the same time though, unemployment was beginning to skyrocket as manufacturing jobs were lost in the millions. Empire was on the rise, and thus so were poverty and inequality.[33]

As we saw in Chapter 1, Ronald Reagan invented the trope of the welfare queen amidst this growing economic crisis to win consent for trickle-down economics. However, it was Clinton who fully neoliberalized welfare with his passage of the Personal Responsibility and Work Opportunity Reconciliation Act in 1996. In the name of promoting personal responsibility and empowerment through work, the Act dismantled the previous public assistance system by instituting a five-year lifetime limit on benefits (although states were free to enact even tougher limits as they saw fit). No matter your circumstances, you would be made to hustle.

For example, Ventura discusses the Welfare to Work Partnership founded in 1997—a public–private partnership between large employers and the Clinton Administration designed to support the new workfare regime and to facilitate the hiring of welfare recipients. Thanks to the lifetime limit on benefits, workers had little choice but to accept more readily available, low-paying, benefit-less jobs. These flexible jobs come with no protection, stability, or security; thus, being forced to work them only exacerbates the daily realities and hardships of being poor. However, the companies involved in this public–private partnership reaped massive benefits: they received detailed information on their new, cheap labor force from the state, as well as big tax breaks for hiring "off the rolls." What is more, this new cheap labor was instrumental in further undermining the power of unions, as these workers couldn't expect, much less demand, more than what they were being offered by employers. In this way, welfare today is synonymous with accumulation by dispossession.[34] The neoliberal state helps multinational corporations get rich by (1) dismantling social protections and supports, (2) lessening their tax responsibilities, and (3) forcing the poorest workers into highly exploitative hustles.

It is important to see that the privatization of welfare is not only about accumulation by dispossession. It is also about criminalizing poverty. Unlike early regimes of social welfare, which were also punitive and degrading, new policies and programs are premised on the idea that poverty was completely the fault of the individual rather than a systemic feature of capitalism. Since welfare recipients are regarded as morally deficient for their failures to assume personal responsibility, they aren't entitled to the same rights as other citizens. Thus, applicants for, and recipients of, benefits are positioned as criminals just for being in need in the first place. The implication of this criminalization of poverty is that it makes basic social need a matter of individual moral deficiency rather than a social problem to be dealt with in common. Thus, state programs don't necessarily need social workers to help mitigate the injustices and brutalities of poverty, but rather criminal investigators who are charged with policing the poor—rooting out fraud and protecting taxpayers against allegedly deviant and immoral poor people. Consequently, welfare applicants and recipients live under constant state surveillance and moral suspicion, where everything they do becomes potential grounds for a fraud investigation. As journalist Matt Taibbi learned in his research into contemporary welfare programs,

> The entire world becomes a legal minefield. If you're poor and on public assistance, just about anything you do that defines you as a living human being can turn into the basis of a fraud case. Getting laid can be fraud. Getting sick can be fraud. Putting your kids in daycare can be fraud. Not "sounding poor" can be fraud.[35]

Being on welfare is risky, demoralizing, punishing, and socially isolating. Put a little differently, welfare today exists not as part of our infrastructures of social reproduction, but as part of the broader criminal industrial complex discussed in Chapter 2. Ultimately, this criminal industrial complex serves two functions, one political-economic and the other cultural. First, as discussed above, it provides a way to deal with the disposable populations in ways that are nonetheless profitable for the state and corporations (i.e., cheap labor, tax breaks, shrinking welfare rolls). Second, this system performs the work for neoliberal governmentality by creating a culture of social division and disposability, where lines can be easily drawn between those who are "free" to hustle and those who must be forced to hustle. In other words, while the hustle should unite us, thanks to state hustles like welfare and the broader criminal industrial complex, it operates as a key axis of disconnection and disimagination. Indeed, criminalizing poverty and forcing poor people into highly exploitative hustles authorizes and sustains a deeply racialized culture of personal responsibility and self-enterprise that keeps most everyone isolated and alienated from one another.

Debt Sentences

The second state hustle I want to introduce has to do with the creditocracy, Andrew Ross' take on the neoliberal world of global finance that we also encountered in Chapter 2. The creditocracy is the consequence of financialization: specifically, it is the economic structure constructed by increasing re-regulation of the financial industries, which works to create a world of mass indebtedness. We are all what Ross calls "revolvers," caught up in unending cycles of credit and debt that generate huge profits for banks and other outfits of global finance. For in a world of precarization and privatization, ordinary people rely on access to credit to support their daily lives, from cars to homes to health to furniture to food to education. The creditocracy sentences us to a life of indebtedness, which means we are constantly paying a surcharge to the financial industries, just to keep on living and reproducing ourselves. In this way, despite how "free" we may feel, we are always, to a certain extent, being forced to hustle.

While the criminal industrial complex creates a mass of *criminals* who can be exploited by the state and private corporations, the creditocracy works to create a mass of *debtors* who can also be readily exploited by these same entities. Here's how it works. The creditocracy is set up to keep folks in debt and to protect the financial markets that profit off this debt. Revolvers must always repay and take personal responsibility for their debts; they are subject to what Ross calls the "payback morality"—to be made to feel like bad, immoral people if we can't make good on our repayments. Meanwhile, the big banks are anything but moral or responsible. After wrecking the global economy in 2008, they were bailed out by the neoliberal state. This is because they function as the center of financial capitalism, so they must be made whole regardless of morality.[36]

The arm of the creditocracy that probably hits closest to home for you right now is student debt. Student debt is a state hustle that operates as a subtly pernicious form of accumulation by dispossession and disimagination. Instead of providing young people access to affordable education, neoliberal policy delivers students to the financial industries as debtors, shifting more and more of the responsibility for financing education to the private sector. Higher education, which is increasingly touted as a requisite for a "good job," becomes a means to enrich banks, lenders, and the state itself, who make billions annually off student loan interest.

However, privatizing educational financing is not only an economic process of accumulation by dispossession, as the condition of indebtedness means that young people's futures have been mortgaged. Not only do young people's future wages and earnings belong to the banks and the neoliberal state, but students have to build a life under the weight of mounting interest, making decisions and life plans on the basis of the moral demand to repay. In this sense, debt disciplines and controls, ensuring debtors stay focused on self-appreciation through personal responsibility for repaying one's loans. In other words, student debt effectively sentences young people to a life of hustling for the state and corporate firms, stripping them of an open future and setting them up for a life of disimagination.[37]

And just think: these student debt sentences are what privilege looks like in enterprise culture! Indeed, we must see that life in the creditocracy is even more cruel for poor people, especially poor folks of color.

For example, many people are unable to qualify for a bank account and, therefore, are made to rely on payday loans and cash-checking services, which charge astronomical fees. You must pay big to get paid your measly check, which constitutes an even more directly consequential and exploitative form of wage theft than student debt.

So, as we have been exploring throughout this chapter, we hustle, and get hustled, divided. While the creditocracy is a material form of exploitation and dispossession we all share, our experience of it is defined by inequality.

CRITICAL PRACTICE

- Consider how debt transforms your identity as a student. What are the consequences of this state hustle in your own life? How might you approach your education, and your life more generally, if you weren't worried about repaying future debts? What does debt do to your future?

KNOCKING THE HUSTLE

As we have seen, we are all hustling, but we remain divided by entanglements of class, race, and gender. We are all working our butts off in the social factory, but we can't see our commonalities thanks to the norms of self-enterprise, de-proletarianization, and the entwined systems of inequality and exploitation that undergird neoliberal culture. However, now more than ever, we all have much to gain from "knocking the hustle." I often wonder what would happen if we poured all our hustling energies into common ventures that are directed toward a more democratic and egalitarian society?

It is important to see that, across the world, people are knocking the hustle. For example, worker cooperatives in Europe, South America, and the United States, among other places, allow members to collectively own and govern their workplaces. New models of social enterprise, where the goal is not profit, but common goods and collective caretaking, are also on the rise. Communities are experimenting with new, collective financing models where credit is extended to ventures that promise to redistribute wealth in more socially productive ways, not extract wealth through accumulation by dispossession. Folks are also organizing around the issue of debt. For example, Ross is involved with the Strike Debt movement, "a nationwide movement of debt resisters fighting for economic justice and democratic freedom." As their website states, "We want an economy in which our debts are to our friends, families, and communities—and not to the 1%."

Ultimately, the promises of these challenges to neoliberal culture will never be realized if we don't confront the systems of hustling that keep us in our lanes on the neoliberal highway, suffering alongside each other, though radically divided. *Really* knocking the hustle will require not only new forms of collective social doing, but also a broad-based movement against precarization. This movement, built on our commonalities and a shared class consciousness, would be a sort of re-proletarianization that is both feminist and antiracist. It would be rooted in a new, bold vision not only of labor, but also of society as a whole. If we want to knock the hustle, in other words, we must find ways to produce and reproduce our lives in common, to take care of each other collectively, and to create a world that is rid once for all of the biopolitics of disposability.

NOTES

1 Pierre Dardot and Christian Laval, *The New Way of the World: On Neoliberal Society* (New York: Verso, 2014), 255.
2 Lester Spence, *Knocking the Hustle: Against the Neoliberal Turn in Black Politics* (New York: Punctum Books, 2015), 2.
3 Wendy Brown, *Undoing the Demos: Neoliberalism's Stealth Revolution* (New York: Zone Books, 2015), 31.
4 See Brown, *Undoing the Demos*, 35–40.
5 Dardot and Laval, *New Way of the World*, 255.
6 Angela McRobbie, *Be Creative: Making a Living in the New Cultural Industries* (Cambridge: Polity Press, 2016), 15.
7 McRobbie, *Be Creative*, 11.
8 Dardot and Laval, *The New Way of the World*, 260.
9 Nick Dyer-Witheford and Greig de Peuter, *Games of Empire: Global Capitalism and Video Games* (Minneapolis: University of Minnesota Press, 2009), 4.
10 See Arlie Hochschild, *The Managed Heart: Commerialization of Human Feeling* (Los Angeles: University of California Press, 2012).
11 See Dyer-Witheford and de Peuter, *Games of Empire*, 35–68.

12 Karen Ho, *Liquidated: An Ethnography of Wall Street* (Durham: Duke University Press, 2009), 11.

13 Ho, *Liquidated*, 76.

14 Ho, *Liquidated*, 105.

15 Thanks is owed here to Arianna O'Connell and Hayley Anderson for their research.

16 Alison Hearn, "'John, A 20-Year-Old Boston Native With a Great Sense of Humor': On the Spectacularization of the 'Self' and the Incorporation of Identity in the Age of Reality Television," in *The Celebrity Culture Reader*, ed. P. David Marshall (New York: Routledge, 2006), 621–622.

17 Hearn, "'John, A 20-Year-Old Boston Native," 622.

18 Alison Hearn, "'Meat, Mask, Burden': Probing the Contours of the Branded Self," *Journal of Consumer Culture* 8 (2008): 197–217.

19 Laurie Ouellette and James Hay, *Better Living Through Reality TV: Television and Post-Welfare Citizenship* (Malden: Blackwell, 2008), 127–128.

20 Dardot and Laval, *The New Way of the World*, 267.

21 Laurie Ouellette, "*America's Next Top Model*: Neoliberal Labor," in *How to Watch Television*, eds. Ethan Thompson and Jason Mittell (New York: New York University Press, 2013), 172.

22 Ouellette and Hay, *Better Living through Reality TV*, 103.

23 Ouellette and Hay, *Better Living through Reality TV*, 115.

24 Brenda Weber, *Makeover TV: Selfhood, Celebrity, and Celebrity* (Durham: Duke University Press, 2009), 38.

25 Nancy Fraser, "Contradictions of Capital and Care," *New Left Review* 100 (2016), https://newleftreview.org/II/100/nancy-fraser-contradictions-of-capital-and-care

26 See Wendy Brown, *States of Injury* (Princeton: Princeton University Press, 1995)

27 See Angela McRobbie, *The Aftermath of Feminism: Gender, Culture, and Social Change* (London: Sage, 2008); *New Femininities: Postfeminism, Neoliberalism, and Subjectivity*, eds. Rosalind Gill and Christina Scharff (New York: Palgrave Macmillan, 2011).

28 See Anita Harris, *Future Girl: Young Women in the Twenty-First Century* (New York: Routledge, 2003).

29 Angela McRobbie, "Postfeminism and Popular Culture," *Feminist Media Studies* 4.3 (2004): 255–264.

30 Julie Wilson and Emily Yochim, *Mothering Through Precarity: Women's Work and Digital Media* (Durham: Duke University Press, 2017), 68–72.

31 Wilson and Yochim, *Mothering Through Precarity*, 94–98.

32 Wilson and Yochim, *Mothering Through Precarity*, 97.

33 Patricia Ventura, *Neoliberal Culture: Living with American Neoliberalism* (New York: Routledge, 2016), 90–91.

34 Ventura, *Neoliberal Culture*, 98–99.

35 Matt Taibbi, *The Divide: American Injustice in the Age of the Wealth Gap* (New York: Spiegel and Grau, 2014), 328.

36 Andrew Ross, *Creditocracy and the Case for Debt Refusal* (New York: Or Books, 2013), 30–67.

37 Ross, *Creditocracy*, 103–143.

5

THE MOODS OF ENTERPRISE
NEOLIBERAL AFFECT AND THE CARE OF THE SELF

CHAPTER OVERVIEW

What are the sensibilities that undergird our everyday lives as neo-liberal subjects? What does it *feel like* to inhabit enterprise culture? What mood does the hustle put us in? What mood do we need to be in to hustle? In this chapter, we are going to tackle these questions by exploring the affective worlds of neoliberalism and the structures of feeling that accompany enterprise culture. As we will see, the norm of self-enterprise and the four *D*s create an all-too common (and col-lective) sense of depression, anxiety, and illness. However, instead of resisting and transforming the shared structures that condition our everyday lives and make us sick, we are encouraged to engage in indi-vidualized and privatized practices of self-care that shut down our critical capacities for social interconnection and political intervention.

The majority of the chapter focuses on two primary, intertwined dimensions of neoliberal self-care: (1) *the financialization of the self and social relationships*; and (2) *the privatization of happiness.*

These distinctly neoliberal approaches to self-care are focused on self-appreciation in the market and operate in everyday life as powerful status-quo stories that sustain our disaffected consent. More specifically, we examine how these forms of neoliberal self-care invite **cruel optimism**, as they ask us to invest our hopes and desires for health and happiness in the very structures that are making us sick in the first place.

In the final section, we consider how the care of the self might also be mobilized as a site of radical critique, resistance, and social transformation. Through alternative practices of self-care animated by feminist senses of commonality, collective caretaking, shared vulnerability, and equality, we might cultivate capacities for imagining, inhabiting, and building a world beyond neoliberalism.

THE CARE OF THE SELF

As we know, neoliberal biopolitics hold individuals, and individuals alone, personally responsible for their lives. It is up to each individual to maintain and optimize their bodies, mind, health, and well-being in the market. If we cannot, we are disposable. In this sense neoliberal governmentality hinges on biopolitical regimes of self-governmentality— on individual and privatized practices of self-care. To be clear, the care of the self is nothing new. However, what *is* new about contemporary self-care is how fundamental it is to neoliberal social order and the production of neoliberal subjects.

More specifically, in enterprise culture, our everyday lives come to hinge on what Foucault called **technologies of the self**. Technologies of the self are operations that we perform on our selves in order to manage, care for, or know it more fully. As such, these technologies of the self "permit individuals to effect by their own means, or with the help of others, a certain number of operations on their own bodies and souls, thoughts, conduct, and way of being, so as to transform themselves."[1] Generally speaking, technologies of the self are wonderful things. Meditation and mindfulness help folks to cultivate peace of mind. Yoga enables folks to feel healthy and centered. Self-help programs encourage self-reflection, self-awareness, and self-empowerment.

Undoubtedly, practices of self-care have a long history and permeate myriad cultural contexts. However, neoliberalism governs through technologies of the self, and so self-care becomes central. It is the primary medium of biopolitics, and as we will see, it is also how we maintain our disaffected consent. Thus, although technologies of the self may well be empowering and even figure as a crucial means of surviving neoliberalism, they also often operate as powerful status-quo stories that keep us tethered to our neoliberal conjuncture by inciting us to turn inward and focus on transforming our individual selves. Therefore, it is vitally important to critique them, especially their cultural power to shape our affects and senses of social possibility.

Recall the discussion of self-branding and makeovers from the previous chapter. We can think of these practices as distinctly neoliberal technologies of the self, where self-care becomes first and foremost about self-appreciation. In other words, shows like *What Not to Wear* convert technologies of the self (fashioning the self) into technologies of self-appreciation (growing one's human capital for market competition). In what follows, we are going to explore more fully the neoliberal care of the self, and what happens to our identities and social relationships when self-care becomes directed toward self-appreciation and dictated by the demands of the hustle. First though, we explore what it *feels* like, day in and day out, to inhabit enterprise culture, where we have to take personal responsibility for our lives and health in the market.

ANXIOUS AND "OUT OF GAS"

7 Cups of Tea is an "on-demand emotional health and well-being service" that connects depressed individuals to a diverse online network of "trained, compassionate" listeners. According to the company's site,

> People connect with listeners on 7 Cups of Tea for all kinds of reasons, from big existential thoughts to small, day-to-day things that we all experience. Unlike talking to family or friends, a 7 Cups of Tea listener doesn't judge or try to solve problems and say what to do. Our listeners just listen. They understand. They give you the space you need to help you clear your head.

In addition to providing listeners, 7 Cups of Tea offers online therapy and referrals, self-care exercises, as well as group chats and support forums. Importantly, 7 Cups of Tea promises to value you no matter your station in life. "We are living in a world with an immense love deficit, which means that none of us is receiving the love we need to reach our true potential, to truly thrive," explains the site's mission page.

> Our goal is to build a support system, a web that can hold every member of our world. We believe that we can fill that love-gap for every person in the world, either because they are an active member of our community or because they are touched personally by someone who has been empowered by 7 Cups of Tea.

As we know, living in competition breeds social alienation and disconnection at both the individual and social level. 7 Cups of Tea promises to compensate for this "love deficit" with networked compassion and connection.

Notably, 7 Cups of Tea peddles services tailored to specific groups, including colleges and universities. As the site explains to prospective users (i.e., college administrators):

- **64%** of young adults who are no longer in college are not attending college because of a **mental health-related reason**
- **25%** of college students have been diagnosed with a **mental health condition** within the past year
- **72%** of students living with a mental health condition have experienced a **mental health crisis on campus**
- **31%** have felt so depressed that it was "difficult to function"
- **50%** have experienced "overwhelming anxiety"
- **45%** of college students felt things were "hopeless"

The site promises anonymous, convenient, always-on services that are alleged to diffuse valuable life skills (technologies of the self) into campus culture, while extending the reach of counseling centers that often fail to connect with those most in need.

7 Cups of Tea highlights two entwined developments connected to the rise of neoliberal culture: the widespread diagnoses of mental health conditions, most notably, depression and anxiety, and the growth of a marketplace for health and wellness products. The latter is what Carl Cederstrom and Andre Spicer call "the wellness

syndrome." They argue that wellness has emerged as a powerful ideological force within neoliberal culture, becoming all the rage in recent years among public and private institutions alike—from government agencies to global corporations to college campuses. For example, Google employs a "chief happiness officer" whose job it is to optimize the health and happiness of its employees. The company monitors employee moods and behaviors and uses the data to identify and solve potential issues that might negatively impact their well-being.

While affects like depression and anxiety have long been experienced by individuals in different historical contexts, today they have become more general social conditions that are widespread among the population, as diagnoses of depression and anxiety began to skyrocket in the late 1970s. William Davies suggests that this rise in mental unhealth is the inevitable outcome of the rise of neoliberal culture and the norm of competition: "Whenever we measure our self-worth relative to others, as all competitions force us to do, we risk losing our sense of self-worth altogether."[2] Similarly, other scholars like Dardot and Laval link the rise of depression to the neoliberal hustle and its demand of constant performance, explaining that "Depression is in fact the obverse of performance—a response by the subject to the injunction to realize and be responsible for himself, to surpass himself ever more in the entrepreneurial adventure."[3] According to Alain Ehrenberg, the depressed subject is one who is out "out of gas": "Depression presents itself as *an illness of responsibility* in which the dominant feeling is that of failure. The depressed individual is unable to measure up; he is tired of having to become himself."[4] In her memoir, *Depression: A Public Feeling*, cultural theorist Ann Cvetkovich puts her own affective collapse to words:

> As soon as the shadow of anxiety begins to fall over you, you start to panic, and the panic brings you down fast—it wakes you bolt upright in the morning, makes you sweat, leaves you unable to think about anything else. You're caught in the downward spiral of feeling bad about feeling bad. Whatever you thought you might have learned about staying out of this trouble has clearly proven inadequate, so now what are you going to do? And if you come up with a plan (doubtful, but let's try to imagine for a moment that it might be possible), how are you even going to begin to execute it when depression's stealth destroys your agency?[5]

As Davies explains, "It is only in a society that makes generalized, personalized growth the ultimate virtue that a disorder of generalized, personalized collapse will become inevitable."[6] Put a little differently, neoliberalism not only creates a crisis of care in the family (as suggested in the previous chapter), but it also creates a crisis of self-care.

CRITICAL PRACTICE

- How does neoliberal culture's command to be constantly performing, producing, and growing impact your own affective world? Do you identify with the feeling of being "out of gas"? How do you experience neoliberalism's crisis of self-care?

Crucially, the "generalized, personalized collapse" precipitated by a culture of "generalized, personalized, growth" opens up the space for the emergence of a marketplace of products promising to help folks get back on the neoliberal highway. Neoliberalism's competitive social world breeds widespread depression and anxiety; in response to this crisis of self-care, the market steps in, offering a sprawling array of individualized wellness products. For example, signing up for 7 Cups of Tea is presented as a vital win-win situation for both students and schools, as, according to the site, "Each lost student costs your school approximately $15,000 per year in revenue and significantly reduces that student's chance of success in life." Indeed, 7 Cups is presented as good for students' human capital, as well as for the institution's bottom line.

There is a powerful paradox at work here. Therapeutic products like 7 Cups of Tea help to mitigate the daily hurts of life in a competitive society, providing vital forms of support, care, and perhaps even love. For their users, they are certainly sites of coping, getting by, and, at times, survival. However, these practices of self-care encourage us to internalize, and thereby live by, the very same neoliberal logics of privatization, self-enclosed individualism, and personal responsibility that are causing all these hurts in the first place.

As Davies' work shows, since the rise of neoliberalism and the generalization of depression and anxiety, psychiatry has been redirected toward the scientific management of unhappiness, morphing into a dispassionate, quantified field where diagnoses are identified, classified, and observed, and drugs are developed, marketed, and prescribed. "Psychiatric insight into the recesses and conflicts of the human self was replaced by a dispassionate, scientific guide for naming symptoms," Davies explains. "And in scrapping the possibility that a mental syndrome might be an understandable and proportionate response to a set of external circumstances, psychiatry lost the capacity to identify problems in the fabric of society or economy."[7] Contemporary psychiatric discourses diagnose and locate social problems in individuals, in particular, in individual chemical imbalances or genetic codes. Psychotropic drugs target individual affects, promising to regulate objective chemical imbalances and help suffering selves return to their "true" selves, that is, selves that are in a better mood for enterprise.

In working at a molecular level rather than a social or political one, contemporary psychiatric discourses become part of the disimagination machine, stripping us of our capacities for radical critique and getting to the roots of our problems. We stay stuck in neoliberal horizons, unable to hear what our affects are trying to tell us about what's currently wrong and what world we're yearning for.

More pointedly, Kristin Swenson argues that contemporary psychiatry is part of what she calls an *affective state apparatus*. As we already know, the neoliberal state aims to govern conducts and behaviors through the imposition of competition and personal responsibility; however, this approach creates widespread depression and anxiety. Consequently, the state must develop new biopolitical regimes for governing affect in order to keep "out of gas" subjects in gear and on the road. For example, Swenson analyzes the George W. Bush Administration's New Freedom Commission on Mental Health that was constituted to study mental health services and delivery systems. The commission's final report, *Achieving the Promise: Transforming Mental Health Care in America*, cited alarming statistics about mental disabilities and suicide from the World Health Organization and called for expanded, readily accessible, consumer-driven mental health services. Tellingly, the justification for getting drugs to more children and families was individual productivity and not social well-being. Allegedly, the state was losing $79 billion annually in lost productivity, which included estimates regarding those who committed suicide young and therefore could not work a full life.[8]

Indeed, in a neoliberal culture, what is at stake in feeling depressed or being ill is ultimately one's ability to be productive and hustle. Wellness thus operates as both an economic *and* moral demand to optimize our bodies, souls, and minds so as to prove our merit in the market. Cederstrom and Spicer are scathing in their critique of contemporary wellness ideology, especially when it comes to young people in college like you. With the wellness syndrome, "Self-exploration and self-discovery is morphed into self-actualization and self-enhancement."[9] Instead of experimenting with the boundaries of identity and politics, the self becomes consumed in the project of growing its human capital. Toward the end of their book, Cederstrom and Spicer argue that it is time "to stop obsessively listening to our bodies, to give up fixations with our own health and happiness and to abandon the illusion of limitless human potential."[10]

However, we need to think carefully about the politics of wellness. To be sure, striving for wellness makes us disciplined and docile subjects of enterprise. But at the same time, and this is key, our health—or lack thereof—is where many feel the mundane brutalities of neoliberal precarity most acutely, making our bodies and affects sites not only of neoliberal oppression, but also of potential resistance and social interconnection. Of course, it is not surprising that we tend to treat depression and other "bad" affects as deeply personal problems to be managed on our own. In a culture that exalts boundless productivity, being immobilized by depression is understandably a source of shame and stigma. However, it is important to understand that *affects are social*; they don't emerge organically from individuals, although we feel their effects on our individual bodies in profound ways. Hopefully, by seeing mental unhealth as symptomatic (at least in part) of neoliberal culture, and not simply of some natural defect, we can start to sense not only a bit of personal relief, but also our commonalities and the new political horizons these commonalities are capable of opening up.

Before we turn more fully to the idea of the care of the self as a site of potential resistance, we need to understand the dominant discourses, practices, and structures of feeling of neoliberal self-care. How does neoliberal governmentality incite us to care for ourselves and keep hustling? What technologies of the self circulate in the markets of enterprise culture? What platforms are available to us? What does the neoliberal care of the self look like and mean in everyday life?

THE FINANCIALIZATION OF THE SELF AND SOCIAL RELATIONSHIPS

The first dimension of the neoliberal care of the self that we are going to explore is what Randy Martin calls the **financialization of daily life**. As discussed in Chapter 2, financialization is a key component of neoliberalism and has to do with the growing significance of global financial markets within contemporary regimes of wealth accumulation and value production. However, as Martin suggests, the logics and effects of financialization seep deep into the nooks and crannies of everyday life. As walls between the speculative global economy and individuals come tumbling down, neoliberal citizens are invited, and compelled, "to live by finance." "Finance, the management of money's ebbs and flows, is not simply in the service of accessible wealth, but presents itself as a merger of business and life cycles, as a means for the acquisition of self," explains Martin. Living by finance becomes a template for self-care and growth—a "proposal for how to get ahead, but also a medium for the expansive movements of body and soul."[11] In other words, financialization is more than a political-economic reality; it is a technology of the self, a path for obtaining the good life, as it "promises a way to develop the self" in a precarious, competitive world.[12]

More specifically, Martin shows how the financialization of daily life brings risk management to the center of subjectivity. The financialized self is, first and foremost, a manager of risk, someone who is always speculating—gathering information and calculating odds. After all, if the self is nothing but human capital that must be appreciated over time, it only follows that it must simultaneously be at risk for depreciation and thus must be vigilantly monitored. Potential threats lurk everywhere, so individuals thus must always be managing risk, parsing potentials for good and bad outcomes in order to optimize future returns on the self.

Importantly, the financialization of daily life encourages individuals to embrace the personal management of risk as a commonsense and empowering condition of citizenship; for, as Martin suggests, "To be risk averse is to have one's life managed by others, to be subject to their miscalculations, and therefore to be unaccountable to oneself."[13] To not be able to manage risk is to be a dependent, stalled subject in need of government intervention. Indeed, in the context of neoliberalism, certain populations and groups are regularly singled out for being "at risk" and targeted by social programs aimed to increase their prospects for self-care and the hustle.

In a world of privatized risk, where the burdens of risk-bearing are increasingly offloaded from the state and employers onto individuals and families, it is not surprising that the care of the self would become synonymous with the work of risk management. Yet, it's vital to consider the psychic and social costs of these technologies of the self. The financialization of daily life and its incitement to risk management produces highly *reflexive* selves. According to Eva Illouz, "A reflexive self has internalized strong mechanisms of self-control to maintain its self-interest, not through the blatant display of competitive selfishness, but through the art of mastering social relationships."[14] Reflexive selves engage in ongoing surveillance and evaluation of themselves and their social environments, as well as ongoing reflection and rationalization on their decisions and behaviors. Put differently, reflexive selves are regularly auditing their lives, just like accountants audit their firms. In turn, even our social relationships become subject to the logics and dictates of finance.

As Todd May argues,

> Neoliberal relationships are economic ones. They are centered on consumption and investment . . . the idea of gain and loss has seeped into our approach to relationships with one another. Whether the gain be instantaneous consumption or future return, we are encouraged to look upon one another in economic terms. We are accountants in our relationships.[15]

Relationships are to be assessed, evaluated, and rationalized according to their potential return and impact on one's human capital. "Rather than seeing others with whom we share this world as equals, neoliberalism encourages us instead to see them as resources or competitors or objects of entertainment," suggests May.[16]

Hence, financialized relationships are highly instrumental and premised on inequality, as even friends and lovers come to matter only in terms of what they are imagined to contribute (or not) to one's self-enterprise. Put a little differently, financialization necessitates narcissism, but a narcissism that is not about excessive self-love, but self-fragility: for "[a] narcissistic personality is a personality so fragile that it needs constant support."[17] It relates to others instrumentally; what matters is what other people can provide to a self that needs to be held together. When individuals come to depend on others for narcissistic reasons—that is for their own self-appreciation—deep, reciprocal relationships based on trust and equality are difficult to cultivate.

Risk management might certainly feel empowering as it offers sensibilities of control, but it also keeps us in a state of disimagination, as we are unable to critique the root structures of the world we live in, much less envision an alternative future. We become stuck in the rules and norms of the neoliberal conjuncture. You see, risk management is about speculating on an unknowable future by embedding oneself in the realities and knowledges of the present. The financialization of daily life asks us to constantly fold the future into our present, to think and live as if every decision, action, or relationship is directly creating a particular future. However, we sense that risk is everywhere and ultimately uncontrollable, so this constant, highly speculative integration of the future into our present only breeds more anxiety and uncertainty, as failure might ensue at every turn despite our best laid plans. This anxiety and uncertainty leads to stronger urges to double down on the present by working harder to manage risk and appreciate one's human capital.

CRITICAL PRACTICE

- How does the financialization of daily life—specifically the way it asks us to be always be calculating and managing risk—shape your own social world and sense of possibility?

- Consider the various social relationships that make up your social world, including friends, lovers, family, peers, co-workers, etc. What relationships are financialized ones? How do they work? To what extent are these relationships characterized by competition and narcissism? Do they feel mutual and equal? Why or why not?
- Can you think of people and opportunities that you shied away, or even actively disconnected, from due to their potential to depreciate your human capital?

The Financialization of Daily Life in Digital Culture

In so many ways, digital technologies program financialization, as well as its psychic and social consequences, into our lives and relationships. After all, risk management requires data, and when wired, information and opportunities for speculation are always at one's fingertips, ever-churning and readily accessible. Apps for managing risk, from weather to one's finances, are just waiting to be downloaded and put to work, while Google promises access to a global, ever-expanding, always available world of knowledge.

Nowhere perhaps is the financialization of the self more clear than in the rise of the quantified self movement. Self-quantifiers relentlessly track their bodily processes, moods, steps, sleep, caloric intake, etc. The goal is to know the self in order to optimize it, that is, to calibrate the body for optimal outcomes. As movement leader and *Wired* editor/writer Gary Wolf explained in his popular TED Talk on the topic,

> We know that numbers are useful for us when we advertise, manage, govern, search. I'm going to talk about how they're useful when we reflect, learn, remember, and want to improve. . . . If we want to act more effectively in the world, we have to know ourselves better.

The idea here is that one's performance and wellness can be simultaneously gauged and guided by the data gathered about oneself through constant self-surveillance of one's body. Optimal physical health is reduced to a series of inputs and outputs. If we eat this many calories, walk this many steps, get so many grams of protein, carbs, and fats, we can achieve any goal we set our minds to. Since we sense our ultimate lack of control in a world of privatized risk, we seek to control ourselves by relying on neutral data to inform our choices and to define growth. Detailed and exhaustive information is imagined to enable the structuring of one's life for optimal results in all arenas, thereby fortifying the self against potential depreciation; as Cederstrom and Spicer put it, "It is not so much about amending various flaws as reconfiguring the entire self, reforming it into a streamlined business."[18]

At this point, it is important to think back the Hayek's theory of the human discussed in Chapter 2. According to Hayek, humans are fundamentally ignorant when it comes to society as a whole, but they contribute to a greater social truth by pursuing and maximizing their opportunities in the market. The quantified self thus epitomizes the human in Hayek's sense; they represent fundamental ignorance taken to its logical extreme. Self-quantifiers reduce self-knowledge to data collection and reflexivity so as to enhance their performance in market society. At this point, the self is fully financialized in body and soul.

While the quantified self movement might seem like an extreme case, thanks to the surge in popularity of wireless, self-tracking devices like Fitbit, self-quantification has emerged as a more mundane and pervasive cultural phenomenon. Self-surveillance and data collection are increasingly coded into our everyday lives, programming users to relate to their bodies as financial assets to be monitored and optimized.

In addition to programming users to financialize their relationship to the self, digital culture also exacerbates the narcissism required to structure one's life around risk management and self-appreciation. Indeed, in many popular online environments, users are programmed to actively financialize their social relationships. As Sherry Turkle puts it, digital technologies and platforms "tempt [users] into narcissistic ways of relating to the world."[19] Online, friends and community exist to validate one's own human capital, to affirm and bear witness to one's practices of self-appreciation. Just think about what it is like to participate on Facebook or Instagram. These platforms encourage users to engage in self-branding by prompting them to construct a media image of the self that is available for consumption by one's network of friends and followers. You share a clever status update, a link to an article, a photo, and through notifications, you are actively training yourself to monitor your self-appreciating feedback which comes in the form of likes, comments, and shares. Narcissism is built into these media systems, as users' identities come to hinge on ongoing positive feedback from their audiences.[20]

CRITICAL PRACTICE

WayBetter is a digital platform that offers a range of tools promising to help people develop healthy habits.[21] For example, WayBetter's app DietBet features three dieting games: KickStarter, Transformer, and Maintainer. KickStarter is a game where the players must lose 4% of their initial weight in one month; in Transformer, the players must lose 10% of their initial weight in six months, with individual percentage goals each month. The Maintainer game lasts a full year, and contestants must weigh in between −4% and +2% of their initial weight every month of the year. Here's how it works. Contestants pay to enter into games with other players. All the players pay the same set amount, and at the end of the game, after the company takes a cut, the money in the pot is split amongst the winners (a.k.a. those who accomplished the goals given to them). As the site explains,

> "We make games that motivate people to achieve their goals. Imagine a game that makes it fun to lose weight, to exercise more, to quit smoking. Could a game change your life? Yes! We call all our games bets because we use money to hold you accountable. But it's not about betting. Our games are about believing in yourself, investing in your health, and sticking to your commitments."

• How does WayBetter exemplify the financialization of daily life? How does this example help us to see the entangled

Figure 5.1 WayBetter's DietBet Game

affective and economic dimensions of neoliberal self-care and wellness?

- Consider your own participation on popular social media, dating apps and sites, and/or other digital platforms connected to your personal practices of self-care and daily living. How do the digital platforms that you engage with on a daily basis promote the financialization of friendship and other social relationships?

THE PRIVATIZATION OF HAPPINESS

As we have seen, the financialization of daily life is a powerful structure of feeling, as it provides what Martin describes as "a highly elastic mode of self-mastery that channels doubt over uncertain identity into fruitful activity."[22] When the self and its social relationships are financialized, folks are always tracking, always calculating, always reflecting, always speculating, and thus, necessarily, always anxious and insecure deep down. However, everyday life in neoliberal culture is profoundly contradictory. While depression and anxiety are generalized across the population, discourses of happiness proliferate. We are told constantly to be happy, or more accurately, *to work to be happy*. This incitement to be happy is the second dimension of neoliberal self-care that warrants our careful consideration.

Self-help books comprise a huge share of the publishing industry and peddle a wide array of technologies of the self, all of which promise, in one way or another, to increase our happiness so long as we are willing to put in the work required to transform our affective lives. For example, in an article published at *Elite Daily,* Dean Bokhari describes his post-college journey through over 450 self-help books. After realizing he had no desire to pursue the parent-approved, "safe job" in law, Bokhari turned to the world of self-help in hopes of discovering a more meaningful life path. Explaining to readers that most of what he read "sucked," Bokhari offers up fifteen "science backed" books that actually "stuck." These included classics like Marcus Aurelius' *Meditations* and Dale Carnegie's *How to Win Friends and Influence People,* as well as more recent takes on self-care and development like Stephen Covey's *The Seven Habits of Highly Effective People,* which helps readers cultivate habits for achievement in all areas of life; Roy Baumeister and John Tierney's *Willpower: Rediscovering the Greatest Human Strength,* which teaches readers how to enhance their impulse control; Sam Harris' *Waking Up*, which explores connections between the brain, consciousness, and spirituality; and Adam Grant's *Give and Take: Why Helping Others Drives Our Success,* which explores the importance of giving for individual success.

We can think of this sprawling market of self-help in terms of what Jennifer Silva calls the *mood economy*. The mood economy is the correlate of global neoliberal economy: privatizing risk requires privatizing happiness. Silva explains, "Just as neoliberalism teaches young people that they are solely responsible for their economic fortunes, the mood economy renders them responsible for their emotional fates."[23] Indeed, in a world without public infrastructures and safety nets, daily personal hardships and uncertainties must be met with individualized and marketized practices of self-care. Broadly speaking, **the privatization of** happiness refers to a range of technologies and practices whereby individuals come to not only assume more material responsibility, but also more psychic responsibility for the condition of their lives. In the mood economy, people learn to look inward and to focus on changing their own attitudes, behaviors, affects, and dispositions. Here, ongoing precarization requires ongoing affective resilience—the cultivation and maintenance of a capacity for bouncing back and living through tough times. The mood economy engenders this affective resilience by offering a range of technologies for finding and creating happiness on one's own, that is, for privatizing happiness.

A central discourse of the mood economy is the power of positive thinking. Allegedly, thinking positive thoughts is the key to unlocking privatized happiness. As Barbara Ehrenreich explores in her book *Bright-Sided: How the Relentless Promotion of Positive Thinking Has Undermined America,* "[T]here is no kind of problem or obstacle for which positive thinking or a positive attitude has not been proposed as a cure."[24] Positive thinking is a general, elastic form of mind-cure, whereby changing one's attitude and outlook is presented as the solution to all of life's dilemmas, from trying to lose weight to finding a mate to landing that dream job. This discourse suggests that being a positive individual leads to positive outcomes (i.e., wealth, love, health). Thus, expelling "negative" people, affects, and other influences from one's life becomes a crucial requisite of neoliberal self-care.

For example, *The Secret,* a best-selling, multi-media self-help brand founded by Rhonda Byrne.[25] Insisting that each and every person deserves to live a life of abundance and happiness, *The Secret* promises "to bring joy to billions" through "life-transforming tools" that will help you be the best you can be. As the book states at the outset,

> As you travel through its pages and you learn the Secret, you will come to know how you can have, be, or do anything you want. You will come to know who you really are. You will come to know the true magnificence of all that awaits you.[26]

So, what is the big secret? According to Byrne, the secret to happiness and living the life you choose is the Law of Attraction. "Like attracts like," which, in this case, means that the thoughts you send out into the Universe attract the very things you are thinking about. According to the law of attraction, positive people attract positive outcomes. Thoughts and mental attitudes are magnets: in other words, whatever frequency your thoughts emit will, without fail, attract corresponding results. All of this translates to a simple reality. You create your own life. You have attracted everything that has happened to you and will ever happen to you, good or bad. You are in control. You have the power to transform your life into whatever you put your thoughts, feelings, and intentions to. "Create the most magnificent version of you!" exclaims Byrne.[27] "The universe exists to do your bidding, if only you can learn to harness the power of your desires," Ehrenreich describes of this logic.[28] Talk about a neoliberal status-quo story!

Happiness as Work Ethic

While some might be tempted to dismiss New Agey, self-help programs like *The Secret* as just pop psychology, it is important to see that these fundamental ideas about the power of positive affect to create greater levels of individual happiness have a long history in U.S. thought and have been legitimated in recent decades within the academic field of psychology. Indeed, positive psychology—the scientific study of happiness—is a burgeoning area of inquiry within universities and research labs.

Let's take a closer look at how this more scientific facet of the discourse works. Happify is an online program and app designed to help you "Break Old Patterns" and "Form New Habits." The program's website proclaims, "How you feel matters! Whether you're feeling sad, anxious, or stressed, Happify brings you effective tools and programs to help you take control of your feelings and thoughts." According to the website, Happify has built its program on the best scientific research in positive psychology and cognitive behavioral theory, research that understands how happiness is a habit of mind. The idea is that our brains can be changed "by adopting new thought patterns, by training our brain as if it were a muscle, to overcome negative thoughts." With just a "few simple and even entertaining mental diversions," we can rewire our brains to push back against negative thoughts and feelings and not allow them to overrun our life. Happiness is both a science and work ethic.

Importantly, the goal of Happify is not for users to be happy all of the time, which allegedly diminishes our capacities for happiness, but rather to cultivate resilience and the *capacity* for happiness. As the site explains, "Positive psychology doesn't turn a blind eye to suffering or psychological illness, but it does encourage individuals and even communities to adopt practices that can boost optimism, increase resilience, and live happy, engaged lives." In other words, programs like Happify aren't interested in the root causes of suffering and unhappiness; instead they want us to focus on producing positive, optimistic affects by transforming our relationship to the often miserable and brutal social worlds we inhabit.

The rise of positive thinking, psychology, and apps like Happify are part of what Sam Binkley calls "a new discourse on happiness."

> Through the lens of this new discourse, life is viewed as a dynamic field of potentials and opportunities, and happiness is presented both as a goal and a 'monetary instrument,' realized through a strategic program of emotional well-being. In other words, the new discourse on happiness proposes a certain transformation in one's relation to the world and to oneself: as one incorporates the new program into one's outlook, one abandons the world of static states and stable ontologies for one of dynamic possibilities, risks, and open horizons.[29]

According to Binkley, happiness is not simply an endpoint; rather, it is, first and foremost, a "work ethic" through which we transform ourselves into enterprising, self-responsibilized, resilient, and self-appreciating subjects. Through honing one's mind for happiness, individuals come to actively embrace the hardships of precarity as an opportunity for self-appreciation and emotional enterprise. Happiness' work ethic, as it were, encourages folks to actively disembed themselves from "the world of static states and stable ontologies" (which are associated with the social welfare state of embedded liberalism) and to construct *for oneself* an affective world of "dynamic possibilities, risks, and open horizons" more suitable to neoliberalism's enterprise culture.

It is important to see that digital culture not only offers apps like Happify; it also provides readily accessible programs and platforms for displaying one's happy work ethic. For example, Antonia Eriksson is a personal trainer who struggled with anorexia and documented her journey to health on Instagram, a practice that ultimately transformed her into a popular and successful fitness micro-celebrity. During her recovery, Eriksson shared every meal and workout with her followers.

In one post in particular she shared two pictures five years apart that showcased her successful journey to health and happiness:

> Facebook-memories reminded me of this picture today, taken 5 (!!!) years ago and I just had to find a picture from now to compare it with! In between these two pictures I have been a real party girl, I have had anorexia, orthorexia, problems with binge eating and also depression. I sure have fought my battles but I have kept going and kept working towards becoming a better version of myself—and now I am here! It's easy to forget your progress and journey. On the first picture I was a con-fused 16 year old girl who had no idea who she was. Today I am a strong, healthy and independent woman who knows what she wants out of life and isn't afraid to ask for it. Today I am the best version of myself so far and I am going to keep working towards becoming better and bet-ter. Never give up darlings, things can always ALWAYS get better, and in the end it's the journey that really matters and changes us.(Oh and for the record—there's just about a 6–8 kg weight gain between the two pictures)

For Eriksson, documenting her efforts to heal on social media is an empowering project of self-care and vital technology of the self that undoubtedly inspired other young women who were struggling with eating disorders. In image after image tracking changes in her affect, mood, and body, she gives visual form to her own triumphant processes of becoming well, while also gaining constant affirmation and positive feedback from her followers. However, this meticulously documented path to health and happiness reproduces ideologies of self-appreciating individualism. What falls out of view are the roots of our unhappiness, not to mention all of those people who, unlike Eriks-son, don't have the capital—economic, media, cultural, political, or otherwise—to appreciate their self on their own. In other words, cir-culating images of successful individual projects of privatized happi-ness participate in neoliberal governmentality, reproducing ideologies of meritocracy and the freedom to choose and thereby rationalizing the biopolitics of disposability in our everyday lives.

As we can see with Eriksson, the privatization of happiness pres-ents itself as an empowering project of personal growth and self-care. What is more, it also figures as a vital means to achieving neoliberal citizenship, especially for working-class folks, as Silva documents. Gaining control over one's emotions and affects comes to substitute for previous templates of citizenship that are no longer readily available. Neoliberalism undercuts traditional paths to adulthood (public education, a stable job, a family); consequently, young adults must pioneer alternative routes to growing up. These new paths often have less to do with outward markers of success and stability (marriage, a career, a home) and more to do with internal, psychic development and emotional transformation. In this way, the mood economy provides alternative roads to citizenship and belonging as the always-elusive "American Dream" of homeownership and a happy nuclear family become further and further out of reach for more and more people.

Accordingly, for many of the working-class people in Silva's study, adulthood has become a therapeutic process of "self-realization gleaned from denouncing a painful past and rebuilding an emancipated self."[30] Privatizing happiness and disembedding oneself from one's social world brings with it self-worth and value. Even if you don't have it all materially, you've proven yourself to be a worthy, self-enclosed, and self-reliant person: you may not be rich, but you've overcome suffering and hardship on your own, and that counts for something.

Privatizing happiness is immensely seductive. After all, who doesn't want to be happy, especially when one's happiness is a sign of one's individual merit, morality, and citizenship? Ultimately though, the privatization of happiness like the financialization of daily life, comes at a steep social cost. As Silva's work shows, this approach to self-care often leads individuals to form "hardened selves," "turning inward as a way to steel themselves against the possibility of disappointment and hurt." In everyday life, privatizing happiness often means making "a virtue out of not asking for help" and living a life of rugged individualism, where relationships with others are often regarded too risky to pursue.

The privatization of happiness also guides individuals to draw hard and fast lines between the self and friends or family members who, from within the mood economy, are perceived to be "negative" influences and not able to privatize happiness on their own. In this context, solidarity becomes next to impossible, as painful experiences and everyday struggles are interpreted as deeply personal and privatized and, therefore, cannot be recognized as part of a broader, shared social experience of systemic oppression. As people take personal responsibility for their lives by focusing on their own emotional transformation, past solidarities that were based on collective understandings of class, gender, and racial identity are broken. Like we saw previously with the financialization of daily life, the privatization of happiness is thus a process of disimagination, whereby our capacities for radical critique, commonality, and interconnection are replaced with neoliberal capacities for self-appreciation, privatized self-care, and affective resilience.

CRITICAL PRACTICE

- How does the privatization of happiness figure in and come to shape your everyday life? What does it look like it? How do you enact and perform it? Who and/or what does privatized happiness bring into your world? Who and/or what does it encourage you to exclude?
- What are the broader implications and consequences of these practices of privatizing happiness? What social worlds are they constructing? What alternative worlds are they shutting down?

CRUEL OPTIMISM

As we have seen in the previous two sections, both the financialization of daily life and the privatization of happiness operate as powerful structures of feeling; they provide templates for the care of the self that are germane to enterprise culture. Moreover, they offer a vast array of technologies of self-appreciation, thereby inviting folks to live highly instrumentalized and individualized lives. However, by asking us to be constantly speculating about ourselves and social relationships, of daily life the financialization and the privatization of happiness lead us to disimagination; they have us actively constructing self-enclosed social worlds built on inequality, narcissism, personal responsibility, and loneliness, where all we can do is double down on our present reality in the hope of optimizing a future return on our self.

We can think of neoliberal self-care in terms of what Lauren Berlant calls **cruel optimism**. In order to live, we need optimism, that is, we need to be affectively invested and attached to our social world to get out of bed in the morning and to keep moving through our everyday lives. Living itself is undergirded by fantasies that sustain our optimism in the social world. Yet, one of the most quietly detrimental features of neoliberal culture is the way that its status-quo stories encourage cruel fantasie. For, in order to live, we have to attach to and invest in the very fantasies (i.e., privatized risk and happiness) that are threatening our lives in the first place. Here's how Berlant explains cruel optimism:

> I define "cruel optimism" as a kind of relation in which one depends on objects that block the very thriving that motivates our attachment in the first place.
>
> All attachment is optimistic. But what makes it cruel is different than what makes something merely disappointing. When your pen breaks, you don't think, "This is the end of writing." But if a relation in which you've invested fantasies of your own coherence and potential breaks down, the world itself feels endangered.
>
> A destructive love affair is my favorite example: if I leave you I am not only leaving you (which would be a good thing if your love destroys my confidence) but also I [am] leaving an anchor for my optimism about life (which is why I want to stay with you even though I'm unhappy, because I am afraid of losing the scene of my fantasy itself).
>
> So this double bind produces conflicts in how to proceed, because massive loss is inevitable if you stay or if you go.[31]

Ultimately, with the idea of cruel optimism, Berlant is asking, "Why is it so hard to leave those forms of life that don't work? Why is it that, when precariousness is spread throughout the world, people fear giving up on the institutions that have worn out their confidence in living?"[32] For Berlant, cruel optimism is a fraught affective relation to the present situation where folks come to stay attached to precarization, even though this attachment is hurting them. Put a little differently, cruel optimism is ultimately what prevents us from "losing confidence" in our world despite our disaffected consent. We cannot actually manage risks, and we cannot actually privatize happiness. Yet we keep trying, living as if we could, trapped in the affective impasses of cruel optimism and the moods of enterprise.

AGAINST THE MOODS OF ENTERPRISE

While the financialization of daily life and privatized happiness engender cruel optimism, does that imply that the care of the self must too? Might the care of the self be a site of resistance and transformation, of counter-conduct and common reason? Might it unlock our critical imaginations and help us to sense new possibilities for self- and collective caretaking? Might it be a place where we see and claim our shared vulnerabilities and interconnections?

Self-Care as Warfare

Black feminist and activist Audre Lorde famously wrote that, "Caring for myself is not self-indulgence, it is self-preservation, and that is an act of political warfare." It is important to see that self-care is not inherently neoliberal, especially for those who have been and continue to be systematically oppressed and marginalized. For while precarization unravels previous systems of advantage, privilege remains, acting as a sort of privatized material and affective support system for navigating an uncertain and competitive world. To put it another way, thanks to various forms of privilege, some people are more primed to engage in the highly privatized and marketized forms of self-care required by neoliberal governmentality and biopolitics. For these folks, optimism need not feel all that cruel. Indeed, as we saw in the previous chapter, people don't feel the brunt of neoliberal precarity and the impossibilities of self-appreciation equally: while some are allegedly "free" to hustle, others are channeled into highly exploitative and violent systems of institutionalized hustling. In other words, for the growing populations of disposable people, self-care is more than self-appreciation. As Sara Ahmed insists, "selfcare is warfare."[33] It is about surviving a world that you are not necessarily meant to survive. It is about pushing back against the biopolitics of disposability and their assaults on our dignity, health, and capacities for individual and collective life.

While the previous sections have focused on the neoliberal care of the self in digital culture, it's important to see that alternative practices of self-care are proliferating too, opening up spaces for alternative forms of resilience, well-being, identity formation, and happiness. In "'Live Through This': The Feminist Care of the Self 2.0," Laurie Ouellette and Jacquelyn Arcy build on the idea of self-care as warfare in their analysis of *Rookie,* an interactive website for teenage girls founded by Tavi Gevinson in 2011. More specifically, they show how *Rookie* offers a distinctly feminist version of self-care, where young women are enjoined "to practice care of the self as an ethical obligation to oneself, as a form of resistance, as a survival strategy, and as a way of forging non-hierarchical support networks with others."[34] In this way, *Rookie* is less about reinscribing neoliberal governmentality and more about cultivating resources and practices for surviving it *together.* For example, the interactive site encourages the formation of "subjugated knowledges," which enable the site's young users "to consider different explanations and explore different possibilities for themselves. On *Rookie,* girls' own stories, drawings, and anecdotes about eating disorders, racism, harassment, body image anxiety, sexual violence, and economic hardship challenge the legitimacy of recognized knowledges."[35]

As Ouellette and Arcy suggest, the affordances of digital culture are not completely dominated by the individualizing logics of financialization and privatized happiness. In other words, digital culture does not only program users to be self-appreciating subjects, but it is also a place where folks come together to wage war on the moods of enterprise and struggle for social *and* emotional justice. In many ways, emotional justice is the opposite of cruel optimism. For, as Yolo Akili explains in her post on *Crunk Feminist Collective,* "Emotional justice is about working with [the] wounding. It is about inviting us into our feelings and our bodies, and finding ways to transform our collective and individual pains into power."[36]

Consider the popular hashtag #MyDepressionLooksLike (Figure 5.2), which highlights shared sensibilities and experiences of depression. Here depression is no longer simply a private disorder, as users' collective contributions transform individualized feelings into common

Beautifully Weird. @beautweird · 8 Nov 2016
Churned up soul, mind of shattered glass, hung on loosest thread, wrapped in layers of dread, wanting to be dead. #MyDepressionLooksLike

↩   ↻   ♥ 3   •••

andy @andy · 7 Nov 2016
#MyDepressionLooksLike me crying in laundry room because doing my laundry feels so overwhelming.

↩   ↻ 1   ♥ 10   •••

Kam @kam · 7 Nov 2016
#MyDepressionLooksLike me sitting on the couch or in my bed, doing absolutely nothing but hating myself for it.

↩   ↻ 4   ♥ 14   •••

Queer Xicana Chrome @QueerXChrome · 7 Nov 2016
#MyDepressionLooksLike celebrating my first trip to the grocery store in 6 weeks cuz I know how much energy it's taken me to get here 😊🎉

↩   ↻ 1   ♥ 25   •••

Work Hard Like Kenny @work · 7 Nov 2016
#MyDepressionLooksLike the blank stare I have while I get lost in my own head over all my responsibilities & inability to complete them all

↩   ↻ 8   ♥ 18   •••

Figure 5.2 #MyDepressionLooksLike

experience. When posted to the #MyDepressionLooksLike feed, depression is no longer just privatized and clinical, but shared and cultural: a yearning to be in a different sort of relation to ourselves, to our world, and to others.

Perhaps "bad" affects like depression and sadness need not only be things we have to fix by ourselves. They might also be constructed as sites of radical critique, social interconnection, and political intervention. For example, artist Audrey Wollen develops Sad Girl Theory, explaining that "Girls' sadness is not passive, self-involved or shallow; it is a gesture of liberation, it is articulate and informed, it is a way of reclaiming agency over our bodies, identities, and lives." Specifically, Woolen uses Instagram and selfies to explore the cultural politics of sadness in a time where "if we don't feel overjoyed about being a girl, we are failing at our own empowerment." Wollen views her Sad Girl theory as "a permission slip" to resist neoliberal feminism (which we will explore in the next chapter). She explains,

> feminism doesn't need to advocate for how awesome and fun being a girl is. Feminism needs to acknowledge that being a girl in the world right now is one of the hardest things there is—it is unimaginably painful—and that our pain doesn't need to be discarded in the name of empowerment. It can be used as a material, a weight, a wedge, to jam that machinery and change those patterns.[37]

Sad girl theory rejects the injunction to be happy and insists on sadness as a shared, gendered sensibility and practice of emotional justice that registers the broader structures and material realities shaping young women's lives.

Similarly, Johanna Hedva writes "sick woman theory," taking her own struggles with chronic illness and pain as a lens for looking outward and interrogating the biopolitical brutalities of neoliberal precarity. Weaving together descriptions of her own experiences with insights from political and cultural theorists like Cvetkovich, Hedva concludes:

> The most anti-capitalist protest is to care for another and to care for yourself. To take on the historically feminized and therefore invisible practice of nursing, nurturing, caring. To take seriously each other's vulnerability and fragility and precarity, and to support it, honor it, empower it. To protect each other, to enact and practice community. A radical kinship, an interdependent sociality, a politics of care.[38]

What Hedva is suggesting is that learning to care for ourselves *with* others may not only allow us to form potent critiques of the social worlds that are making us sick. Self-care might also inspire new ways of being in common with one another, new practices of community and solidarity, in short, a new world that honors and centers the labors of social reproduction and allows us to actually take care of each other together.

Perhaps we don't have to "own" our sicknesses; they can belong to the structures that make us sick. Perhaps our "bad" affects don't have to be managed by us alone; they can be mobilized to form new social bonds, sensibilities, attachments, and political horizons. Perhaps the care of the self doesn't have to be where we financialize our selves and social relationships; as the place where we often feel the problems of neoliberal culture most acutely, it might be a common place where, together, we start to recover from neoliberalism by learning to un-privatize the labors of social reproduction and care.

Friendship and Affirmative Speculation

To conclude, let's consider the sorts of friendships that might emerge in the context of the feminist forms of self-care outlined above. In his book, *Friendship in the Age of Economics,* May explores the contours and potentials of friendships in neoliberal culture. As we have already seen, thanks to the neoliberal care of the self, contemporary friendships are readily reduced to economized, narcissistic relationships. The parties involved are never on equal and common ground, as relationships are premised on competition and self-appreciation. However, May also sees radical possibility in friendship and the potential for building new senses of interdependency and equality that disrupt neoliberal modes of optimism. He explains, that

> Everyone is on her own, and so everyone is in competition with everyone else. This aloneness breeds a sense of insecurity. In a society in which people were more deeply tied to one another, this insecurity might lead to social solidarity.[39]

Friendship is a potential pathway to social solidarity because it is where we might nurture affective capacities for equality and collective caretaking, in other words, new fantasies and sensibilities of what might make for a good life. May explains further:

> I am struck by how many of my students feel that there is something wrong with the world, resonate with discussions like Marx's treatment of alienation, recognize the emptiness of lives of consumption, but insist that there is nothing to be done about it. They feel alone; solidarity is not a possibility they recognize. What friendship, which these students do recognize as a possibility for them, provides is a model

that will give us the concept of equality in a way that is relevant for constructing collective resistance to the domination of neoliberalism.[40]

In other words, the ability to have non-self-appreciating friendships is a condition of possibility for the social transformation of our disaffected consent. In these friendships, self-enclosed individualism melts away. Boundaries between self and other become porous as people in a friendship come to trust one another with their vulnerabilities and fragilities and thus to depend on one another in sustained ways. As May puts it,

> In having a close friendship, I learn to trust another human being, to place myself in her hands in important ways. This teaches me that I can approach others as more than centers of competition or objects of personal gain or entertainment.[41]

These capacities for connection, trust, and equality are a prerequisite for developing capacities for collective doing and political intervention, that is, for a more radically democratic future and a world beyond the cruel optimism of living in competition.

We can think of these transformative, deep friendships as representing a new practice of speculation, what the authors of the collectively-authored *Speculate This!* call **affirmative speculation**. The neoliberal mode of speculation is *firmative* speculation. It operates according to the logics of financialization and thus seeks to calculate and contain risk in the service of self-appreciation and market competition. Simply put, firmative speculation seeks to firm the future, to lock it down through the management and control of risk. Affirmative speculation is different:

> Affirmative speculation is founded on a paradox: it functions and thrives by concerning itself with an uncertainty that must not be reduced to manageable certainties. By definition, affirmative speculation lives by thinking in the vicinity of the unthinkable (rather than by asserting that the unthinkable is in principle always thinkable, knowable, calculable, and so on). As a mode of radical experimentation with the future, it experiments with those futures that are already here and now and yet are different from the here and now. Paradoxically, in affirmative

speculation—and hence at a moment of potent self-affirmation—what we affirm is something that has the potential to undo us: this is not, in other words, a self-congratulatory affirmation of what we are; it is, rather, an affirmation of what we might become.[42]

Affirmative speculation transforms our disaffected consent and cruel optimism by tapping the potential for other worlds and realities. For example, in non-self-appreciating friendship, we cease to relate to one another through competition. Rather, we risk ourselves and our self-enclosed individualism, opening up to the potentialities of equality and being in common with another. Indeed, affirmative speculation is a mode of living and approach to self-care that wagers on, and thereby pries open, new fantasies, forms of optimism, and social relations that are waiting to be imagined and constructed. These worlds are not certain; they cannot be known or calculated in advance. We can only get there by risking ourselves and "losing confidence" in the world as we know and experience it.

CRITICAL PRACTICE

- What do you think about Berlant's theory of cruel optimism as the primary affective structure of feeling of precarization? Does this concept help to explain your experiences of everyday life in enterprise culture? If so, how specifically?
- Do you experience "self-care as warfare"? Why or why not? How is your experience of neoliberal self-care connected to your social position?
- In addition to the examples of struggles for emotional justice described above, can you think of other ways that we might collectively push back against the moods of enterprise and their cultural power?
- At what other sites in your everyday life, in addition to friendship, might you practice affirmative speculation? Why did you chose these sites? What potential futures are you trying to open up?

NOTES

1 Michel Foucault, "Technologies of the Self," in *The Essential Foucault*, eds. Paul Rabinow and Nikolas Rose (New York: The New Press, 1994), 146.

2 William Davies, *Happiness Industry: How the Government and Big Business Sold Us Well-Being* (London: Verso, 2015), 143.

3 Pierre Dardot and Christian Laval, *The New Way of the World* (London: Verso, 2013), 292.

4 Alain Ehrenberg, *The Weariness of the Self: Diagnosing the History of Depression in the Contemporary Age* (Montreal: McGill-Queen's University Press, 2010), 4.

5 Ann Cvetkovich, *Depression: A Public Feeling* (Durham: Duke University Press, 2012), 64.

6 Davies, *The Happiness Industry*, 177.

7 Davies, *The Happiness Industry*, 174.

8 Kristin Swenson, "Affective Labor and Government Policy: George W. Bush's New Freedom Commission on Mental Health," *Baltic Journal of Law & Politics* 4 (2011): 1–23. doi:10.2478/v10076–011–0010–7

9 Carl Cederstrom and Andre Spicer, *The Wellness Syndrome* (Cambridge: Polity Press, 2015), 12.

10 Cederstrom and Spicer, *The Wellness Syndrome*, 134.

11 Randy Martin, *The Financialization of Daily Life* (Philadelphia: Temple University Press, 2002), 3.

12 Martin, *The Financialization of Daily Life*, 9.

13 Martin, *The Financialization of Daily Life*, 106.

14 Eva Illouz, *Saving the Modern Soul: Therapy, Emotions, and the Culture of Self-Help* (Berkeley: University of California Press, 2008), 93.

15 Todd May, *Friendship in the Age of Economics: Resisting the Forces of Neoliberalism* (Lanham: Lexington Books, 2012), 108.

16 May, *Friendship in the Age of Economics*, 133.

17 Sherry Turkle, *Alone Together: Why We Expect More From Technology and Less From Each Other* (New York: Basic Books, 2011), 177.

18 Cederstrom and Spicer, *The Wellness Syndrome*, 104.

19 Sherry Turkle, *Alone Together*, 179.

20 Sarah Banet-Weiser, *Authentic TM: The Politics of Ambivalence in a Brand Culture* (New York: New York University Press, 2012), 88.

21 Thanks to Chelsea Rogozinski for providing this example.

22 Martin, *The Financialization of Daily Life*, 9.

23 Jennifer Silva, *Coming Up Short: Working-Class Adulthood in the Age of Uncertainty* (Oxford: Oxford University Press, 2013), 21.

24 Barbara Ehrenreich, *Bright-Sided: How the Relentless Promotion of Positive Thinking Has Undermined America* (Detroit: Thorndike Press, 2009), 76.

25 Thanks to Nadiya Wahl for developing this example for me.

26 Rhonda Byrne, *The Secret* (New York: Atria Books, 2006), xii.

27 Byrne, *The Secret*, 23.

28 Ehrenreich, *Bright-Sided*, 98.

29 Sam Binkley, *Happiness as Enterprise: An Essay on Neoliberal Life* (Albany: State University of New York Press, 2014), 1.

30 Silva, *Coming Up Short*, 115.

31 Lauren Berlant, "Interview," *Rorotoko,* June 5, 2012, http://rorotoko.com/interview/20120605_berlant_lauren_on_cruel_optimism/

32 Berlant, "Interview."

33 Sara Ahmed, "Selfcare as Warfare," *feministkilljoys*, August 25, 2014, https://feministkilljoys.com/2014/08/25/selfcare-as-warfare/

34 Laurie Ouellette and Jacquelyn Arcy, "Live Through This: Feminist Care of the Self 2.0," *Frame* 28 (2015): 111.

35 Ouellette and Arcy, "Live Through This," 107.

36 Yolo Akili, "The Immediate Need for Emotional Justice," *Crunk Feminist Collective*, November 16, 2011, www.crunkfeministcollective.com/2011/11/16/the-immediate-need-for-emotional-justice/

37 Audrey Wollen, "How Girls Are Finding Empowerment Through Being Sad Online," *Dazed*, www.dazeddigital.com/photography/article/28463/1/girls-are-finding-empowerment-through-internet-sadness

38 Johanna Hedva, "Sick Woman Theory," *Mask Magazine*, www.maskmagazine.com/not-again/struggle/sick-woman-theory

39 May, *Friendship in the Age of Economics*, 114.

40 May, *Friendship in the Age of Economics*, 134.

41 May, *Friendship in the Age of Economics*, 138.

42 Uncertain Commons, *Speculate This!* (Durham: Duke University Press, 2013), https://speculatethis.pressbooks.com/chapter/affirmative-speculation/

6

ENTERPRISING DEMOCRACY
NEOLIBERAL CITIZENSHIP AND
THE PRIVATIZATION OF POLITICS

CHAPTER OVERVIEW

While the previous two chapters delved into the everyday worlds of neoliberal labor and affect, this chapter explores the world of neoliberal politics and the implications of enterprise culture for democracy. Enterprise culture not only privatizes our working lives and our moods, but also the horizons of politics and citizenship. Here we ask: What happens to democracy in an enterprise culture? What happens to political struggles and citizenship when market logics and competition define how we think about and practice collective action?

We begin this chapter by thinking about the privatization of our political horizons. We revisit Wendy Brown's theory of de-democratization and consider the new political players that are enabled by the enterprising of democracy. These include corporations, non-governmental organizations, philanthropists, marketers, celebrities, and media audiences, as well as individual donors and consumers.

Once we have wrapped our heads around the privatization of politics more generally, we turn our attention to two primary and intertwined dimensions of neoliberal politics and its processes of de-democratization. First, we engage with Sarah Banet-Weiser's work on *brand culture*, and consider how the logic of branding comes to define the field of political and social action and what the critical consequences of this development are for democracy, as well as of our capacities for democracy. Second, we will explore the *neoliberal politics of identity*. As we will see, neoliberal governmentality and enterprise culture turn citizenship and equality into a competition, thereby diminishing our desires for commonality, as well as the possibilities for meaningful and transformative political intervention. Indeed, neoliberalism's privatization of our political horizons makes democracy—the process of governing ourselves in common and working toward a more egalitarian future—an increasingly impossible project.

THE PRIVATIZATION OF POLITICS

In Chapter 2, we discussed Wendy Brown's contention that neoliberalism and democracy are, in fact, incompatible, as neoliberalism's investment in market order is irreconcilable with popular sovereignty and the idea that people should collectively rule their lives. More specifically, Brown argues,

> the neoliberal triumph of *homo oeconomicus* as the exhaustive figure of the human is undermining democratic practices and a democratic imaginary by vanquishing the subject that governs itself through moral autonomy and governs with others through popular sovereignty. The argument is that economic values have not simply supersaturated the political or become predominant over the political. Rather, a neoliberal iteration of *homo oeconomicus* is extinguishing the agent, the idiom, and the domains through which democracy—any variety of democracy—materializes.[1]

The loss of democratic agency might also suggest the loss of politics, but that's not the case. Indeed, Brown's point is not that the market is superseding the political but rather that, in typical neoliberal fashion, it is remaking politics in its own image: that is, neoliberal reason is "enterprising" democracy. Politics still happens, but it is a politics where democracy has been, as Brown puts it, "hollowed out." We are still interpellated as citizens; we still have elections; we still have state institutions, programs, and processes. However, increasingly these foundations of liberal democracy have been reoriented by neoliberal reason toward enterprise and competition in both theory and practice. Our desires for self-determination and autonomy, for social connection and democratic life, come to be subject to the logics and workings of economic growth.

Consequently, politics is no longer primarily a struggle over how best to order society. Within neoliberalism, politics is not the exercise of popular sovereignty, that is, a shared process of governing through participation in public life and institutions. Instead, politics is primarily about growing "market share" for a cause, campaign, or candidate, as the logics and practices of finance define the field of political action, citizenship, and activism. For example, take democratic elections in the United States. Campaigns are competitive brands, each of which is trying to out-maneuver the other through strategic communication practices to win the largest market share of the electorate. Like brands, campaigns are oriented toward building an authentic image of the candidate that voters will connect with affectively. We track poll numbers like stock values. Citizens are consumers of these brands and investors in particular social or political causes. Nothing more. Nothing less. In this hollowed-out version of democracy, the most pressing role for citizens is electing the nation's CEO every four years. This is the big one, where one mega-brand battles against the other for the right to steer the nation's brand for global competition.

In this sense, the field of political and civic engagement exists as a marketplace, where one certainly has choices to make and action to take, but not usually as a practice of democracy, as the contours of collective life have already been decided for us: global competition and self-appreciation. The horizons of politics are privatized; they lead us toward spontaneous order, where citizen-consumers are competing human capitals, and acts of citizenship figure as input into the giant information processor of the market. Ultimately, when politics are privatized, every social problem we face as individuals, communities, the nation, or the world becomes something to be addressed, imagined, and solved within the context of the market.

Neoliberal Political Actors

Within this world of privatized politics, there are new key players; with the hollowing out of public, democratic processes, the field of politics opens to a range of new and old agents, institutions, and organizations from the private sector. These include the following:

- **Corporations** and their practices of corporate social responsibility
- **Philanthropists** and their efforts to solve the world's pressing problems through good business practice
- **Non-governmental organizations** and the growing market for international aid and social welfare provision
- **Marketers** and their promotion of particular causes and campaigns
- **Celebrities** and their media promotion of particular causes and campaigns
- **Consumer citizens** and their "buying into" particular causes and campaigns
- **Individual donors** who fund particular causes and campaigns

Each of these is discussed more fully below.

Corporations

Increasingly, corporations shape and intervene in the field of political action through their *corporate social responsibility* (CSR) efforts. In a world where the corporate brand is the primary measure of market value, social and political causes, which used to be outside the scope of business practice, can emerge as "good business" to the extent that they might enhance a firm's brand value. As Sarah Banet-Weiser explains of the logic of CSR:

> It is not the logic of social justice, or what a corporation might do beyond the confines of its own bottom line to create a more equitable market. Rather, the logic of CSR is about the various ways in which a corporation's support of social issues—be they sweat-free labor, the environment, or funding for AIDS or breast cancer research—can build the corporation's brand and thus bring in more revenue and profit.

> The attention to social issues is a "value add"; saving the world, in the language of the corporation, can be profitable.[2]

Increasingly, we see corporations acting as political "citizens" in the market to grow and/or manage their brand. In doing so, CSR provides a corporate context for consumers to undertake social action and civic engagement. Of course, this is a privatized form of politics; it happens within the movements and demands of the global market.

Philanthropists

While philanthropists have long played an active role in public research institutions and programs, neoliberal governmentality has ushered in what Matthew Bishop and Michael Green enthusiastically call the age of *philanthrocapitalism*. Philanthrocapitalists seek to solve the world's most entrenched and pressing problems through the application of business methods and logics. Bishop and Green explain, "Their philanthrophy is 'strategic,' 'market conscious,' 'impact oriented,' 'knowledge based,' often 'high engagement,' and always driven by the goal of maximizing the 'leverage' of the donor's money."[3] As we saw in the examination of education in Chapter 3, philanthrocapitalists like Bill Gates come to wield enormous power as their promises of efficiency and measurable outputs reshape how we think about, and go about, addressing social problems like education. Similar to the logic of CSR, philanthrocapitalism suggests that saving the world and good business are one and the same. By thinking in terms of return on investment, like only the brightest and most successful capitalists can, we can figure out how to harness market mechanisms to create tangible social change. Again, politics is deeply privatized: placed in the hands of wealthy social entrepreneurs and at a distance from democratic processes of collective governance.

Non-Governmental Organizations (NGOs)

During the 1990s, the number of registered non-governmental organizations skyrocketed from 6,000 to 37,000, as the end of the Cold War and structural adjustment policies opened up a space for the development of what scholars often refer to as global civil society.[4] Today, it is estimated that there are 3.7 million NGOs, some of which operate in specific countries and others that operate transnationally. The largest NGOs are usually rooted in the heart of Empire (i.e., the United States and Western Europe). NGOs are a crucial part of the neoliberal shift to global governance and Empire. These organizations work "in between" the private market and the state to advocate for particular groups and causes and to provide vital social services (i.e., health, food, education) that were once the purview of the state. Unlike public services, these organizations do not rely solely on state distributions, but rather on a mix of state contracts and private support from foundations and individual citizens. This global third sector employs millions and constitutes one of the world's largest economies. Indeed, this sprawling network of NGOs is a competitive marketplace where aid products and services are advocated for, funded, and traded. While NGOs obviously play an enormous role in many people's lives as employers and basic service providers, it is crucial to see that these organizations have little power when it comes to actual state regulation and policymaking. In other words, they are not democratic organizations; they are part of Empire and spontaneous market order—global governance by global capitalism.

Marketers and Communication Specialists

Today marketers and communication specialists are indispensable political operatives. As media scholars have argued, we live in what Andrew Wernick calls a *promotional culture*. Thanks to the privatization and marketization of all of social life, communication, at its core, becomes promotional in nature—that is, designed to sell a specific message, brand, product, idea, or cause. In other words, communication is not primarily informational, but rather strategic, instrumental, and persuasive. While propaganda has long served as a promotional tool of states and corporations, in promotional culture, the entire sphere of public debate and deliberation becomes a promotional space, as political actors focus on the strategic communication of their position within the private market. In this promotional context, PR experts and communication specialists of all sorts become central to the political process, as it is their job to sell particular political causes and market different platforms of social action.[5]

Celebrities

Celebrities are increasingly empowered political actors within promotional culture, as their star image and sway with audiences make them vital, strategic resources to a cause. Marketers routinely tap celebrities to help sell particular campaigns. Celebrities also mobilize their star status to become active political agents in their own right. In a promotional and privatized political culture, celebrity voices come to matter more than those of ordinary citizens, for better or worse. As we will see, as highly visible individuals, celebrities also become prominent cultural sites where privatized politics play out in public.

Consumer Citizens and Media Audiences

In a privatized, promotional culture, consumers and media audiences perform the role of citizens. To be a citizen is to be an engaged and active media user/consumer, responding to the various contexts for participation provided by corporations, NGOs, and other promotional political campaigns. Social action and civic engagement are directed not toward the practice of democracy as collective governing, but rather toward registering one's choices and desires and advocating for one's preferred social investments within the marketplace.

Donors

When the state is no longer dedicated to maintaining public infrastructures, including an open and democratic political process, politics and social action are increasingly funded by private entities and individuals. From rulings like *Citizens United*, which extended First Amendment rights to corporations (thereby enabling the unchecked flow of monied interests into the electoral process), to the provision of humanitarian relief in the wake of disasters (whereby emergency, life-saving aid is contingent in large part on successful media campaigns), our political context is driven in powerful ways by the actions of donors and not by the needs, rights, dreams, or desires of ordinary citizens and democratic populations.

CRITICAL PRACTICE

Let's ground this privatized political world and its key players in a concrete example of enterprising democracy. Product (Red) is a licensed brand that was founded by activist rockstar Bono and philanthropist Bobby Shriver in 2006. The (Red) brand partners with popular lifestyle companies like Gap, Apple, American Express, and Coca-Cola to fight HIV/AIDS in African countries. Partner companies produce (Red) branded products and donate a portion of their profits to the Global Fund, an international financing agency that was seeded by Bill Gates and works to raise and distribute resources for fighting deadly, though preventable, diseases like HIV/AIDS, tuberculosis, and malaria.

Take a look at the promotional diagram about how Product (Red) works. Ask yourself the following questions:

HOW (RED) WORKS

Shoppers note that when you buy (RED) products, up to 50% of profits from those sales will go to fight AIDS.

Shoppers buy (RED) and the manufacturers of the (RED) products send a contribution directly to the Global Fund - not to (RED).

The Global Fund uses 100% of this money - with no overhead taken out - to finance HIV/AIDS programs.

Figure 6.1 Product (Red)

- How is Product Red indicative of neoliberalism's privatization of the political, especially the new political agents that privatization and enterprise culture empower?
- What potential problems, both practically and philosophically, do you see with making the public health issue of HIV/AIDS in African countries something that can be addressed by and within the market? Who has power and voice as citizens in this case? Who does not?

In the remainder of this chapter, we will examine two primary dimensions of neoliberalism's privatization of the political and their consequences for democracy and citizenship. The *first* is what Sarah Banet-Weiser calls brand culture, where marketing increasingly provides "the cultural contexts for everyday living, individual identity, and affective relationships."[6] Brands are "platforms of living" and templates for identity. Crucially, the brand is also a pervasive logic for imagining and creating social change. The *second* dimension of the privatization of the political is the neoliberal politics of identity and its transformation of political struggle into a competition for equality. As we will see, neoliberalism reorients past identity-based political struggles (e.g., feminism, LGBTQ rights, antiracism) for equality and downward distribution towards marketized struggles for recognition and inclusion. At the same time, neoliberalism activates hate and discrimination against historically marginalized groups, as politics becomes a cutthroat market competition fueled by cruelty and resentment.

BRAND CULTURE

The first way to approach neoliberalism's privatization of the political is through the lens of brand culture. In *Authentic™: The Politics of Ambivalence in a Brand Culture*, Banet-Weiser argues that the logics of branding now permeate all sectors of society, from art and religion to citizenship and politics: "Branding in our era has extended beyond a business model; branding is now both reliant on, and reflective of, our most basic social and cultural relations."[7] Nowadays, brands come to do much more than help to sell products; they form our cultural, social, and political contexts; they shape our senses of belonging, community, and political possibility. Simply put, **brand culture** transforms the logic of branding into a ubiquitous cultural language and structure of feeling, encompassing not just our acts of purchasing goods but also our practices of identity formation and citizenship.

Commodity Activism and Consumer Citizenship

In brand culture, politics and citizenship are facilitated by ongoing engagements with brands. Thus, social action and civic engagement are increasingly animated by the logics of media promotion and marketing. Banet-Weiser and Roopali Mukherjee propose the term **commodity activism** to capture how, within neoliberalism, "realms of culture and society once considered 'outside' the official economy are harnessed, reshaped, and made legible in economic terms."[8] "Social activism," they suggest, "may be shifting shape into a marketable commodity."[9] Consequently, acts of citizenship and cultural resistance are now a market interaction; they are about the consumption and circulation of goods and meanings.

It is important to note that commodity activism is not specific to neoliberalism. Since the rise of consumer culture, consumption has been a site of political struggle. For example, early welfare rights activists organized around the idea that poor people should have the right to participate in consumer culture; citizenship meant being able to consume the same goods as others. Later on, much of the civil rights movement was staged in the realm of consumer culture, as organizers led bus boycotts, occupied lunch counters, and picketed department stores to protest Jim Crow and the systemic exclusion and marginalization of African-Americans within consumer capitalism. Therefore, to understand the rise of *neoliberal* brand culture, Banet-Weiser traces three distinct moments of **consumer citizenship** and commodity activism that paved the way for the contemporary context.

The first moment is Fordist mass consumption. During the post-World War II period of embedded liberalism, consumption emerged as the new context for democratic citizenship. An expanding economy built on the mass production and consumption of goods, coupled with the growth of television and the suburbs, rearticulated the American Dream away from the pursuit of a better life for immigrants to the attainment of a particular, middle-class lifestyle. The means to achieve this lifestyle was consumer culture; hence, one's citizenship and belonging came to hinge on the ownership and display of goods and products. This is what Lizabeth Cohen calls "the consumer's republic," where, as Banet-Weiser argues, "political and social values previously tied to more abstract political ideologies, such as freedom, democracy, and equality, were understood as accessible specifically through the promises of consumer capitalism."[10] What's crucial about this moment is the idea of the good life is now linked to the cultivation of a specific consumer identity; in other words, "consumer choices could be political choices."[11]

The second moment of commodity activism has to do with the transition from Fordism to post-Fordism and the emergence of branding as the central accumulation strategy of capitalism, a development discussed in Chapter 4. During this period, marketing shifts its focus. Instead of selling a mass of goods to a mass of consumers, a practice that obscured social differences between consumers, marketers began carving up audiences into niche groups based on social identity and consumer lifestyle, targeting specific audiences with products customized for them. Consequently, differences proliferated in consumer and media culture, and crucially, authenticity became a central concern of marketing, as products needed to reflect the "real" values and beliefs of different social groups. It is important to see that this shift from mass to niche marketing was a double-edged sword from the perspective of expanding inclusion and representation. On the one hand, it recognized communities who had long been excluded from popular media and consumer culture, as well as broader political processes. On the other hand, it commodified identities, translating historical and political struggles for social justice into market practices. Struggles for equality became fodder for marketers and their quest to create authentic, niche representations and brands.[12]

According to Banet-Weiser, these two moments paved the way for our contemporary moment of neoliberal commodity activism and consumer citizenship, where the consumer becomes an active participant in enhancing specific brands. Rather than targeting consumer groups with authentic products, marketers now seek to interpellate individual entrepreneurs of the self by providing the context for an authentic brand relationship. "The trick for contemporary marketers," Banet-Weiser explains, "is how to create engagement that feels authentic while still privileging the market exchange."[13] The idea here is to appeal to consumers' sense of self-appreciating individualism. The brand presents itself as an ethical and social "platform for living";[14] participation in the brand promises to enhance one's overall human capital as a citizen of the neoliberal state.

Crucially, the contemporary marketing of authentic brand relationships and platforms takes place within interactive and participatory digital environments, where there is a constant tension between individualism and collective action. In the era of big data, marketers know more about *individual* users and can target them accordingly (as opposed to a mass or a niche). Yet, the networked character of digital culture also means that individual participation is always happening within a social collectivity. Thus, neoliberal commodity activism comes to *feel* democratic, even though it is not. Banet-Weier puts it this way:

> The individual entrepreneur is encouraged to participate in collective action through brands . . . just as citizens have been encouraged throughout U.S. history to exercise civic behavior such as voting and organizing (some citizens far more than others, of course). The contemporary moment, however, is characterized by the fact that brand culture profit will always trump collective politics and social issues, so that these same collective politics are authorized by the brand itself.[15]

In brand culture, where the logics and practices of marketing and promotion guide most social processes, digital forms of commodity activism become the predominant language of and framework for political engagement. Today, as Banet-Weiser shows, we inhabit *branded political cultures*, where logics of brand expansion and practices of self-appreciation and self-enterprise become the taken-for-granted ground of politics and citizenship. In other words, causes and campaigns become brands, and we dedicate ourselves to expanding them in the promotional and participatory networks of digital culture.

Critical Consequences

You might be thinking, So what? What are the problems with brand culture? Even if politics are increasingly privatized and branded, don't they still make a difference and help bring about social change? After all, don't brands like Product (Red) raise awareness and mobilize audiences to take action on important social issues? I want to suggest that there are three major problems with brand culture and its privatization of our political horizons, each of which contributes to de-democratization and the hollowing out of public institutions and our capacities for collective governing. We can see these critical consequences if we consider the impact of brand culture on struggles for environmental justice.

1. Political struggle becomes oriented toward spontaneous market order, not democracy. In brand culture, politics comes to be defined not necessarily by the pressing issues for democracy and collective life, but rather by the spontaneous order of the market. In other words, politics is reduced to causes and campaigns that are conducive to branding and the generation of brand value. Certainly, when thinking about environmental action, the most obvious example of branded politics is the rise of "green" brands and commodities. Eager to capitalize on public concerns about environmental destruction and climate change, countless companies have branded themselves and their products as eco-friendly. In turn, consuming green products and associating with green brands become the context for displaying one's environmental citizenship. As critics of this green market have suggested, however, all of this market-based environmentalism amounts to little more than "greenwashing," that is, covering over a firm's own contributions to environmental degradation through branding oneself as a socially responsible corporation.

However, it is important to see that brand culture and its privatization of politics is more complicated than the critiques of greenwashing suggest. At issue is not simply the marketization of environmentalism, but also the ways in which brand logics come to shape how we think about the nature and content of political action itself. When politics becomes limited to what will sell, only certain problems become legible. Banet-Weiser writes, "If the market structures and determines what is defined as political, then market logic applies to politics: if an issue does not have a large enough consumer base, or is seen as too alienating or offensive to consumers, then it will not become a branded political culture. Thus, some issues cannot readily be made into a brand, because branding logic cannot be easily integrated or applied. If certain politics do not add value to a brand, and thus are not "brandable," a brand community will not form around and within these politics.[16]

Simply put, those causes that cannot generate brand value within the market become disposable political investments. In brand culture, the only politics that become viable are those that can circulate within the existing *economies of visibility*.[17] Politics becomes constricted to what will circulate online and garner an active media audience. What becomes possible to struggle for is thus limited to what is imagined to activate particular affects and actions privileged by brand logic and digital culture. As Banet-Weiser explains, "brand logic appeals to consumers through emotive and affective relationships that structure privatized management and state deregulation and privilege the consumer citizen."[18] In other words, brand culture enacts the "hollowing out" of democracy by enclosing citizenship within the horizons of the market's spontaneous order. Politics, activism, and citizenship are themselves deregulated—privatized and given over to the market, untethered from the common work of collective governing.

The theory of social change undergirding this vision of citizenship is simple: if enough competing, self-appreciating human capitals input their political preferences and social desires into the market, justice will materialize spontaneously. Our political horizon is thus spontaneous order. Thanks to brand culture, it seems that all we can do is to publicize our desires in the context of the private market.

2. Citizenship is oriented toward self-appreciation, not the practice of democracy. At its core, democratic citizenship is a practice of collective governing, the exercise of popular sovereignty. Recall Brown's concept of "bare democracy" discussed in Chapter 2. In its basic form, democracy is the idea—and, most importantly, the commitment to the idea—that the people should rule. While practices of democratic citizenship (e.g., voting) are usually undertaken by individuals, they are oriented toward a collective process of deliberation and determination of the contours of common life. My point is not that neoliberal citizenship is self-motivated, as, of course, all democratic participation is self-motivated to an extent. Rather, what I want to suggest is that neoliberal citizenship is not about collective governing but about self-appreciation.

In brand culture, for example, where citizenship is guided by brand logic, citizens become, first and foremost, social entrepreneurs, dedicated to expanding a brand's political causes, which in turn, works to establish and nurture one's own self-brand. Put another way, citizenship and brand activism figure as facets of human capital. In the context of environmental justice and activism, for instance, brand culture provides ample opportunity for self-expression and consciousness-raising amongst one's digital networks, as green brands and organizations promote their causes online and enjoin their followers to do the same. However, it is important to think carefully about the horizons of political action and citizenship here. To what extent is our online promotion of environmental causes a practice of collective governing? What is actually being accomplished in these acts of branded online activism?

I want to suggest that brand culture converts our democratic desires and practices of citizenship into self-appreciating activity, as the practice of citizenship is oriented away from collective life and toward the interior state of the self, thanks to the narcissistic structures of digital culture discussed in the previous chapter. Put differently, political participation within brand culture offers an "ethical and moral context in which one can 'take care of the self'" by demonstrating one's "social responsibility" as human capital.[19] Unlike the forms of self-care and appreciation discussed in the previous two chapters (i.e., makeovers, happiness apps), what is happening here is the "maintenance of a politically virtuous self" who displays their personal morality and social commitments through promotional participation in digital culture.[20]

It is important to see how this separates one's political horizons from others'. Those with the means to buy "green" become good ethical consumer citizens, which, in turn, devalues those who can't afford to be so socially responsible. Indeed, it is important to consider who gets excluded from citizenship when citizenship becomes about consumer activism and self-appreciation in brand culture.

3. When politics are branded, we lose the interconnectedness of the issues we are facing. It is important to see that brand culture becomes a powerful force in the neoliberal disimagination machine; it strips us of our critical capacities for radical critique. When the world of politics is animated by brand logic, it becomes difficult, if not impossible, to sense "the interconnectedness of political issues."[21] Causes and campaigns are organized to mobilize discrete political actions and affects connected to particular brand cultures, making it difficult, at best, to see a broad, historical, and interconnected political field. Mapping the conjuncture (the aim of this book!) thus becomes increasingly challenging. For in enterprise culture, foundational issues of political economy and governmentality fall out of view, as it is only those distinct, self-enclosed causes that register in the digital market and its economies of visibility which can be articulated and addressed. In this context, how can we govern collectively if we can't see the interconnect-edness of our politics? How can we imagine and move toward an alternative future if we can't map our conjuncture? How can we work to transform the conditions of our lives if we remain ignorant of them?

Let's consider the problem of climate change. In her book, *This Changes Everything: Capitalism vs. the Climate,* Naomi Klein argues that we cannot, in fact, do anything about climate change without dismantling neoliberal capitalism and its financialization of our social world. Climate change is not simply an environmental issue; it is a political issue that touches and intersects with myriad other political issues, including inequality, health, and capitalism. Yet, as we have already seen, the predominant forms of activism available within brand culture (e.g., buying green, spreading aware-ness of environmental issues via one's social networks) do nothing to disrupt market order and neoliberal logics, much less allow us to see the interconnectedness of issues that must simultaneously be considered.

Truly addressing climate change hinges on large-scale resistance and the rapid development of new governmentalities and counter-conduct. However, enterprise culture and its disimagination and struc-tural ignorance work together to render neoliberal subjects incapa-ble of these tasks. As Klein's research documents, people all over the world are resisting the devastating effects of fossil fuels. They are organizing to protect vital natural resources, blockading extraction sites, even as state/corporate powers threaten harm and arrest. How-ever, these ongoing and interconnected political struggles barely regis-ter in brand culture and the neoliberal world of enterprised democracy. In the end, collectively resisting and realizing new governmentalities requires conjunctural critique. They require new political sensibilities of interconnection and interdependence, not market enterprise and self-appreciation.

CRITICAL PRACTICE

- Consider another political issue, one that is close to your heart. Now think about how this issue appears in brand culture (if at all). How is it promoted? What affects does it seek to activate and capitalize on? What practices of citizenship and commodity activism does it encourage? Now trace the three critical consequences outlined above. Does brand culture privatize your political horizons and practices of citizenship? If so, how specifically?

THE NEOLIBERAL POLITICS OF IDENTITY

The second dimension of neoliberalism's privatization of our political horizons is the neoliberal politics of identity, more specifically, the new politics of equality and disposability. Recall from Chapter 1 that neoliberalism represents a new hegemony, and as such, it redraws the horizons of political struggle. What comes to be at stake in neoliberal politics is not the public function of the state, but rather the best way to create a market society rooted in competition and private enterprise. Thus, we see new political antagonisms and conflicts. More specifically, a left neoliberalism and a right neoliberalism emerge to duke out how to best create a market order. At the heart of *both* sides are a new politics of equality and disposability.

As we know, neoliberalism imposes a world of competition fueled by the ideology of meritocracy. Consequently, equality emerges not as something guaranteed by the state, but as something that must be competed for in the market. In *Twilight of Equality: Neoliberalism, Cultural Politics and the Attack on Democracy*, Lisa Duggan explores these new politics of equality and disposability by tracing how neoliberalism's political-economic agenda of upward wealth redistribution and privatization advances *through* the politics of identity.[22] As Duggan makes clear, identity categories and social hierarchies of class, race, gender, sexuality, and nationality have long been key axes of oppression, exploitation, power, and inequality within liberalism.

However, the ongoing construction of a competitive, enterprise society, where people must assume more and more personal responsibility for their lives, hinges on new and profoundly contradictory mobilizations of identity and difference. On the one hand, previously excluded groups are granted inclusion into market society, so long as they conform to the norms of self-enterprise and privatized self-care. These are the politics of *left* neoliberalism. On the other hand, social hierarchies of race, gender, sexuality, ability, and citizenship are seen as irrelevant and, increasingly, retrenched in brutal ways. These are the politics of *right* neoliberalism. More specifically, as we saw previously with the criminal industrial complex, right neoliberalism mobilizes an aggressively Social Darwinist view of competition that works to render vulnerable populations and historically marginalized groups disposable in order to maintain the social hierarchies and regimes of dispossession from which its constituents benefit.

As we will see, in both left and right neoliberalism, **competing for equality** becomes the horizon of the political. Thus, democracy as a practice of collective governing rooted in the idea of equality becomes increasingly unviable. Thanks to the competitive structure of feeling that neoliberalism brings to political life, individual or group equality is felt to come at the expense of others'. Regardless of our politics, we become caught up in that oppositional consciousness bred and required by living in competition. Consequently, we lose our capacities to see and forge interconnections, as neoliberal governmentality and the enterprising of democracy have us all competing for equality in a world where equality is fundamentally impossible. Thus, as we will see, right and left neoliberalism feed off each other, especially in digital, brand culture, keeping us all stuck within the devastations of the current political horizons of our neoliberal conjuncture.

Left Neoliberalism and Marketized Equality

As we explored in Chapter 3 in reference to *Waiting for Superman,* neoliberal governmentalities and ideologies often appear as progressive political struggles for racial and gender equality. In the film, the charter school push to economize and privatize public education appears as a political struggle for greater equality and inclusion. Underprivileged kids with big dreams seem to benefit from neoliberal reform; because the current state-run system is broken, it must be fixed to create a true meritocracy where all kids have equal opportunity to choose and compete regardless of their circumstance.

This progressive, left version of neoliberal politics is premised on what Duggan calls the new equality politics that emerged in the post-Cold War context of the 1990s. For example, Duggan traces what happened to LBGTQ struggles during this time. Organizing by groups like ACT UP around the AIDS pandemic was radical. In the wake of so many lost lives, in relation to which the state and companies sat silently by, activists insisted that queer bodies, sexualities, and lives be protected. They demanded downward redistribution of resources and power. However, around the same time, a more moderate group primarily comprised of wealthy, white men were developing a different political horizon for gay rights and activism. In stark contrast to AIDS activism, which embraced the vulnerable and marginalized, these groups reoriented activism toward inclusion in the burgeoning enterprise culture. The bodies that mattered here were what Duggan calls "homonormative" ones, those that conformed to dominant cultural ideals of the nuclear family, bodily modesty and control, self-care, and enterprise in the market. The rights to marry and to serve in the military—inclusion within two of the most conservative institutions—were adopted as the primary fronts of political struggle. In these new equality politics, struggles for inclusion and social protection were not about changing the power structures of capitalist society but rather furthering the neoliberal project of creating a privatized, market order of self-appreciating individuals and families. According to Duggan, this is a "trickle-down vision of equality," where the empowerment and expansion of the market through the inclusion of more self-enterprising individuals is alleged to further the prospects of all. However, this "trickle-down" idea of equality, devoted to empowering the homonormative bodies of self-enterprise, actually works to render queer, non-conforming bodies disposable, while pulling the rug out from under more radical and democratic movements for queer visibility, inclusion, and social protection.[23]

Accordingly, in the new equality politics of left neoliberalism, equality is marketized. It is about the right to compete in the market. Here are the key feature of **marketized equality**:

1. Marketized equality is self-enclosed and individualized; it is animated by the norm of self-enterprise.
2. Marketized equality seeks inclusion and recognition within the meritocratic market order and its economies of visibility.
3. Marketized equality does not challenge neoliberal governmentality; it expands neoliberal governmentality.
4. Marketized equality actively produces disposability and inequality.

Ultimately, marketized equality privatizes collective struggle, as these forms of equality lead to new, neoliberal forms of *individualized solidarity*. In these forms of solidarity, collectivity is about securing access to self-appreciation for the self and others in the market. Here, inclusion is not about democracy, collective governing, or a more egalitarian distribution of economic, social, and cultural power and resources. Rather, collectivity is about private individuals' participation in and recognition by the market. As we know, neoliberal inclusion and recognition don't—and, in fact, can't—include everyone, but only those who merit their place through self-enterprise and competition. Thus, individualized solidarities do the work of neoliberal governmentality, as these political struggles for equality now participate in doing the work of sorting the winners from the losers.

To understand the power of marketized equality within our political imaginations, we need to consider briefly neoliberalism's complicated relationship to the social movements for racial and gender justice of the 1960s and 1970s. On one hand, neoliberalism represented a swift and decisive backlash against these movements that demanded—and in large part won—emancipation and extended rights to participate in public life. Indeed, as we saw in Chapter 1, neoliberal hegemony was established in part through the rejection of these identity-based movements for downward redistribution of power and resources. At the same time, we can't ignore the extent to which the rise of left neoliberalism rides on the backs of these movements, specifically their critiques of the state and its historical exclusion of marginalized groups. While neoliberal governmentality vehemently rejects the collectivist and democratic aspects of these social movements, it nonetheless draws energy from their critique of the social welfare state—which, as we know, relied heavily on racial and gender exploitation and oppression—and channels these political energies toward neoliberal struggles for marketized equality. Let's turn now to some examples to see how this all plays out in cultural practice and discourse.

Postfeminist Sensibilities and Neoliberal Feminism

As we explored in Chapter 4, the neoliberal crisis of care required new gender ideologies and sensibilities, as women once primarily scripted for a life of domesticity were now expected to participate in the dual-income society of flexible, insecure work. Post-feminism thus became a prominent, deeply individualized discourse of gender empowerment rooted in self-enterprise; it proclaimed women could have it all—a successful career and a happy family—if they worked hard and made good choices. Postfeminism thus incorporated feminist ideas of equal participation in paid work as commonsense, while also reinscribing heteronormative, patriarchal regimes of family and care work.

As Catherine Rottenberg argues, these postfeminist sensibilities of individualized gender empowerment have given rise to new, seemingly progressive forms of **neoliberal feminism** that are exemplified by Facebook executive Sheryl Sandberg's popular book *Lean In: Women, Work, and the Will to Lead* and the social movement it has generated since its publication. Within the discourses of *Lean In*, feminism as a collective, democratic struggle for gender justice is redefined as a personal practice of neoliberal self-governmentality. While earlier feminist movements critiqued gender exclusion and exploitation at the heart of liberalism and pressed for redistributions of power and resources, neoliberal feminism offers up more inclusion in market competition as the answer to entrenched gender inequality. In other words, neoliberal feminism hollows out the democratic project that was at the heart of liberal feminism and replaces it with an individualized, marketized struggle for equality.

More specifically, Rottenberg shows how *Lean In* interpellates a highly privatized feminist subject who must confront entrenched systems of gender inequality with proper technologies of self-appreciation:

> Individuated in the extreme, this subject is feminist in the sense that she is distinctly aware of current inequalities between men and women. This same subject is, however, simultaneously neoliberal, not only because she disavows the social, cultural and economic forces producing this inequality, but also because she accepts full responsibility for her own well-being and self-care.[24]

CRITICAL PRACTICE

Check out this image from Leanin.org.

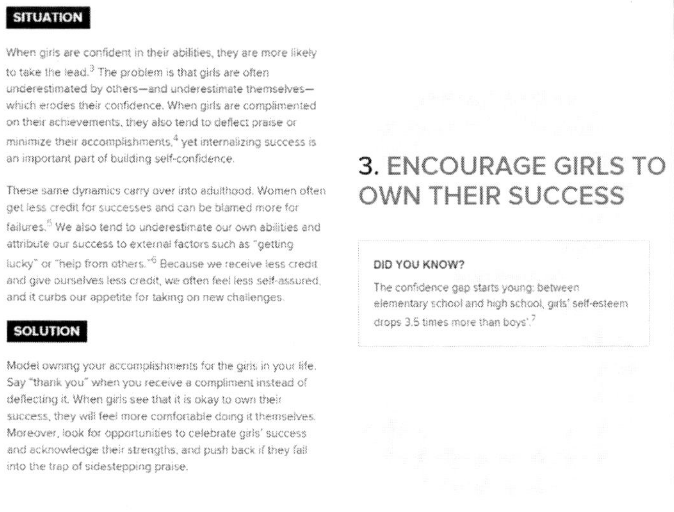

SITUATION

When girls are confident in their abilities, they are more likely to take the lead.[3] The problem is that girls are often underestimated by others—and underestimate themselves—which erodes their confidence. When girls are complimented on their achievements, they also tend to deflect praise or minimize their accomplishments,[4] yet internalizing success is an important part of building self-confidence.

These same dynamics carry over into adulthood. Women often get less credit for successes and can be blamed more for failures.[5] We also tend to underestimate our own abilities and attribute our success to external factors such as "getting lucky" or "help from others."[6] Because we receive less credit and give ourselves less credit, we often feel less self-assured, and it curbs our appetite for taking on new challenges.

SOLUTION

Model owning your accomplishments for the girls in your life. Say "thank you" when you receive a compliment instead of deflecting it. When girls see that it is okay to own their success, they will feel more comfortable doing it themselves. Moreover, look for opportunities to celebrate girls' success and acknowledge their strengths, and push back if they fall into the trap of sidestepping praise.

3. ENCOURAGE GIRLS TO OWN THEIR SUCCESS

DID YOU KNOW?

The confidence gap starts young: between elementary school and high school, girls' self-esteem drops 3.5 times more than boys'.[7]

Figure 6.2 Tip #3 for "How to Be a Role Model for Girls"

• How does the Lean In movement operate as a form of neoliberal gender governmentality for both women and young girls?

> • How does Lean In's feminism exemplify marketized equality and individualized solidarity?
> • How does this version of feminist equality politics contribute to the biopolitics of disposability?

Post-Race Sensibilities and Neoliberal Antiracism

Left neoliberalism also authorizes its own version of antiracism rooted in **post-race** sensibilities. When President Obama was elected in 2008, many commentators jumped to the conclusion that the United States had finally entered a truly "post-racial" era. Allegedly, the election of the first African-American president signaled the end of the residual effects of past racisms, from slavery to Jim Crow; for, clearly, race placed no limits on hard-working, capable individuals like Obama. What distinguishes these post-racial discourses from those of colorblindness (where we shouldn't see race) is that post-race actively embraces race (Obama's racial identity is celebrated rather than negated) in order to then disavow the effects of racism (race no longer matters for personal outcomes).

Roopali Mukherjee argues that these post-racial sensibilities are crucial to neoliberal governmentality. They act as a form of "official antiracism" that helps to legitimate the neoliberal state and its programs of governing through self-enterprise and meritocracy in the market. As Mukherjee puts it,

> Discourses of post-race valourize marketized modes of racial reform, which, on one hand, must weed out 'at risk' individuals who are inferior in terms of their life capacities and ill-equipped to participate in the commercialization of life . . . and, on the other, 'good risks' who are available to be channelled into privatized, and profitable, circuits of inclusion, advancement, and civic care.[25]

In other words, **neoliberal antiracism** works to *erase and redraw* lines between citizens according to who is capable of privatized citizenship and who is not virtuous when it comes to prospects for productive market agency. In one fell swoop, it extends racial equality to those who merit it (e.g., President Obama), while simultaneously relegating those who are deemed incapable of self-appreciation to a life of disposability and institutionalized hustling.

In his article, "'A Postgame Interview for the Ages': Richard Sherman and the Dialectical Rhetoric of Racial Neoliberalism," Joe Tompkins pulls apart the logics of neoliberal antiracism through an analysis of the media controversy sparked by NFL star cornerback Richard Sherman. After a game-saving pass deflection that secured his team the 2014 National Football Conference (NFC) championship and a trip to the Super Bowl, an excited Sherman engaged in some run-of-the-mill trash talk in his postgame interview with Fox sportscaster Erin Andrews, inadvertently setting off a national discussion about race. The first part of the conversation was ugly; Twitter users responded to Sherman's interview with a wide and vicious range of overtly racist epithets (e.g., "thug" and much worse). The racist attacks on Sherman reflect long-standing white supremacist discourses that, as we will discuss soon, continue to be mobilized to rationalize the disposability of poor black communities. However, at the same time, the swift and broad movement to denounce this overt racism exemplifies neoliberal antiracism. Commentators from across the media world jumped to defend Sherman and condemn the racists on Twitter. Specifically, commentators highlighted how Sherman was a "man of enterprise," "a kid from Compton, surrounded by bad circumstances who made good grades and worked hard to create a new life for himself."[26] Sherman had competed for his equality and won. Therefore, he was not, in fact, disposable—in other words, he was not one of those "thugs" who warrant aggressive policing and institutionalized hustling—but rather a worthy citizen. In this way, neoliberal antiracism's marketized vision of equality rationalizes and produces the biopolitics of disposability.

Critiquing struggles for marketized equality is tricky. Certainly, the inclusion of previously marginalized groups within existing structures and systems represents important social and cultural progress. And to be absolutely clear, the work of creating an egalitarian and democratic world beyond neoliberalism will not be possible without real and transformative commitments to inclusion, diversity, recognition, and the coalitions and common sensibilities that these struggles make possible. However, as Jo Littler explains, marketized equalities and the meritocratic ideologies that animate them do little to challenge neoliberalism's culture of upward redistribution and the fundamental inequalities on which it is premised. She writes that meritocracy

> has become a key ideological means by which plutocracy—or government by a wealthy elite—perpetuates itself through neoliberal culture. It is not, in other words, merely a coincidence that the common idea that we live, or should live, in a meritocratic age co-exists with a pronounced lack of social mobility and the continuation of vested hereditary economic interests.[27]

In short, the age of meritocracy and marketized equality is also the age of precarity, inequality, and Empire.

CRITICAL PRACTICE

- Should our political goal really be just a more diverse elite, while the vast majority lives the four *D*s? What other ways might we think about struggles for and the politics of equality? How might we expand our political imaginations and horizons to create more widely shared visions of social inclusion?

Right Neoliberalism and the Culture of Cruelty

While left neoliberalism seeks to expand access to the enterprise society through marketized equality, right neoliberalism feels and works differently. Right neoliberalism tends to be authoritarian and socially conservative. As described in Chapter 1, right neoliberalism initially cohered through new coalitions between conservative Christians, anti-communists, and free marketers. These coalitions were forged in the post-World War II era in opposition to labor unions, social movements, and the social welfare policies of the liberal state. While both right and left neoliberalism are invested in creating market order, right neoliberalism is far less invested in the diversity of this order.

Instead, right neoliberalism embraces the Social Darwinism at the heart of neoliberal social ontology fully and aggressively, seeing the lack of inclusion as an economic advantage to be exploited. Thus, right neoliberalism ends up explicitly working through existing social hierarchies.

Put another way, right neoliberalism openly works through the biopolitics of disposability. As we already know, the biopolitics of disposability relegates individuals and entire populations to social death. While liberalism long deemed certain people unworthy of social protection by the state, within regimes of neoliberal govern-mentality, where everyone is now subject to precarity, sharp *cultural* lines must be drawn between, on the one hand, meritocratic citizens who have competed for and won their equality and, on the other, disposable human beings who have failed to accept personal respon-sibility for their lives. As we saw above, left neoliberalism's new equality politics tend to obscure the biopolitics of disposability on which their marketized promise of empowerment is premised; how-ever, right neoliberalism overtly mobilizes the biopolitics of dispos-ability in order to legitimate and extend regimes of oppression and accumulation by dispossession. Individuals and entire groups (e.g., poor people, welfare recipients, prisoners) become "dead weight" that can, and should, be disposed of for the benefit of those deemed worthy and valuable to the market.[28]

Furthermore, while neoliberal precarization inspires rage at the political-economic system, the right neoliberal politics of identity works to channel political anger into privatized resentment, where cer-tain individuals and social groups (e.g., immigrants, women, queers, racial minorities of all sorts, youth, white trash, homeless people) are easily scapegoated for the misery and insecurity produced by neolib-eral elites. In a de-democratized world where competition becomes a structure of feeling embedded in our lifeworlds, political anger has nowhere to go except private individuals and vulnerable groups imag-ined to be the source of precarization for others. For example, con-sider the harsh stance on immigration that Donald Trump successfully took during the 2016 presidential election. Thanks to precarization, voters were easily interpellated to scapegoat immigrants, especially so-called illegal immigrants, as they were made to represent increased competition for scarce jobs and resources. Despite the fact that immigrants undoubtedly share the same desires for economic security, good jobs, and social protection as many of Trump's supporters, these common desires are channeled into divisive forms of oppositional politics that mobilize and reproduce the biopolitics of disposability. In effect, the widespread social crises that are generated by neoliberalism get actively attributed to, and sorted out on, specific bodies who are not imagined to merit belonging in the nation. In this way, unlike left neoliberalism, right neoliberalism openly performs the work of normalizing social inequality as a functional and fundamental feature of neoliberal society.

In this way, right neoliberalism engenders and relies upon a broader *culture of cruelty*. With its active fueling of resentment and competition for equality, right neoliberalism operates in everyday life as a sadistic form of cultural politics. As Henry Giroux puts it, this version of neoliberalism

> creates an unbridled individualism that embodies a pathological disdain for community, produces a cruel indifference to the social contract, disdains the larger social good, and creates a predatory culture that replaces compassion, sharing and a concern for the other. As the discourse of the common good and compassion withers, the only vocabulary left is that of the bully—one that takes pride in the civic-enervating binary of winners and losers.[29]

This sadistic culture of cruelty and bullying is perhaps nowhere more clear than in the phenomenon of internet trolling and harassment, where women, people of color, and other marginalized voices are viciously attacked and threatened when they appear within and disrupt the existing economies of visibility and market inclusion. For example, consider the case of Anita Sarkeesian, a media critic and blogger who is the founder of *Feminist Frequency*, a website dedicated to critical analysis of gender representation in popular culture, and the host of *Tropes vs. Women in Video Games,* a web series that hones in specifically on women's representation in video games. After launching a highly successful Kickstarter campaign to support her show, Sarkeesian became the target of intense attacks, receiving graphic rape and death threats. Or consider another example. When the popular film franchise *Ghostbusters* was rebooted in 2016 with a multiracial and all female cast, many fans, particularly male fans, took to social media to object to the gender reorientation of the franchise. However, it was African-American cast mate Leslie Jones that ultimately took the most overt abuse, as she was subject to vicious, racist attacks on Twitter. Since competition necessarily entails winners and losers, when someone like Jones ostensibly "wins" by being included and recognized within economies of visibility—in this case, a Hollywood blockbuster—others (e.g., white men who feel excluded) fight back in order to assert their power and status, often with overt racism, homophobia, and misogyny. Indeed, this competition for equality even helps to explain, or at least situate conjuncturally, the recent rise in so-called men's rights groups, as well as increased neo-Nazi activities and hate crimes.

It is important to see that marketized equalities of left neoliberalism offer very little when it comes to substantively challenging right neoliberalism's culture of cruelty and its politics of resentment. This is *not* to say that competition levels the playing field between different social groups. Rather, competing for equality—whether in the terms of diversity or identity-based resentment—retrenches and intensifies existing social hierarchies and power relationships. By making competition and its oppositional consciousness a general norm of politics, neoliberalism welcomes both a diversification of the elite (marketized equality) and the ongoing exploitation and oppression of historically marginalized groups (the biopolitics of disposability). Thus, in ways that might feel incredibly paradoxical, the diverse, progressive structures of feeling of left neoliberalism and the cruel, bullying cultures of right neoliberalism end up working together to sustain a hollowed-out democracy, built on competition between citizens.

When equality is something we have to compete for privately, we lose the capacities for radical critique and the ability to map the conjuncture; instead, politics becomes reduced to bullying and efforts to fight the bully back. We can't see, and perhaps don't desire to see, our commonalities and shared fates. Instead, we get entangled in the neoliberal culture of competition, where competing for equality operates as a toxic and divisive structure of feeling, one that channels our affects, capacities, and desires toward social division and even hate.

As a result, if we want to move beyond neoliberalism and construct a new world, we must abandon *both* the politics of right and left neoliberalism and their mutually reinforcing chokehold on our political imaginations. We have to stop inhabiting the oppositional consciousness of competing for equality and start telling new stories of interconnection and commonality that will enable the transformative political interventions we collectively need and desire.

COMPETING FOR EQUALITY IN BRAND CULTURE

Let me try to connect all the dots with a final example of neoliberal politics. On February 6, 2016, Beyoncé premiered the music video "Formation." Hailed as a rallying cry for black political activism and, specifically, #blacklivesmatter, the video remixes histories of oppression and exploitation, old and new. From shots of the singer on the hood of a New Orleans police car surrounded by post-Katrina flood waters to exuberant dance sequences shot in mansions from the antebellum South, Beyoncé's video represents a playful, provocative, and deeply political statement, best encapsulated perhaps in one shot: "STOP SHOOTING US." Beyoncé went on to perform the song the next evening at the 2016 Super Bowl halftime show. The live performance evoked the same political spirit as the video, as the singer was backed up by a troop of dancers dressed as militant members of the Black Panther Party, while the performance concluded dramatically with raised fists, a sign of black power and resistance.

"Formation," and particularly the Super Bowl performance, were widely interpreted as a brave, feminist, antiracist challenge to the status quo. For a few critical moments, Beyoncé was imagined to disrupt business-as-usual on one of the biggest, most conservative stages, and to force audiences to confront both her own power as a woman artist and the entrenched, pressing issues facing the black community. Not surprisingly however, while many praised Beyoncé for her political intervention, others were outraged by the audacity of her performance. Debates raged on cable news and proliferated on social media, amplifying heated conversations about racial injustice in the United States.

In so many ways, Beyoncé's Super Bowl performance of "Formation" and the media controversy it sparked encapsulates what happens to our political horizons when democracy is enterprised. Beyoncé is celebrated, on the one hand, as a powerful brand that embodies the existence and utopian promise of meritocracy and competitive market society; she represents the cream of the crop, a self-made entrepreneur who's been able to rise to the top. On the other hand, "Formation" also shows how struggles for market inclusion are at the heart of contemporary political culture, as what is imagined to matter so much about Beyoncé's work is the way it appears to fight for and facilitate media recognition on behalf of black lives. Here struggles for inclusion are not struggles for participation in popular sovereignty, but rather struggles for circulation and appreciation within the economies of visibility of brand culture. Simply put, with Beyoncé, brand politics meets neoliberal commodity activism in the wider competition for equality.

CRITICAL PRACTICE

Now let's see if *you* can put all of the knowledge we've built throughout the chapter to work, using theories of both brand culture and the neoliberal politics of identity to analyze what's happening to our political horizons.

The Black Lives Matter movement is certainly one of the most vital and important social movements of the day. Emerging out of the neoliberal biopolitics of disposability, Black Lives Matter seeks to end the criminal industrial complex discussed in previous chapters and its state-sanctioned violence against and dispossession of black and brown people and their communities. In this way, Black Lives Matter represents a crucial political front in the struggle against neoliberal governmentality.

• However, what happens when this movement to build a new world is taken up within existing economies of visibility, where brand logic, marketized equality, and competition structure the field of progressive, political action? How do online arguments between #Blacklivesmatter and #Alllivesmatter exemplified by this meme speak to the various problems of competing for equality in brand culture discussed above?

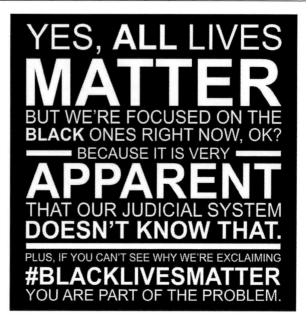

Figure 6.3 "Black Lives" vs. "All Lives"

THE POWER OF ORGANIZING

I imagine you might be getting frustrated at this point. You might be asking yourself: what are we supposed to do? Isn't branded political engagement better than none at all? We shouldn't eschew politics just because it's competitive, right? After all, hasn't democratic politics always been about competing ideas? Isn't that what public deliberation is all about? And we certainly have an obligation to act and fight back against the bully even if our political horizons are privatized, right? Yes. Absolutely! But, at the same time, we have to be able to imagine forms of political and social action that are not rooted in enterprise and competition and that might actually have a chance to challenge the cultural powers of neoliberalism.

One distinction that I have found useful in this regard is the distinction that Astra Taylor draws between activism and organizing.[30]

Thanks to brand culture and its participatory environments, lots of us are activists, as we regularly express our political views on social media, commit to living particular sorts of lifestyles, and participate in political protests against various forms of inequality and oppression. However, very few of us are organizers. Organizing requires taking the long-view when it comes to effecting social and political change and engaging in hard-nosed power analysis to determine how to achieve concrete ends. Crucially, organizing also requires coalition-building across different social groups and political causes. And, most of all, organizing requires a speakable vision of the world we want to see: a new political horizon.

As we saw in Chapter 1, neoliberal hegemony was won through organizing. If we want a new world, we're going to have to imagine, organize, and fight like hell for it. Of course, organizing needs the energy and support of activism, especially when you're up against entrenched regimes and interests. However, as we have seen throughout this chapter, activism in brand culture without organizing is liable to keep us stuck within the confines of our neoliberal conjuncture, competing for equality.

Indeed, organizing will require us to abandon our attachments to right *and* left neoliberalism and traverse the field of privatized politics in new ways. Organizing asks us to work across difference to find common ground and sense a new future. Simply put, organizing is how we get back our capacities for interconnection, equality, imagination, and democracy and open up those new worlds we're all yearning for.

If we can start organizing, I actually think we will find that neoliberalism is sowing the seeds of its own destruction. In privatizing our social worlds and insisting that we take personal responsibility for our lives and communities, neoliberal hegemony is begging us to experiment, improvise, create, cooperate, and innovate in order to get by and survive. What is more, left neoliberalism has undoubtedly honed our collective capacities for inclusion, diversity, and recognition, which are central ingredients in coalition-building and organizing. The big question is if we can take these new political opportunities and capacities and channel them into the production of more egalitarian and democratic worlds—that is, toward a future of living in common.

NOTES

1 Wendy Brown, *Undoing the Demos: Neoliberalism's Stealth Revolution* (New York: Zone Books, 2015), 79.

2 Sarah Banet-Weiser, *Authentic: The Politics of Ambivalence in a Brand Culture* (New York: New York University Press, 2012), 144.

3 Matthew Bishop and Michael Green, *Philanthrocapitalism: How the Rich Can Save the World* (New York: Bloomsbury Press, 2008), 6.

4 See for example David Bornstein, *How to Change the World: Social Entrepreneurs and the Power of New Ideas* (Oxford: Oxford University Press, 2008).

5 See Graham Knight, "Activism, Branding, and the Promotional Public Sphere," in *Blowing up the Brand: Critical Perspectives on Promotional Culture*, eds. Melissa Aronczyk and Devon Powers (New York: Peter Lang, 2010), 173–194.

6 Banet-Weiser, *Authentic*, 4.

7 Banet-Weiser, *Authentic*, 4.

8 Sarah Banet-Weiser and Roopali Mukherjee, *Commodity Activism: Cultural Resistance in Neoliberal Times* (New York: New York University Press, 2013), 1.

9 Banet-Weiser and Mukherjee, *Commodity Activism*, 2.

10 Banet-Weiser, *Authentic*, 23.

11 Banet-Weiser, *Authentic*, 23.

12 Banet-Weiser, *Authentic*, 33.

13 Banet-Weiser, *Authentic*, 38.

14 See also Adam Arvidsson, *Brands: Meaning and Value in Media Culture* (London: Routledge, 2006).

15 Banet-Weiser, *Authentic*, 37–38.

16 Banet-Weiser, *Authentic*, 147.

17 See Sarah Banet-Weiser, "Keynote Address: Media, Markets, Gender: Economies of Visibility in a Neoliberal Moment," *The Communication Review* 18 (2015): 53–70. See also Herman Gray, "Subject(ed) to Recognition," *American Quarterly* 65 (2013): 771–798.

18 Banet-Weiser, *Authentic*, 142.

19 Banet-Weiser, *Authentic*, 146.

20 Banet-Weiser, *Authentic*, 146.

21 Banet-Weiser, *Authentic*, 164.

22 Lisa Duggan, *The Twilight of Equality: Neoliberal Cultural Politics, and the Attack on Democracy* (Boston: Beacon Press, 2003), xx.

23 See Duggan, *Twilight of Equality*, 43–66.

24 Catherine Rottenberg, "The Rise of Neoliberal Feminism," *Cultural Studies* 28.3 (2014): 418–437, doi:10.1080/09502386.2013.857361

25 Roopali Mukherjee, "Antiracism Limited: A Pre-History of Post-Race," *Cultural Studies* 30.1 (2016): 47–77, doi:10.1080/09502386.2014.935455

26 Joe Tompkins, "'A Postgame Interview for the Ages': Richard Sherman and the Dialectical Rhetoric of Racial Neoliberalism," *Journal of Sport and Social Issues* 40.4 (2016): 291–314. doi:10.1177/0193723515615180

27 Jo Littler, "Meritocracy as Plutocracy: The Marketising of 'Equality' within Neo-liberalism," *New Formations: A Journal of Culture/Theory/Politics* 80–81: 52–72. doi:10.3898/NewF.80/81.03.2013

28 Greg Bras provided valuable insights and contributions here.

29 Henry Giroux, "The Authoritarian Politics of Resentment in Trump's America," *Truthout*, November 13, 2016, www.truth-out.org/opinion/item/38351-the-authoritarian-politics-of-resentment-in-trump-s-america

30 See Astra Taylor, "Against Activism," *The Baffler* 3 (2016), https://thebaffler.com/salvos/against-activism.

CONCLUSION
LIVING IN COMMON

THE CRISIS OF NEOLIBERALISM

In Chapter 1, we traced the rise of our neoliberal conjuncture back to the crisis of liberalism during the late nineteenth and early twentieth centuries, culminating in the Great Depression. During this period, huge transformations in capitalism proved impossible to manage with classical laissez-faire approaches. Out of this crisis, two movements emerged, both of which would eventually shape the course of the twentieth century and beyond. The first, and the one that became dominant in the aftermath of the crisis, was the conjuncture of embedded liberalism. The crisis indicated that capitalism wrecked too much damage on the lives of ordinary citizens. People (white workers and families, especially) warranted social protection from the volatilities and brutalities of capitalism. The state's public function was expanded to include the provision of a more substantive social safety net, a web of protections for people and a web of constraints on markets.

The second response was the invention of neoliberalism. Deeply skeptical of the common-good principles that undergirded the emerging social welfare state, neoliberals began organizing on the ground to develop a "new" liberal governmentality, one rooted less in laissez-faire principles and more in the generalization of competition and enterprise. They worked to envision a new society premised on a new social ontology, that is, on new truths about the state, the market, and human beings. Crucially, neoliberals also began building infrastructures and institutions for disseminating their new knowledges and theories (i.e., the Neoliberal Thought Collective), as well as organizing politically to build mass support for new policies (i.e., working to unite anti-communists, Christian conservatives, and free marketers in common cause against the welfare state). When cracks in embedded liberalism began to surface—which is bound to happen with any moving political equilibrium—neoliberals were there with new stories and solutions, ready to make the world anew.

We are currently living through the crisis of neoliberalism. As I write this book, Donald Trump has recently secured the U.S. presidency, prevailing in the national election over his Democratic opponent Hillary Clinton. Throughout the election, I couldn't help but think back to the crisis of liberalism and the two responses that emerged. Similarly, after the Great Recession of 2008, we saw two responses emerge to challenge our unworkable status quo, which dispossesses so many people of vital resources for individual and collective life. On the one hand, we witnessed the rise of Occupy Wall Street. While many continue to critique the movement for its lack of leadership and a coherent political vision, Occupy was connected to burgeoning movements across the globe, and our current political horizons have been undoubtedly shaped by the movement's success at repositioning class and economic inequality within our political horizon. On the other hand, we saw the rise of the Tea Party, a right-wing response to the crisis. While the Tea Party was critical of status-quo neoliberalism—especially its cosmopolitanism and embrace of globalization and diversity, which was perfectly embodied by Obama's election and presidency—it was not exactly anti-neoliberal. Rather, it was *anti-left neoliberalism*; it represented a more authoritarian, right version of neoliberalism.

Within the context of the 2016 election, Clinton embodied the neoliberal center that could no longer hold. Inequality. Suffering. Collapsing infrastructures. Perpetual war. Anger. Disaffected consent. There were just too many fissures and fault lines in the glossy, cosmopolitan world of left neoliberalism and marketized equality. Indeed, while Clinton ran on status-quo stories of good governance and neoliberal feminism, confident that demographics and diversity would be enough to win the election, Trump effectively tapped into the unfolding conjunctural crisis by exacerbating the cracks in the system of marketized equality, channeling political anger into his celebrity brand that had been built on saying "f*** you" to the culture of left neoliberalism (corporate diversity, political correctness, etc.). In fact, much like Clinton's challenger in the Democratic primary, Bernie Sanders, Trump was a crisis candidate.

Both Sanders and Trump were embedded in the emerging left and right responses to neoliberalism's crisis. Specifically, Sanders' energetic campaign—which was undoubtedly enabled by the rise of the Occupy movement—proposed a decidedly more "common-good" path. Higher wages for working people. Taxes on the rich, specifically the captains of the creditocracy. Universal health care. Free higher education. Fair trade. The repeal of *Citizens United*. Trump offered a different response to the crisis. Like Sanders, he railed against global trade deals like NAFTA and the Trans-Pacific Partnership (TPP). However, Trump's victory was fueled by right neoliberalism's culture of cruelty. While Sanders tapped into and mobilized desires for a more egalitarian and democratic future, Trump's promise was nostalgic, making America "great again"—putting the nation back on "top of the world," and implying a time when women were "in their place" as male property, and minorities and immigrants were controlled by the state.

Thus, what distinguished Trump's campaign from more traditional Republican campaigns was that it actively and explicitly pitted one group's equality (white men) against everyone else's (immigrants, women, Muslims, minorities, etc.). As Catherine Rottenberg suggests, Trump offered voters a choice between a multiracial society (where folks are increasingly disadvantaged and dispossessed) and white supremacy (where white people would be back on top). However, "[w]hat he neglected to state," Rottenberg writes,

> is that neoliberalism flourishes in societies where the playing field is already stacked against various segments of society, and that it needs

only a relatively small select group of capital-enhancing subjects, while everyone else is ultimately dispensable.[1]

In other words, Trump supporters may not have explicitly voted for neoliberalism, but that's what they got. In fact, as Rottenberg argues, they got a version of *right* neoliberalism "on steroids"—a mix of blatant plutocracy and authoritarianism that has many concerned about the rise of U.S. fascism.

We can't know what would have happened had Sanders run against Trump, but we can think seriously about Trump, right and left neoliberalism, and the crisis of neoliberal hegemony. In other words, we can think about *where* and *how* we go from here. As I suggested in the previous chapter, if we want to construct a new world, we are going to have to abandon the entangled politics of both right and left neoliberalism; we have to reject the hegemonic frontiers of both disposability and marketized equality. After all, as political philosopher Nancy Fraser argues, what was rejected in the election of 2016 was progressive, left neoliberalism.[2] While the rise of hyper-right neoliberalism is certainly nothing to celebrate, it does present an opportunity for breaking with neoliberal hegemony. We have to proceed, as Gary Younge reminds us, with the realization that people "have not rejected the chance of a better world. They have not yet been offered one."[3] Mark Fisher, the author of *Capitalist Realism,* put it this way:

> The long, dark night of the end of history has to be grasped as an enormous opportunity. The very oppressive pervasiveness of capitalist realism means that even glimmers of alternative political and economic possibilities can have a disproportionately great effect. The tiniest event can tear a hole in the grey curtain of reaction which has marked the horizons of possibility under capitalist realism. From a situation in which nothing can happen, suddenly anything is possible again.[4]

I think that, for the first time in the history of U.S. capitalism, the vast majority of people might sense the lie of liberal, capitalist democracy. They feel anxious, unfree, disaffected. Fantasies of the good life have been shattered beyond repair for most people. Trump and this hopefully brief triumph of right neoliberalism will soon lay this bare for everyone to see. Now, with Trump, it is absolutely clear: the rich rule the world; we are all disposable; this is no democracy. The question becomes: How will we show up for history? Will there be new stories, ideas, visions, and fantasies to attach to? How can we productively and meaningful intervene in the crisis of neoliberalism? How can we "tear a hole in the grey curtain" and open up better worlds? How can we put what we've learned to use and begin to imagine and build a world beyond living in competition? I hope our critical journey through the neoliberal conjuncture has enabled you to begin to answer these questions. More specifically, I hope our journey has helped to clarify *what* we need to build and *how* we might get there.

WHAT WE NEED

What do we need to transform the conditions of our lives and realize the new worlds we long for? What can a cultural studies perspective on neoliberalism teach us about social change? If we really understand that the neoliberal conjuncture has been socially constructed—and thus is not necessary, natural, or inevitable—then what we need becomes clear: we need critical and theoretical resources that will enable us to imagine and build a future beyond living in competition; we need resources for moving toward a world of living in common.

Common Stories

As we have seen, neoliberalism relies on a host of entwined status-quo stories: self-enclosed individualism, personal responsibility, the utopian promise of meritocracy, the self as enterprise, privatized happiness, marketized equality. In their own ways, each of these stories keeps us attached to living in competition. Many of these stories prompt us to turn our disaffected consent inward toward ourselves, to double down on the present in order to protect and secure ourselves against others. Other status-quo stories provide templates for social action and citizenship that de-democratize and work to further neoliberalism's privatization of our political horizons. Thanks to these status-quo stories, we approach life, relationships, our environments and citizenship with an oppositional consciousness, and thus are unable to recognize, much less act upon, our commonalities—our shared dreams and desires, visions and vulnerabilities. We hustle, and get hustled, divided.

We need new stories, ones that will enable us to "lose confidence" in this culture of competition and social division. In the face of hate, disconnection, and inequality, we must insist on our commonality. Specifically, we need stories that can explain how and why our individual and collective lives feel so wrong. Crucially, these common stories must be ones that hold *different* experiences and situations of precarity together in ways that do not obscure and reinscribe inequalities of class, gender, sexuality, race, ability, and citizenship. Indeed, just because we are all subject to neoliberal precarity does not mean that we experience neoliberalism in the same way: that histories of oppression and exploitation go away, or that social hierarchies no longer exist and matter. However, we must be careful not to tell stories that exaggerate, reify, and sharpen our differences at the expense of our commonalities. Doing so is likely to lead us back into competing for equality in the terms of neoliberal hegemony. Put differently, we need critical stories of the conjuncture, stories that enable us to map our differences at points of social interconnection and commonality; stories that allow us to see ourselves as part of a broader social whole that threads our lives together; stories that enable us to claim our interdependency, interconnection, and shared vulnerabilities.

Common Reason

Crucially, our new stories should inspire new visions of governing. They should intimate new possibilities, new cultures, and new forms of cultural power adequate to holding new social worlds together. In other words, they should produce new "mentalities" of governing, new political reason. I have suggested that developing new sensibilities for common reason is a good place to start.

As we have explored, neoliberalism is, at heart, a mentality of governing for and through markets. It is based on the political reason of competition. It says that the best way to order society is through the promotion of private enterprise in all arenas of social life. We are thus, always and everywhere, *homo oeconomicus*—nothing more and nothing less than human capital. As we have seen, this governmentality is at the root of our anxieties; it contributes to the rampant cruelty, violence, and "crisis ordinariness" that defines our lives.

However, common reason looks not to protect and secure the self-enclosed individual of liberal and neoliberal social ontology, but the individual in the whole, who is always already vulnerable to and dependent upon others and their environments. Common reason is premised on a social ontology that is radically different from neoliberalism's social ontology. Indeed, self-appreciating individualism makes no sense from the perspective of common reason. For common reason is rooted in the radical interconnectivity of all of life, human and non-human. Common reason is about mutuality and interdependency; it invites us to think and act relationally, to define parts and wholes, the individual and collective together, one through the other.

Common Horizons

As we know, the rise of neoliberal hegemony was organized, resourced, and coordinated politically to reinvent individual-liberty liberalism and create a new market society. The Neoliberal Thought Collective actively promoted an enterprise culture with new norms and rules for individual life rooted in competition. In other words, the neoliberal project was not focused on one issue; it was about the creation of a new society—a new social totality. As we have seen, however, a central paradox of neoliberal theory is that individuals are to remain ignorant market actors, while the neoliberal state works to construct and police the conditions for this new society of spontaneous market order.

Throughout the twentieth and early twenty-first century in the U.S. context, the common-good side has never really been as intentional and ambitious, organized and coordinated. All told, it has been decidedly more modest and defensive, pouring energies and resources into discrete political struggles (e.g., racial justice, gender justice, environmentalism, labor), each of which is fundamental to building a new, egalitarian world, but on their own, they are not able to articulate a new hegemony, to bring about a new conjuncture. In short, *common-good sensibilities and movements are alive and well*, but they tend to be captured by neoliberal hegemony.

More specifically, in recent decades, especially since the end of the Cold War, our common-good sensibilities have been channeled into neoliberal platforms for social change and privatized action, funneling our political energies into brand culture and marketized struggles for equality (e.g., charter schools, NGOs and non-profits, neoliberal antiracism and feminism). As a result, despite our collective anger and disaffected consent, we find ourselves stuck in capitalist realism with no real alternative. Like the neoliberal care of the self, we are trapped in a privatized mode of politics that relies on cruel optimism; we are attached, it seems, to politics that inspire and motivate us to action, while keeping us living in competition.

To disrupt the game, we need to construct common political horizons against neoliberal hegemony. We need to use our common stories and common reason to build common movements against precarity—for within neoliberalism, precarity is what ultimately has the potential to thread all of our lives together. Put differently, the ultimate fault line in the neoliberal conjuncture is the way it subjects us all to precarity and the biopolitics of disposability, thereby creating conditions of possibility for new coalitions across race, gender, citizenship, sexuality, and class. Recognizing this potential for coalition in the face of precarization is the most pressing task facing those who are yearning for a new world. The question is: How do we get there? How do we realize these coalitional potentialities and materialize common horizons?

HOW WE GET THERE

Ultimately, mapping the neoliberal conjuncture through everyday life in enterprise culture has not only provided some direction in terms of what we need; it has also cultivated concrete and practical intellectual resources for political intervention and social interconnection—a critical toolbox for living in common. More specifically, this book has sought to provide resources for thinking and acting against the four *D*s: resources for engaging in counter-conduct, modes of living that refuse, on one hand, to conduct one's life according to the norm of enterprise, and on the other, to relate to others through the norm of competition. Indeed, we need new ways of relating, interacting, and living as friends, lovers, workers, vulnerable bodies, and democratic people if we are to write new stories, invent new governmentalities, and build coalitions for new worlds.

Against Disimagination: Educated Hope and Affirmative Speculation

We need to stop turning inward, retreating into ourselves, and taking personal responsibility for our lives (a task which is ultimately impossible). Enough with the disimagination machine! Let's start looking outward, not inward—to the broader structures that undergird our lives. Of course, we need to take care of ourselves; we must survive. But I firmly believe that we can do this in ways both big and small, that transform neoliberal culture and its status-quo stories.

Here's the thing I tell my students all the time. You cannot escape neoliberalism. It is the air we breathe, the water in which we swim. No job, practice of social activism, program of self-care, or relationship will be totally free from neoliberal impingements and logics. There is no pure "outside" to get to or work from—that's just the nature of the neoliberalism's totalizing cultural power. But let's not forget that neoliberalism's totalizing cultural power is also a source of weakness. Potential for resistance is everywhere, scattered throughout our everyday lives in enterprise culture. Our critical toolbox can help us identify these potentialities and navigate and engage our conjuncture in ways that tear open up those new worlds we desire.

In other words, our critical perspective can help us move through the world with what Henry Giroux calls educated hope. Educated hope means holding in tension the material realities of power *and* the contingency of history. This orientation of educated hope knows very well what we're up against. However, in the face of seemingly totalizing power, it also knows that neoliberalism can never become total because the future is open. Educated hope is what allows us to see the fault lines, fissures, and potentialities of the present and emboldens us to think and work from that sliver of social space where we do have political agency and freedom to construct a new world. Educated hope is what undoes the power of capitalist realism. It enables affirmative speculation (such as discussed in Chapter 5), which does not try to hold the future to neoliberal horizons (that's cruel optimism!), but instead to affirm our commonalities and the potentialities for the new worlds they signal. Affirmative speculation demands a different sort of risk calculation and management. It senses how little we have to lose and how much we have to gain from knocking the hustle of our lives.

Against De-democratization: Organizing and Collective Governing

We can think of educated hope and affirmative speculation as practices of what Wendy Brown calls "bare democracy"—the basic idea that ordinary people like you and me should govern our lives in common, that we should critique and try to change our world, especially the exploitative and oppressive structures of power that maintain social hierarchies and diminish lives. Neoliberal culture works to stomp out capacities for bare democracy by transforming democratic desires and feelings into meritocratic desires and feelings. In neoliberal culture, utopian sensibilities are directed away from the promise of collective governing to competing for equality.

We have to get back that democractic feeling! As Jeremy Gilbert taught us, disaffected consent is a post-democratic orientation. We don't like our world, but we don't think we can do anything about it. So, how do we get back that democratic feeling? How do we transform our disaffected consent into something new? As I suggested in the last chapter, we organize. Organizing is simply about people coming together around a common horizon and working collectively to materialize it. In this way, organizing is based on the idea of radical democracy, not liberal democracy. While the latter is based on formal and abstract rights guaranteed by the state, radical democracy insists that people should directly make the decisions that impact their lives, security, and well-being. Radical democracy is a practice of collective governing: it is about us hashing out, together in communities, what matters, and working in common to build a world based on these new sensibilities.

The work of organizing is messy, often unsatisfying, and sometimes even scary. Organizing based on affirmative speculation and coalition-building, furthermore, will have to be experimental and uncertain. As Lauren Berlant suggests, it means "embracing the discomfort of affective experience in a truly open social life that no one has ever experienced." Organizing through and for the common "requires more adaptable infrastructures. Keep forcing the existing infrastructures to do what they don't know how to do. Make new ways to be local together, where local doesn't require a physical neighborhood."[5] What Berlant is saying is that the work of bare democracy requires unlearning, and detaching from, our current stories and infrastructures in order to see and make things work differently. Organizing for a new world is not easy—and there are no guarantees—but it is the only way out of capitalist realism.

Against Disposability: Radical Equality

Getting back democratic feeling will at once *require* and *help us to move beyond* the biopolitics of disposability and entrenched systems of inequality. On one hand, organizing will never be enough if it is not animated by bare democracy, a sensibility that each of us is equally important when it comes to the project of determining our lives in common. Our bodies, our hurts, our dreams, and our desires matter regardless of our race, gender, sexuality, or citizenship, and regardless of how much capital (economic, social, or cultural) we have. Simply put, in a radical democracy, no one is disposable. This bare-democratic sense of equality must be foundational to organizing and coalition-building. Otherwise, we will always and inevitably fall back into a world of inequality.

On the other hand, organizing and collective governing will deepen and enhance our sensibilities and capacities for radical equality. In this context, the kind of self-enclosed individualism that empowers and underwrites the biopolitics of disposability melts away, as we realize the interconnectedness of our lives and just how amazing it feels to live and work in common. For when we act in common, even when we fail, we affirm our capacities for freedom, political intervention, social interconnection, and collective social doing.

Against Dispossession: Shared Security and Common Wealth

Thinking and acting against the biopolitics of disposability goes hand-in-hand with thinking and acting against dispossession. Ultimately, when we really understand and feel ourselves in relationships of interconnection with others, we want for them as we want for ourselves. Our lives and sensibilities of what is good and just are rooted in radical equality, not possessive or self-appreciating individualism. Because we desire social security and protection, we also know others desire and deserve the same.

However, to *really* think and act against dispossession means not only advocating for shared security and social protection, but also for a new society that is built on the egalitarian production and distribution of social wealth that we all produce. In this sense, we can take Marx's key critique of capitalism—*that wealth is produced collectively but appropriated individually*—to heart. Capitalism was built on the idea that one class—the owners of the means of production—could exploit and profit from the collective labors of everyone else (those who do not own and thus *have* to work), albeit in very different ways depending on race, gender, or citizenship. This meant that, for workers of all stripes, their lives existed not for themselves, but for others (the appropriating class), and that regardless of what we own as consumers, we are not really free or equal in that bare-democratic sense of the word.

If we want to be *really* free, we need to construct new material and affective social infrastructures for our common wealth. In these new infrastructures, wealth must not be reduced to economic value; it must be rooted in social value. Here, the production of wealth does not exist as a separate sphere from the reproduction of our lives. In other words, new infrastructures, based on the idea of common wealth, will not be set up to exploit our labor, dispossess our communities, or to divide our lives. Rather, they will work to provide collective social resources and care so that we may *all* be free to pursue happiness, create beautiful and/or useful things, and to realize our potential within a social world of living in common. Crucially, to create the conditions for these new, democratic forms of freedom rooted in radical equality, we need to find ways to refuse and exit the financial networks of Empire and the dispossessions of creditocracy, building new systems that invite *everyone* to participate in the ongoing production of new worlds and the sharing of the wealth that we produce in common.

It's not up to me to tell you *exactly* where to look, but I assure you that potentialities for these new worlds are everywhere around you.

Now let's get to work tearing holes and opening up futures of living in common.

NOTES

1   Catherine Rottenberg, "Trumping it Up: Neoliberalism on Steroids," *Aljazeera*, December 18, 2016.

2   Nancy Fraser, "The End of Progressive Neoliberalism," *Dissent Magazine*, January 2, 2017.

3   Gary Younge, "The Right is Emboldened, Yes. But it's Not in the Ascendancy," *The Guardian*, December 30, 2016.

4   Mark Fisher, *Capitalist Realism* (Winchester, UK: Zero Books, 2009), 80–81.

5   Lauren Berlant, "Big Man," *Social Text* (January 19, 2017). https://socialtextjournal.org/big-man/

BIBLIOGRAPHY

Ahmed, Sara. "Selfcare as Warfare." *feministkilljoys*, August 25, 2014.
———. "Losing Confidence." *feministkilljoys*, March 1, 2016.
Akili, Yolo. "The Immediate Need for Emotional Justice." *Crunk Feminist Collective*, November 16, 2011.
Alexander, Michelle. *The New Jim Crow: Mass Incarceration in the Age of Colorblindness*. New York: The New Press, 2012.
Arvidsson, Adam. *Brands: Meaning and Value in Media Culture*. London: Routledge, 2006.
Aschoff, Nicole. *New Prophets of Capital*. London: Verso, 2015.
Banet-Weiser, Sarah. *Authentic: The Politics of Ambivalence in a Brand Culture*. New York: New York University Press, 2012.
———. "Keynote Address: Media, Markets, Gender: Economies of Visibility in a Neoliberal Moment." *The Communication Review* 18.1 (2015): 53–70.
Berlant, Lauren. *Cruel Optimism*. Durham: Duke University Press, 2011.
———. "Interview." *Rorotoko*, June 5, 2012.
———. "Big Man." *Social Text Online*, January 19, 2017.
Binkley, Sam. *Happiness as Enterprise: An Essay on Neoliberal Life*. Albany: State University of New York Press, 2014.
Bishop, Matthew and Michael Green. *Philanthrocapitalism: How the Rich Can Save the World*. New York: Bloomsbury Press, 2008.
Bornstein, David. *How to Change the World: Social Entrepreneurs and the Power of New Ideas*. Oxford: Oxford University Press, 2008.
Brown, Wendy. *States of Injury: Power and Freedom in Late Modernity*. Princeton: Princeton University Press, 1995.
———. "Booked #3: What Exactly is Neoliberalism?" (interview with Timothy Shenk). *Dissent Magazine*, April 2, 2015.
———. *Undoing the Demos: Neoliberalism's Stealth Revolution*. New York: Zone Books, 2015.
Burchell, Graham. "Liberal Government and Techniques of the Self." In *Foucault and Political Reason: Liberalism, Neo-liberalism, and Rationalities of Government*, edited by Andrew Barry, Thomas Osborne, and Nikolas Rose, 19–36. Chicago: University of Chicago Press, 1996.
Cederstrom, Carl and Andre Spicer. *The Wellness Syndrome*. Cambridge: Polity Press, 2015.
Cvetkovich, Ann. *Depression: A Public Feeling*. Durham: Duke University Press, 2012.
Dardot, Pierre and Christian Laval. *The New Way of the World: On Neoliberal Society*. New York: Verso, 2014.
Davies, William. *Happiness Industry: How the Government and Big Business Sold Us Well-Being*. London: Verso, 2015.

Dean, Mitchell. *Governmentality: Power and Rule in Modern Society*. London: Sage, 2009.

Duggan, Lisa. *Twilight of Equality: Neoliberalism, Cultural Politics, and the Attack on Democracy*. Boston: Beacon Press, 2003.

Dyer, Richard. *Heavenly Bodies: Film Stars and Society*. London: Palgrave Macmillan, 1986.

Dyer-Witheford, Nick and Greig de Peuter. *Games of Empire: Global Capitalism and Video Games*. Minneapolis: University of Minnesota Press, 2009.

Ehrenberg, Alain. *The Weariness of the Self: Diagnosing the History of Depression in the Contemporary Age*. Montreal: McGill-Queen's University Press, 2010.

Ehrenreich, Barbara. *Bright-Sided: How the Relentless Promotion of Positive Thinking Has Undermined America*. Detroit: Thorndike Press, 2009.

Erickson, Megan. *Class War: The Privatization of Childhood*. London: Verso, 2015.

Feher, Michel. "Self-Appreciation; or, the Aspirations of Human Capital." *Public Culture* 21.1 (2009): 21–41.

Fields, Karen E. and Barbara J. Fields. *Racecraft: The Soul of Inequality in American Life*. New York: Verso, 2014.

Fisher, Mark. *Capitalist Realism*. Winchester, UK: Zero Books, 2009.

Foucault, Michel. *Power/Knowledge: Selected Interviews and Other Writings*. New York: Harvester, 1980.

———. "Governmentality." In *The Essential Foucault*, edited by Paul Rabinow and Nikolas Rose, 229–245. New York: The New Press, 1994.

———. "So Is It Important to Think?" In *The Essential Foucault*, edited by Paul Rabinow and Nikolas Rose, 170–173. New York: The New Press, 1994.

———. "Technologies of the Self." In *The Essential Foucault*, edited by Paul Rabinow and Nikolas Rose, 145–169. New York: The New Press, 1994.

Fraser, Nancy. "Contradictions of Capital and Care." *New Left Review* 100 (July–August 2016). https://newleftreview.org/II/100/nancy-fraser-contradictions-of-capital-and-care

———. "The End of Progressive Neoliberalism." *Dissent Magazine*, January 2, 2017.

Gilbert, Jeremy. "Disaffected Consent: That Post-Democratic Feeling." *Soundings* 60 (Summer 2015): 29–41.

Gill, Rosalind and Christina Scharff. Eds. *New Femininities: Postfeminism, Neoliberalism, and Subjectivity*. New York: Palgrave Macmillan, 2011.

Giroux, Henry A. "Reading Hurricane Katrina: Race, Class, and the Biopolitics of Disposability." *College Literature* 33.3 (2006): 171–196.

———. "The Politics of Disimagination and the Pathologies of Power." *Truthout*, February 27, 2013.

———. "Beyond Dystopian Visions in the Age of Neoliberal Authoritarianism." *Truthout*, November 4, 2015.

———. "The Authoritarian Politics of Resentment in Trump's America." *Truthout*, November 13, 2016.

Gray, Herman. "Subject(ed) to Recognition." *American Quarterly* 65.4 (2013): 771–798.

Gregg, Melissa and Gregory J. Seigworth. *The Affect Theory Reader*. Durham: Duke University Press, 2010.

Grossberg, Lawrence. *Bringing It All Back Home: Essays on Cultural Studies*. Durham: Duke University Press, 1997.

Hall, Stuart. "The Centrality of Culture: Notes on the Cultural Revolutions of Our Time." In *Media and Cultural Regulation*, edited by Kenneth Thompson, 208–238. London: Sage, 1997.

Hardt, Michael and Antonio Negri. *Empire*. Cambridge: Harvard University Press, 2000.

Harris, Anita. *Future Girl: Young Women in the Twenty-First Century*. New York: Routledge, 2003.

Harvey, David. *A Brief History of Neoliberalism*. Oxford: Oxford University Press, 2007.

Hearn, Alison. "'John, A 20-Year-Old Boston Native with a Great Sense of Humor': On the Spectacularization of the 'Self' and the Incorporation of Identity in the Age of Reality Television." In *The Celebrity Culture Reader*, edited by P. David Marshall, 618–633. New York: Routledge, 2006.

———. "'Meat, Mask, Burden': Probing the Contours of the Branded Self." *Journal of Consumer Culture* 8.2 (2008): 197–217. doi:10.1177/1469540508090086

Ho, Karen. *Liquidated: An Ethnography of Wall Street*. Durham: Duke University Press, 2009.

Hochschild, Arlie. *The Managed Heart: Commerialization of Human Feeling*. Berkeley: University of California, 2012.

Illouz, Eva. *Saving the Modern Soul: Therapy, Emotions, and the Culture of Self-Help*. Berkeley: University of California Press, 2008.

Institute for Precarious Consciousness. "We Are All Very Anxious: Six Theses on Anxiety and Why It Is Effectively Preventing Militancy, and One Possible Strategy for Overcoming It." Reposted on *Plan C*, April 4, 2014. www.weareplanc.org/blog /we-are-all-very-anxious/.

Keating, AnaLouise. *Transformation Now!: Toward a Post-Oppositional Politics of Change*. Champaign: University of Illinois Press, 2012.

Klein, Naomi. *The Shock Doctrine: The Rise of Disaster Capitalism*. New York: Henry Holt and Company, 2008.

———. *This Changes Everything: Capitalism vs. the Climate*. New York: Simon and Schuster, 2014.

Knight, Graham. "Activism, Branding, and the Promotional Public Sphere." In *Blowing up the Brand: Critical Perspectives on Promotional Culture*, edited by Melissa Aronczyk and Devon Powers, 173–194. New York: Peter Lang, 2010.

Lahann, Randall and Emilie Mitescu Reagan. "Teach for America and the Politics of Progressive Neoliberalism." *Teacher Education Quarterly* 38.1 (2011): 7–27.

Lilley, Sasha. "On Neoliberalism: An Interview with David Harvey." http://mrzine. monthlyreview.org/2006/lilley190606p.html

Littler, Jo. "Meritocracy as Plutocracy: The Marketising of 'Equality' within Neoliberalism." *New Formations: A Journal of Culture/Theory/Politics* 80–81 (2013): 52–72. doi:10.3898/NewF.80/81.03.2013

Lorey, Isabell. *State of Insecurity: Government of the Precarious*. London: Verso, 2015.

McRobbie, Angela. "Postfeminism and Popular Culture." *Feminist Media Studies* 4.3 (2004): 255–264.

———. *The Aftermath of Feminism: Gender, Culture, and Social Change*. London: Sage, 2009.

———. *Be Creative: Making a Living in the New Cultural Industries*. Cambridge: Polity Press, 2016.

Martin, Randy. *Financialization of Daily Life*. Philadelphia: Temple University Press, 2002.

May, Todd. *Friendship in the Age of Economics: Resisting the Forces of Neoliberalism*. Lanham: Lexington Books, 2012.

Mirowski, Philip. *Never Let a Serious Crisis Go to Waste: How Neoliberalism Survived the Financial Meltdown*. New York: Verso, 2013.

Mukherjee, Roopali. "Antiracism Limited: A Pre-History of Post-Race." *Cultural Studies* 30.1 (2016): 47–77. doi:10.1080/09502386.2014.935455

Mukherjee, Roopali and Sarah Banet-Weiser. *Commodity Activism: Cultural Resistance in Neoliberal Times*. New York: New York University Press, 2013.

Nealon, Jeffrey and Susan Searls Giroux. *The Theory Toolbox: Critical Concepts for the Arts, Humanities, and Social Sciences*. Plymouth: Rowman and Littlefield, 2012.

Ong, Aihwa. "Neoliberalism as a Mobile Technology." *Transactions of the Institute of British Geographers* 32 (2007): 3–8. doi:10.1111/j.1475–5661.2007.00234.x

Ouellette, Laurie. "*America's Next Top Model*: Neoliberal Labor." In *How to Watch Television*, edited by Ethan Thompson and Jason Mittell, 168–176. New York: New York University Press, 2013.

Ouellette, Laurie and Jacquelyn Arcy. "Live Through This: Feminist Care of the Self 2.0." *Frame* 28 (2015): 95–114.

Ouellette, Laurie and James Hay. *Better Living Through Reality TV: Television and Post-Welfare Citizenship*. Malden: Blackwell, 2008.

Robbins, Alexandra. *The Overachievers: The Secret Lives of Driven Kids*. New York: Hyperion, 2006.

Rose, Nikolas. *Powers of Freedom: Reframing Political Thought*. Cambridge: Cambridge University Press, 2006.

———. *The Politics of Life Itself*. Princeton: Princeton University Press, 2007.

Ross, Andrew. *Creditocracy and the Case for Debt Refusal*. New York: Or Books, 2013.

Rottenberg, Catherine. "The Rise of Neoliberal Feminism." *Cultural Studies* 28.3 (2014): 418–437. doi:10.1080/09502386.2013.857361

———. "Trumping it Up: Neoliberalism on Steroids." *Aljazeera*, December 18, 2016.

Silva, Jennifer. *Coming Up Short: Working-Class Adulthood in the Age of Uncertainty*. Oxford: Oxford University Press, 2013.

Spence, Lester. *Knocking the Hustle: Against the Neoliberal Turn in Black Politics*. New York: Punctum Books, 2015.

Stedman Jones, Daniel. *Masters of the Universe: Hayek, Friedman, and the Birth of Neoliberal Politics*. Princeton: Princeton University Press, 2012.

Swenson, Kristin. "Affective Labor and Government Policy: George W. Bush's New Freedom Commission on Mental Health." *Baltic Journal of Law & Politics* 4 (2011): 1–23. doi:10.2478/v10076-011-0010-7

Taibbi, Matt. *The Divide: American Injustice in the Age of the Wealth Gap*. New York: Spiegel and Grau, 2014.

Taylor, Astra. "Against Activism." *The Baffler* 3 (2016). https://thebaffler.com/salvos/against-activism

Tompkins, Joe. "'A Postgame Interview for the Ages': Richard Sherman and the Dialectical Rhetoric of Racial Neoliberalism." *Journal of Sport and Social Issues* 40.4 (2016): 291–314. doi:10.1177/0193723515615180

Turkle, Sherry. *Alone Together: Why We Expect More From Technology and Less From Each Other*. New York: Basic Books, 2011.

Uncertain Commons. *Speculate This!* Durham: Duke University Press, 2013.

Ventura, Patricia. *Neoliberal Culture: Living With American Neoliberalism*. New York: Routledge, 2016.

Wacquant, Loic. *Punishing the Poor: The Neoliberal Government of Social Insecurity*. Durham: Duke University Press, 2009.

Weber, Brenda. *Makeover TV: Selfhood, Celebrity, and Celebrity*. Durham: Duke University Press, 2009.

Wernick, Andrew. *Promotional Culture: Advertising, Ideology, and Symbolic Expression*. London: Sage, 1991.

Williams, Raymond. *Marxism and Literature*. Oxford: Oxford University Press, 1977.

———. *Keywords: A Vocabulary of Culture and Society Revised Edition*. Oxford: Oxford University Press, 1983.

Wilson, Julie A. and Emily Chivers Yochim. *Mothering Through Precarity: Women's Work and Digital Media*. Durham: Duke University Press, 2017.

Younge, Gary. "The Right Is Emboldened, Yes. But It's Not in the Ascendancy." *The Guardian*, December 30, 2016.

GLOSSARY OF CONCEPTS

Accumulation by dispossession—The process of accumulating wealth through dispossessing others of vital resources. Neoliberalism engages in widespread accumulation by dispossession by transferring wealth from public to the private coffers.

Affect—The potential to affect and be affected. Shaped by broader structures of feeling, affect undergirds our everyday lives and senses of possibility.

Affirmative speculation—A form of speculating on the future that does not aim to control (firm) the future, but rather to open up (affirm) new possibilities for collective life.

Biopolitics—A primary mode of liberal government aimed at regulating the vital lives of citizens and thereby optimizing the health of the nation.

Biopolitics of disposability—The ways in which biopolitics draw lines between valuable bodies who must be "made to live" and disposable bodies who can be "let to die." Within neoliberalism, everyone is potentially disposable, but the biopolitics of disposability draw lines between "winners" and "losers" via market competition.

Brand culture—The dominant culture of neoliberalism where private brands provide the platforms and contexts for everyday life and citizenship. Brand culture privatizes politics by refiguring social activism in terms of market competition and enterprise.

Capitalist realism—The sensibility that we have reached the end of history and that no other reality is possible other than neoliberal capitalism. *See also Disaffected consent.*

Commodity activism—A market-oriented form of social activism where commodity exchange and circulation are the medium of political engagement.

Common reason—A form of political reason premised on equality, democracy, social interconnection, interdependency, and shared vulnerability. Common reason would construct a world of living in common, not competition.

Competing for equality—A powerful structure of feeling within neoliberal culture. Neoliberalism's generalization of competition creates a competition for citizenship. Since inequality is inherent to neoliberalism, equality becomes something that one must compete for and earn in the market.

Conjuncture—The ensemble of cultural, political-economic, and social forces at work in a particular context. The conjuncture is the totality of converging histories and powers that define a historical moment.

Consumer citizenship—A prominent form of citizenship within liberalism and neoliberalism where citizenship is linked to one's status, rights, and practices as a consumer.

Counter-conduct—A mode of everyday living and self-care where one refuses to conduct oneself as a private enterprise and to relate to others through the norm of competition.

Creditocracy—The financial structure that emerged in the wake of neoliberalism's deregulation of banking and finance. The creditocracy is a system of accumulation by dispossession that works to create mass indebtedness in order to generate wealth for the financial industries.

Criminal industrial complex—The neoliberal criminal justice system. To deal with the growing populations of disposable people it creates, the neoliberal state administers a vast and aggressive bureaucracy to police and exploit poor people, especially poor people of color.

Cruel optimism—An affective orientation where the fantasies, attachments, and investments that sustain one's life also work to diminish and endanger one's life.

Culture—The shared beliefs, values, and practices of everyday living that bind a people together, and the specific artifacts and representations produced by and within a culture.

De-democratization—The process of reorienting politics away from participation in collective governing and toward participation in market society. Politics is privatized as the market, rather than the people, comes to rule.

De-proletarianization—The process of getting workers to reimagine themselves as individual self-enterprises with competing interests rather than a class with shared interests.

Disaffected consent—An affective orientation where, although people are deeply dissatisfied with neoliberalism, they acquiesce anyways, often turning inward to find meaning and individual fulfillment. *See also Capitalist realism*.

Disimagination—A cultural process of dismantling people's capacities for critical thinking and social interconnection. Without these capacities, people are unable to imagine alternative ways of being, relating, and producing collective life.

Disposability—*See Biopolitics of disposability.*

Educated hope—An affective orientation that emerges from critical work, where one is able to sense, imagine, and work toward alternative futures.

Embedded liberalism—The hegemonic political-economic system that emerged post-World War II. Embedded liberalism represented a class compromise between capitalists and workers. The market operated within a web of constraints so as to protect national economies, while also enabling international trade.

Empire—The global political-economic system of neoliberalism where a network of international financial institutions, not individual nation-states, exercise sovereignty over the economy. Empire is global rule by global capitalism.

Enterprise culture—The predominant medium of neoliberal governmentality. Neoliberalism advances through the promotion of enterprise culture— the application of an enterprise form to all modes of conduct, even, and especially, those that were previously non-economic.

Financialization—The increasingly prominent role that finance and the financial industries play in the global economy and processes of capitalist accumulation. *See also Creditocracy.*

Financialization of daily life—The increasingly prominent role that the logics and practices of finance (i.e., risk management, speculation on the future, reflexivity) play in everyday practices of identity and self-care.

Four *Ds*—Four prominent consequences of neoliberalism's regime of truth. These include dispossession, disimagination, de-democratization, and disposability.

Good governance—A central linchpin of neoliberal governmentality and process of de-democratization where collective governing is replaced with economized discourses of best practices and benchmarking. Governing is no longer a democratic process but a technical one.

Governmentality—A theory of liberal state power. Governing happens in social and cultural realms where the conducts of citizens are shaped "at a distance" from the state. Governmentality aims to bring individuals' practices of freedom in alignment with the state through the development and dissemination of cultural norms and social knowledges.

Hegemony—A theory of power that argues capitalist dominance is maintained not through direct economic exploitation, but rather through ongoing cultural processes of winning the consent of the governed. Hegemony represents a frontier of politics and is thus always open to contestation.

Human capital—Neoliberalism's reduction of human beings to financial entities. Individuals are first and foremost capital investments. Therefore, in all aspects of life, they must be looking to grow their market value.

Ideology—Commonsensical beliefs and values that are taken-for-granted and thus go unquestioned. Ideology imagines and interprets our social world for us without us knowing it.

Immaterial labor—The leading form of labor in post-Fordist economies. In contrast to manufacturing-based economies, immaterial labor produces immaterial commodities like information, knowledge, culture, feelings, and experiences.

Individual-liberty liberalism—Versions of liberalism committed to the expansion of free markets and private property rights. Laissez-faire capitalism represented an earlier version of individual-liberty liberalism that was premised on a belief that the state should not intervene in the economy. Neoliberalism represents a new version of individual-liberty liberalism that is premised on the state's active promotion of competition and construction of a market society.

Interconnectivity—A social ontology premised on our interconnections, shared vulnerabilities, and inherent interdependencies. This social ontology is thus the opposite of neoliberal social ontology, which is premised on self-enclosed individualism and living in competition.

Labors of self-enterprise—Forms of immaterial labor on the self aimed at increasing one's human capital and capacities for market competition.

Left neoliberalism—The progressive horizon of neoliberal politics. Left neoliberalism is committed to actively constructing a meritocracy where all have equitable access to market competition. *See also Marketized equality.*

Marketized equality—The neoliberal discourse of equality. Equality is not something to be guaranteed or protected by the state, but rather something that must be earned through competition in the market. Within neoliberalism, progressive political struggle is often about expanding marketized versions of equality to previous excluded and marginalized social groups.

Meritocracy—The ideology of social justice as a fair race where the best and most hard-working people come out on top. While this ideology has long played a role in sustaining the fantasy of the American Dream, meritocracy now operates as a powerful facet of neoliberal governmentality, as it rationalizes the state's construction of a market society of winners and losers.

Neoliberal antiracism—Forms of antiracism that expand neoliberal governmentality by helping to draw lines between worthy and unworthy racialized subjects, that is, between those who have earned equality and those who have not. *See also Marketized equality*.

Neoliberal feminism—Forms of feminism that expand neoliberal governmentality by guiding women to confront systemic gender oppression with privatized practices of self-care and empowerment in the market. *See also Marketized equality*.

Neoliberal governmentality—The state's active construction of an enterprise culture through the imposition of competition. Neoliberal governmentality is an aggressive form of governmentality designed to dismantle the social welfare state that emerged in the mid-twentieth century. In neoliberal governmentality, the state and its citizens are remade in the interests of global market competition. The state is no longer a protector of citizens, but a promoter of global profiteering.

Neoliberal hegemony—The establishment of a distinctly neoliberal political-economic field where what is at stake is no longer the state's public role in social life, but its private function in promoting market competition. *See also De-democratization*.

Neoliberal reason—The dominant political reason guiding neoliberal governmentality. Specifically, neoliberal reason is rooted in the generalization of market competition.

Neoliberal social ontology—Neoliberalism's philosophical understanding of the state, the market, humans, and the relationship among these. In neoliberal social ontology, the market is viewed as a giant information processor that computes what is good, true, and valuable, thereby providing a spontaneous order for society; the state is a promoter of private enterprise and market competition; humans are human capital who must be trained to enterprise and appreciate themselves in the market.

Neoliberal Thought Collective—A network of individuals, organizations, and institutions dedicated to maintaining neoliberal hegemony. The Neoliberal Thought Collective can be traced back to 1947 and the establishment of the Mont Pelerin Society, an elite, members-only group that was determined to envision a new liberal society based entirely on free markets and competition.

Personal responsibility—A prominent ideology and reality of neoliberal culture as individuals are both imagined and made to shoulder full responsibility for their successes or failures in life.

Postfeminism—A neoliberal gender ideology and sensibility where women are at once empowered to self-enterprise in the market and expected to remain the primary caretakers at home.

Post-race—A neoliberal racial ideology and sensibility that actively acknowledges past racial oppression in order to show that race is no longer an impediment to one's life chances. In this way, post-racialism is a form of racecraft, as it actively constructs racial meanings and divisions to rationalize neoliberal systems of exploitation and the biopolitics of disposability.

Precarity—The state of being subject to danger and threat. On one hand, precarity is a shared existential condition since our lives are inherently vulnerable to and contingent on others and our environments. On the other hand, precarity is a socially constructed operation of power, where some lives are deemed unworthy of social protection. This latter form of precarity segments and hierarchizes shared precarity along lines of gender, race, class, sexuality, and citizenship, distributing risk differentially among the population.

Precarization—The form of precarity specific to neoliberalism. Within neoliberalism, everyone is increasingly subject to precarity, as neoliberal governmentality and its dismantling of previous systems of social protection and welfare engenders widespread insecurity and volatility. However, precarization is still experienced differentially according to one's social position.

Privatization—The transfer of wealth and state power from public to private sectors through the deregulation of markets and industry and the economization of public resources and social welfare provision.

Privatization of happiness—The process of assuming psychic and emotional responsibility for one's life. Just like individuals must take personal responsibility for risk, they must also take personal responsibility for their happiness, well-being, and success, or lack thereof.

Privatization of risk—The process of transferring responsibility for risk-bearing and management from the state and corporations to individuals. In previous liberal governmentality, risk was distributed across the population. Neoliberalism privatizes risk, condensing it onto the shoulders of individuals and families.

Racecraft—The social construction and mobilization of racial difference in order to rationalize economic exploitation and existing structures of power.

Regime of truth—A theory of how socially constructed knowledges come to be taken as "Truth" by authorities and thus to have material consequences in people's lives. Every conjuncture has a regime of truth, a set of powerful discourses that are taken to be true and thus cannot be readily questioned or challenged.

Right neoliberalism—The conservative horizon of neoliberal politics. Right neoliberalism is far less invested in issues of diversity and equity when it comes to the promotion of market competition, meritocracy, and enterprise. In contrast to left neoliberalism, it seeks to retrench existing social hierarchies of gender, race, class, sexuality, and citizenship.

Self-appreciating individualism—The dominant theory and form of neoliberal individualism. As human capital, individuals must relate to themselves as capital investments that they must work to appreciate in the market. The entire self is thus oriented toward personal growth in the market. The primary relation of the self to itself is one of speculation.

Self-enclosed individualism—Forms of liberal individualism (including both possessive individualism and self-appreciating individualism) where the self is imagined to be radically cordoned off from others and its social world. Hard boundaries between self and others exist and encourage an oppositional consciousness, where people feel like it's them against the world. Self-enclosed individualism is thus fundamental to neoliberal culture and living in competition.

Self-enterprise—The neoliberal norm of subjectivity. Individuals are trained to conduct themselves as private enterprises—entrepreneurs of the self who apply market logics to all aspects of their lives to enhance their position in the market. *See also Labors of self-enterprise.*

Shock doctrine—Neoliberal economist Milton Friedman's belief that the material and affective turmoil of a crisis can be exploited to enact rapid political-economic change. *See also Structural adjustment.*

Spontaneous order—The neoliberal theory of the market as providing the bases for all social relations and processes. Thus, the market is capable of producing social order spontaneously so long as it is actively constructed for competition and private enterprise.

Status-quo stories—Stories that get told, and that we tell ourselves, about who we are, how things work, and why things happen. Status-quo stories cement our relationship to the present, shutting down our capacities for critique and the imagination of alternative worlds.

Structural adjustment—The neoliberal program of enacting radical political-economic change by making much-needed aid and funding contingent on economic restructuring. *See also Shock doctrine.*

Structures of feeling—Raymond Williams' theory that the social sensibilities and feelings that make up everyday life are shaped by broader historical structures and political-economic forces. Feelings are social, historical, and political. *See also Affect.*

Technologies of the self—Operations that one performs on the self in order to manage, care for, or know it more fully (e.g., yoga). In neoliberal culture, where individuals must care for themselves in the market, technologies of the self become vital arms of neoliberal governmentality.

INDEX